EFFECTIVE BUSINESS CORRESPONDENCE

Gennie Vee Gage

EFFECTIVE BUSINESS CORRESPONDENCE

Joel P. Bowman
Bernadine P. Branchaw

Western Michigan University

Canfield Press **cṕ** San Francisco

A Harper & Row Publication
New York, Hagerstown, London

Sponsoring Editor: John A. Woods
Project Editor: Julie Segedy
Production Manager: Marian Hartsough
Cover Artist: Donna Davis
Compositor: Turner, Brown & Yeoman, Inc.
Printer & Binder: Halliday Lithograph
EFFECTIVE BUSINESS CORRESPONDENCE
Copyright © 1979 by Joel P. Bowman and Bernadine P. Branchaw

Library of Congress Cataloging in Publication Data

Bowman, Joel P
  Effective business correspondence.

  Includes index.
  1. Commercial correspondence.   I. Branchaw, Bernadine P., joint
author.   II. Title.
HF5726.B748   651.7'5   78-14313
ISBN 0-06-453713-7

CONTENTS

PREFACE

Effective Business Correspondence has only one goal: to teach students—whether in college or already at work in business—how to write letters that communicate clearly and effectively. Unlike many business communication texts on the market today, *Effective Business Correspondence* concentrates on a single business communication skill of critical importance. The reason that so many business communication classes stress letter writing is that letters provide a business with its principal means of communicating complex ideas to the public and to other businesses.

The ability to write clearly and effectively is a skill that every person in business should have. A major rule of business is that if something is important, it belongs in writing. Because the written language remains much the same whether you are writing letters, memos, or complete analytical reports, solving letter writing problems is an efficient way to develop your writing skills.

In preparing this book, we have emphasized these three central considerations of communicating by letter:

1. How to identify and analyze a letter's business objectives.
2. How to identify and analyze a letter's human objectives.
3. How to present the required information in a way that will help achieve the letter's objectives.

To facilitate the learning of these major aspects of letter writing, we have made liberal use of examples and lists of important techniques and concepts. We have, however, avoided the overly prescriptive approach common to many business communication textbooks. Because no two business letter writing situations are ever identical, we believe that students are better served by learning general principles and the techniques required to apply them in solving a wide variety of business problems.

Our progression is from simple to complex. The opening chapters of Part One establish the importance of letter writing to business and discuss the conventions of letter appearance. Chapters 3, 4, and 5 explain how all letters fit into a communication situation that has a particular past, present, and future that require careful analysis. Step-by-step the text shows you how to think about writing letters, including what you need to know to write effectively, and how to apply the fundamentals of writing to specific kinds of business letters.

Part Two explains the organizational structure, techniques, and principles for writing common business letters. While the examples used are typical of letters actually written in business, we present them as illustrations rather than models and emphasize the uniqueness of each communication situation, even when a particular situation falls into a traditional letter type. Our coverage of the traditional letter types—favorable, unfavorable, and persuasive—leads naturally to a section in Chapter 10, "Mixed Messages." Most business communication textbooks quit after they have covered the frequently written business letters. This book goes a step further and provides the student with a plan for solving business letter writing problems that do not fit neatly into the "frequently written" categories.

We believe that in business, more often than not, it is the exception that proves the rule. Because frequently written letters are often treated as form or guide letters, the letters that students most often have to write from scratch do not fall into one of the "frequently written" categories. To offer students a better opportunity to learn how to analyze business letter writing problems, the chapter covering mixed messages shows students how to solve complex problems for themselves.

The supplemental problems in Part Three are designed to offer students the opportunity to identify, analyze, and solve business letter writing problems without the preconceived ideas that accompany cases at the ends of chapters. For example, when students solve problems at the end of a chapter dealing with negative messages, they make a deliberate effort to look for and find the negative aspect in the problem and to apply the techniques presented in the chapter. Most textbooks do not take students beyond this stage. In *Effective Business Correspondence,* however, we try to teach the student to look for potential difficulties in all communication situations because the business correspondence that will be encountered on the job does not arrive neatly labeled specifying the required reply.

Effective Business Correspondence is specifically designed for use in a one semester or one quarter course that places emphasis on business letter writing. It contains enough material and sufficient cases to keep students busy without the need of supplemental readings or materials. For courses that need to cover more than business letters, we recommend combining *Effective Business Correspondence* with our first book for Canfield Press, *Understanding and Using Communication in Business* (1977). The combination of the texts allows complete coverage of business and organizational communication with an emphasis on letter writing.

Our debts in preparing *Effective Business Correspondence* are many. We owe special thanks to our friends in the American Business Communication Association, most notably Dr. Francis W. Weeks of the University of Illinois, Dr. C.W. Wilkinson of the University of Alabama, and Dr. Patricia J. Marcum of Illinois State University. All provided invaluable advice. We also owe thanks to our colleagues and students, whose advice and criticisms have greatly shaped our thinking about the teaching of business communication. We also thank Mary Ann Bowman for her careful proofreading of the manuscript.

Joel P. Bowman
Bernadine P. Branchaw

PART ONE
General Principles

1. Importance of Letter Writing

Objectives

After you have read this chapter, you should be able to

1. Explain the importance of letter writing to business.
2. Estimate the cost of a typical business letter.
3. List the four main advantages of letter writing.
4. Explain a letter's profit potential.
5. List the four characteristics of a successful letter.

OUR PURPOSE

The main purpose of this book is to show you how to write effective business letters. The ability to write letters that pay for themselves is a skill that everyone needs, and our chief concern is to help you develop that skill. But in addition to presenting the mechanics and principles that will make your letters effective, we also want to show you that letter writing can be a much easier and more pleasurable means of communicating than it's usually thought to be.

Nonverbal and oral communication are usually considered easier and more natural than written communication. And to a certain extent, this is true. It's not accidental that children learn to talk before they learn to write.

WRITING IS WORK

The ability to communicate in writing requires more—and better-developed—communication skills than oral communication usually requires. Also, most of the writing we do as children is associated with school work, and we quickly learn to associate our written messages with our teachers' criticisms. It is no wonder that by the time we're ready to enter the world of business, most of us have learned to be hesitant about writing.

As adults we spend nearly all of our waking lives sending nonverbal and oral messages but comparatively little time writing. Frequently our lack of practice makes letter writing seem a more difficult means of communicating than it actually is.

Correctly approached, letter writing is one of the easiest, most efficient means of communicating. Business letters, however, are frequently considered a bore to read and write. And sometimes the reason is obvious:

```
Dear Sir:

Your letter of the 20th has been received and forwarded
to this office for reply. We have carefully read your letter
and beg to advise you that in accordance with our policy we
are unable to grant your request.

Pursuant to your request, we examined the document which you
find herewith enclosed. Unfortunately, our policy will not
allow us to act on this matter.

We hope that we have been of service in this regard, and if
you have further questions, please do not hesitate to contact
us. We remain,

Yours most sincerely,
```

Yes, the foregoing letter is extreme. Most business letters aren't *that* bad. Letter writers usually manage to say *something* of interest and say it in a warm, natural way. Even so, too many business letters are based on old formulas and contain too many outdated expressions to make interesting reading.

THE EVOLUTION OF BUSINESS LETTERS

The modern business letter is essentially a result of the invention and business use of the typewriter, which occurred in the last quarter of the nineteenth century. Early typewritten letters followed the older forms of handwritten models—hanging paragraphs (in which the first line begins at the left margin and the other lines are indented beneath it; such paragraphs are occasionally still used when a special effect is called for), flowery expressions (especially in the opening and closing), and language that in no uncertain terms indicated the class distinctions between reader and writer.

Around the turn of the century, letters were written in the following style:

```
My dear Sir:

Enclosed herewith you will find our copy of the Brillo report
     that you requested in your letter of recent date.

Regarding the matter of imports, we beg to advise that all our
     exports are taxed. If you have any further questions, feel
     free to contact us at your earliest convenience.

          I beg to remain your most humble and obedient servant,
```

As the modern business letter evolved, the language became less formal and the appearance became more streamlined and efficient. Astute business persons kept track of which letters had the best results, and psychologists and linguists were discovering the effects that language had on people. By the mid-1930s the fundamental principles of modern business writing were set. Progressive businesspersons began to take advantage of these principles.

Untrained letter writers, however, have frequently used a "model" approach to solve their letter writing problems—they go to the files to see what was written before. This technique has been used for years—and it shows. Many letters being written today would sound far more natural to our great grandparents than they do to us. But even trained letter writers are not always able to do their best. Time limitations, interruptions, and other work pressures won't permit the attention to detail that writing the best letters requires. When we are rushed, we all tend to fall back on what we—or someone else—said before. We want you to learn how to write letters without using models. Our goal is to teach you to write the *best* business letter when the circumstances require it and write acceptable letters always—even when your time is limited.

LETTERS ARE IMPORTANT

In spite of the problems many have with writing, letters are one of business's most important means of communicating. Of course, some business communication is nonverbal, and a great deal of it is oral: many words are spoken for each one that is written. But the words that are written are usually the important ones, and no modern business could exist for long without letters and other forms of written communication. Nearly all important business communication is eventually put into writing. Nonverbal communication in business usually communicates status, attitudes, and emotions. Oral communication is usually preliminary. If two businesspersons reach an agreement on the telephone, they will write follow-up letters to make sure that there will be no misunderstandings. If an important meeting is held, someone will take notes and write the minutes. Written communication, including letters, reports, and directives, constitutes a very large part of business activity.

Written communication is important to business—and to civilization in general—because it provides a fairly permanent record. Writing lets people overcome the barriers of time and distance, and it also permits writer and reader to consider carefully the meaning of complex messages. No other means of communication offers this combination of advantages. A telephone call may be much faster than an exchange of letters, but even if the conversation is tape-recorded, the telephone does not leave a readily accessible record.

THE ADVANTAGES AND DISADVANTAGES
OF LETTER WRITING

Letter writing is not important to business by accident or default. The need for efficiency in modern business requires the selection of the best means of communicating in most circumstances. Because the advantages far outweigh the disadvantages of written communcation, business correspondence remains the principal means of nonroutine communication in business.

Communicating by letter has only two real disadvantages:

1. Writing is a more formal means of communicating than speaking, and we tend to be more formal when we write than when we speak. This unnatural formality can result in letters that lack clarity and human warmth.
2. We cannot receive the immediate feedback necessary to alter our message if our receiver doesn't understand what we are saying.

These disadvantages can be overcome by careful writing.

The advantages of communicating by mail make letter writing the single most important means business has to communicate with the public and with other organizations. These advantages are as follows:

1. **Letters provide a permanent record.**   As is true for all written communication, a letter can be filed for future reference. With a letter on file, there can be no question about what was said.
2. **Letters provide proof of agreement.**   An exchange of letters can constitute a contract. If you write to us ordering merchandise at a certain price and we write back agreeing to send it, we have established a contract.
3. **Letters put emphasis on logic.**   Written communication allows for the controlled use of language to present complex ideas. Letters permit the writer to revise the message as often as necessary until it says exactly what is intended. Letters also permit the reader to study the message as long as necessary to understand it. For this reason, letters do a better job of conveying complex information than phone calls or other oral channels of communication.
4. **Letters can be more convenient.**   Letters can usually be written and read at the times most convenient for the writer and reader, whereas phone calls are frequently inconvenient for one party.

Letters—the kind of written communication we are concerned with in this book—are an expensive necessity for business. While the estimates for the cost of an individual letter may vary greatly, it's easy to see that letter writing is expensive enough to deserve every businessperson's attention. In addition to the relatively fixed costs of paper, envelopes, postage, and typewriters, it takes time to write and type a letter.

For example, an executive earning $30,000 a year makes approximately $15 an hour. A secretary earning $12,000 a year makes approximately $6 an hour. The costs of a typical letter for this particular executive and secretary would add up something like this:

Machine dictation time:	15 minutes	$3.75
Transcription time:	20 minutes	2.00
Revising draft:	10 minutes	2.50
Typing final copy:	10 minutes	1.00
Materials and postage:		.40
		$9.65

Some letters, of course, take more time and are more expensive to write than others. Routine, recurring business transactions can usually be written for far less than our hypothetical $9.65. With modern dictation equipment, word-processing centers, power typewriters, and the increased use of standardized paragraphs and form letters, many business writing problems can be solved quickly and easily—over and over again.

Even when you take full advantage of recent letter-writing innovations, your writing skills will remain extremely important. Many business situations still call for individualized letters, and not every company has the latest in time-saving equipment. Also, *you* may be the person in your company selected to write the standardized paragraphs for others to use; and *you* may be assigned the job of ensuring that the paragraphs are current, coherent, correct, and considerate.

THE PROFIT POTENTIAL

To be successful, a letter needs to do a great deal of work. Every letter you will write has what we call a profit potential—that is, the letter represents your investment in a communication process which you make in anticipation of gaining something or of preventing some loss. Many letters can be successful when handled in a simple, routine way. Other letters require more care. Suppose, for example, you must refuse a request made by your company's best customer. If you were careless with your letter, you might offend the customer and lose his or her business. Because the profit potential is high, that letter requires extra care—a larger investment to prevent an even larger loss. While the "profits" of letters cannot always be measured in dollars, letter writers should remember that every business letter will have some impact on the company's profits and that every letter should provide a return for its investment.

Whenever a letter is sent, it represents both the writer and the writer's company. Customers, clients, and associates frequently form their entire impression of you and your company from your letters. A successful letter conveys not only the information you wish conveyed but also the image you wish conveyed. Letters should make their purposes clear and, at the same time, establish empathy between the reader and writer, making the reader feel that the writer is a person with whom it's a pleasure to do business.

SUCCESSFUL LETTERS

It sounds simple enough—to be successful, a letter must make its purpose clear and establish empathy between the reader and writer. But to accomplish these goals, a writer needs to consider the following four variables that will influence the success for a letter:

1. The letter's appearance.
2. The audience's expectations.
3. The purpose of the message.
4. The writing style or language usage.

We will discuss each of these characteristics briefly in Chapters Two through Four before we turn to "Getting Ready to Write" in Chapter Five and to "Specific Message Types" in Part II.

SUMMARY

The main purpose of this book is to show you how to write effective business letters. The ability to communicate in writing requires more and better-developed communication skills than oral communication requires. Correctly approached, however, letter writing is one of the easiest, most efficient means of communicating.

Untrained letter writers frequently use a "model" approach to solve their writing problems—they go to the files to see what was written before. The use of models makes letters dull for both reader and writer. Our goal is to teach you to write the best business letter when the circumstances require it and to write acceptable letters always, even when your time is limited.

Letters are one of business's most important means of communicating. Nearly all important business communication is eventually put into writing because writing provides a fairly permanent record. Writing lets people overcome the barriers of time and distance, and it also permits writer and reader to consider carefully the meaning of complex messages.

The advantages of letter writing are (1) letters provide a permanent record, (2) letters provide proof of agreement, (3) letters put emphasis on logic, and (4) letters can be more convenient.

Every letter you will write has a profit poetntial—that is, the letter represents your investment in a communication process which you make in anticipation of gaining something or of preventing some loss. While the profits of letters cannot always be measured in dollars, letter writers should remember that every business letter will have an impact on the company's profits and that every letter should provide a return for its investment.

A successful letter conveys both the information and the image you wish conveyed. It makes its purpose clear and establishes empathy between the reader and the writer. To achieve these objectives, a writer needs to consider (1) the letter's appearance, (2) the audience's expectations, (3) the purpose of the message, and (4) the writing style or language usage.

EXERCISES

Review

1. Why is letter writing important to business?

2. What single invention had the greatest impact on the modern business letter? Explain.

3. Name the two disadvantages and the four advantages of letter writing.

4. Explain a letter's profit potential.

5. Name the four variables the writer needs to consider to make his or her letter successful.

Problems

1. If an executive earns $50,000 a year and a secretary earns $15,000, what might be the typical letter cost for them?

2. Prepare a brief description of the similarities and differences of communicating orally and by letter.

3. Briefly analyze the letters on page 4 and discuss your reactions.

4. Under what circumstances would you prefer to communicate by telephone? by letter? Explain.

5. What makes writing a more formal means of communicating than speaking?

2. Appearance

Objectives

After you have read this chapter, you should be able to

1. Name the five elements that influence the appearance of a letter.
2. Name the eight major parts of a letter.
3. State the differences between open and mixed punctuation.
4. Type a letter using modified block, block, simplified, and personalized letter formats.
5. Fold a letter properly and insert it into a correctly addressed envelope.
6. State the differences between and similarities of a letter and a memorandum.
7. Type a memorandum using both the horizontal and vertical headings.

LETTERS

By definition a letter is a written message in a particular format—that is, the message is presented using one of several standardized physical presentations, which we generally take for granted. The appearance of a letter is determined primarily by convention—we use a particular form for a letter because over the years a particular form has become accepted as "a letter." As arbitrary as your letter's appearance is, however, appearance plays a vital role in how your reader will react to your message.

The first impression your reader will form of you, your company, and your message will be the result of your letter's appearance. The importance of appearance cannot be overestimated. Readers simply do not give the same respect and attention to a sloppy letter as they do to a neat one. Even if you have done everything else correctly, a messy, unattractive appearance may indicate to your reader that you are a careless, unconcerned person. The opposite is also true: a neat, carefully prepared letter suggests that you are well organized and that you have concern for your reader.

In addition to the neatness of the message—freedom from typographical errors, strikeovers, smudges, and other disorders—you need to consider the impact of stationery, letter layout, and the parts and format of a letter.

The appearance of your letters depends on the following elements:

1. Stationery
2. Letter layout
3. Parts of the letter
4. Punctuation styles
5. Letter formats

STATIONERY

If it is your job to select stationery for your company, do it with care. Choose a paper that will best represent you and your company. You should consider these features:

1. **Quality.** Although paper can be purchased with a rag content of 100 percent, the most widely used paper for letterhead stationery in offices today is 25 percent rag-content paper. Rag-content paper is more durable than wood-pulp paper and makes a better impression. Good quality stationery is worth the investment because it helps create a favorable image for your company.
2. **Size.** The standard size for office stationery is 8½″ x 11″. Some businesses and executives may choose the Monarch-size sheets that measure 7¼″ x 10½″. Half sheets, 5½″ x 8½″, are used by some companies for short notes and intracompany messages.
3. **Watermark.** For added prestige, many companies have a translucent design impressed on the paper during manufacture. This design is called a watermark. Watermarks may be the logo or official emblem of the company.
4. **Weight.** Although paper for office stationery can be purchased in weights from 7 to 32 pounds, the generally accepted weight is from 16 to 20 pounds.
5. **Color.** White is the most acceptable color for business letters; however, pastels are gaining increased acceptance.

LETTER LAYOUT

Your letter should be well balanced. "Picture frame" your message by surrounding it with ample white space. The margins "frame" the message. Although the length of the message generally determines the width of the margins, it's usually best to maintain 1½″ margins, compensating for the loss or gain of space by adjusting the spacing within the parts of the letter. The top margin of a letter is usually 2″; the bottom margin should be about 2″ or more depending again on the length of the message. If the letter is two pages, the bottom margin on the first sheet should be about 1½″.

PARTS OF THE LETTER

The names and positions of the parts of the letter are conventions. Readers expect letters to contain certain elements and to look a certain way. Because an unusual appearance detracts from the content of the letter, your letters should be fairly conventional in appearance. Figure 2-1 illustrates all the parts of a standard, conventional business letter. The parts as shown are correct, but some aspects are changing (especially the salutation) to meet the needs of a changing society.

Letterhead

Almost every business firm uses letterhead stationery for the first page of every letter. The letterhead occupies the top two inches of the paper. In addition to the company's name and address, it may include the telephone number and official emblem of the company. Some firms also include the names of their officers or top executives. Because a company wants to create a favorable impression, it will generally hire a professional designer to create its letterhead.

If you use plain paper for your message, include your return address. Because your name appears at the end of the letter, it should not be included in the return address (See p. 192 for an example).

The succeeding pages of the letter and the envelope should have the same quality, color, and weight as the letterhead page.

Date

Every piece of correspondence requires a date line. The date consists of the day, the month, and the year. Two widely used styles are acceptable:

July 15, 1979 or 15 July 1979

Do not use all figures in the date. Do not abbreviate the month in the date line, though you may abbreviate other dates later in the letter. Depending on the length of the message, type the date line two or more line spaces below the letterhead or the typewritten return address.

Letterhead and Logo   THE MONEY TREE CARD COMPANY
                                               1521 Merriman Drive
                                               Glendale, CA 91202

Date   December 4, 19__

4 Line Spaces

Inside Address   First National Bank of Charleston
Attention Line   Attention: Mr. Charles Schoenknecht
                                        423 South Meridian Drive
                                        Charleston, SC 29408
Double-Space
Salutation   Gentlemen:
Double-Space
Subject Line   SUBJECT: 19__ Calendars
Double-Space
                                        Your order for 1,000 calendars should
Body with single-   arrive by Red Carrier Lines on
  spaced lines in paragraphs.   Thursday, December 14.
Double-Space
  between paragraphs.   The scenes for the various months on
                                        the calendars are reproductions of
                                        original pencil sketches by George
                                        Douglas.
Double-Space
                                        The enclosed brochure shows you our
                                        complete line of greeting cards for
                                        19__. Call our toll free number,
                                        800-789-4500 for prompt delivery.

Double-Space
Complimentary Close   Sincerely yours,
Double-Space
Company Name for   THE MONEY TREE CARD COMPANY
  Legal Signature
4 Line Spaces
Signature   *Karl K. Krammer*
Typed Name   Karl K. Krammer
Title   Sales Manager
Double-Space
Reference Initial   b
Double-Space
Copy Notation   c Vern VanVackren
Double-Space
Enclosure Notation   enc
Double-Space
Postscript   Will I see you at the convention in Chicago?

Figure 2-1. The parts of a letter.

Inside Address

The inside address directs your letter to the recipient. Because envelopes are not retained, the inside address is essential to every letter. The
inside address includes the following:

1. The courtesy title of the addressee. For example: Mr., Mrs., Miss,
    Ms., Dr., Rev., Captain.

2. The addressee's full name.
3. The professional title of the addressee. For example: Dean, Chairperson, Director, President, Consultant.
4. The name of the organization.
5. The street address or mailing address.
6. The city, state, and zip code. The state may be spelled in full or abbreviated using the standard abbreviation or the two-letter ZIP abbreviation. See Figure 2-2 for a complete list of two-letter abbreviations for state, district, and territory names recommended by the U.S. Postal Service. Postal officials recommend only one letter space between the two-letter state abbreviation and the zip code.

If you're not sure how the lines in the inside address should appear, remember that the most specific item—the name—always appears

Alabama	AL	Iowa	IA	North Dakota	ND
Alaska	AK	Kansas	KS	Ohio	OH
Arizona	AZ	Kentucky	KY	Oklahoma	OK
Arkansas	AR	Louisiana	LA	Oregon	OR
California	CA	Maine	ME	Pennsylvania	PA
Canal Zone	CZ	Maryland	MD	Puerto Rico	PR
Colorado	CO	Massachusetts	MA	Rhode Island	RI
Connecticut	CT	Michigan	MI	South Carolina	SC
Delaware	DE	Minnesota	MN	South Dakota	SD
District of Columbia	DC	Mississippi	MS	Tennessee	TN
		Missouri	MO	Texas	TX
Florida	FL	Montana	MT	Utah	UT
Georgia	GA	Nebraska	NE	Vermont	VT
Guam	GU	Nevada	NV	Virgin Islands	VI
Hawaii	HI	New Hampshire	NH	Virginia	VA
Idaho	ID	New Jersey	NJ	Washington	WA
Illinois	IL	New Mexico	NM	West Virginia	WV
Indiana	IN	New York	NY	Wisconsin	WI
		North Carolina	NC	Wyoming	WY

Figure 2-2. Two-letter abbreviations for state, district, and territory names.

first. The most general items—the state and zip code—appear last.

The inside address is typed below the date line. The number of lines between the date and the inside address is determined by the length of the letter. Four to six line spaces are typical.

Whenever possible, direct your letter to an individual rather than to a company. If you don't know the individual's name, then direct the letter to the person's professional title: for example, "Office Manager," "Personnel Director," or "Purchasing Agent."

Personalizing your letters by addressing them to an individual speeds the mail-routing process within the company and will help your letter receive a careful reading.

When you don't know whether a woman prefers "Mrs." or "Miss" for her courtesy title, use "Ms." When you don't know whether the name is masculine or feminine, for example, Kyle, Kim, Jackie, or Erin, use "M." When you address your letter to two or more men, use Mr. Smith and Mr. Adams; to two or more married women, use Mrs. Smith and Mrs. Adams; and to two or more unmarried women, use "Misses." You may choose to use the courtesy title of "Mses." (plural of Ms.) when you are not sure which title the women prefer or when you know that some are married and others are not.

The following are examples of the arrangement of inside addresses:

```
Mr. Gordon Godder
Director of Sales
Godder Guitars Inc.
3802 Karl Avenue
Paw Paw, MI 49079

Wagner Plumbing and Heating Supply Company
Attention Mr. Cris Carpenter
569 Antiago Road
Albuquerque, NM 87105

Mrs. Mary Wells, Controller
3021 Winchell Avenue
Crawfordsville, IN 47711

Dr. James Perkins, Dean
College of Business
Texas A & M University
College Station, TX 77843
```

A simulated inside address is used instead of the inside address in large-scale mailing campaigns to attract the reader's attention. If you are sending the same letter to many people, the cost of typing and addressing each letter individually would probably exceed the increased results the personalization would achieve. Inserting a name and address on a printed form letter is also expensive and usually does not improve the results of a letter.

A simulated inside address retains the traditional appearance of the letter and avoids the use of a salutation based on an obvious mailing list category or the extremely artificial "Dear Friend."

In place of an expensive, personalized address, such as

```
Mr. John A. Woods
1700 Montgomery Street
San Francisco, CA 94111

Dear Mr. Woods:
```

or in place of a less expensive but dull salutation, such as

```
Dear Homeowner:
```

begin the letter with three or four lines personalized for *one* reader and in the usual position of the inside address. For example:

```
You can sleep soundly
When you know your home is
Protected by Sound Alarm...

Because you are
One of Portland's
Busiest executives...
```

Attention Line

Traditionally, the attention line directs a letter to a person; to a professional title, such as Sales Director, Production Manager, or Service Manager; or to a department when the letter is addressed to a company. Modern usage is moving away from the attention line. When you can, address your letter to a particular person, department, or job title.

Traditional:

```
The Williamsburg Hat Company
1492 Columbus Avenue
Ft. Myers, FL 33900

Attention: Director of Personnel
```

Modern:

```
Director of Personnel
The Williamsburg Hat Company
1492 Columbus Avenue
Ft. Myers, FL 33900
```

Should you need to use an attention line, type it on the line after the name of the company (formerly the attention line appeared two line spaces below the inside address). Several styles for typing the attention line are still acceptable:

```
Attention Mr. Joseph Lancaster
ATTENTION: Personnel Department
Attention of the Sales Director
ATTENTION - MS. SARAH SANDSKILL
```

Salutation

The salutation is the conventional greeting which begins the message. Some letter formats, however, omit the salutation. The salutation used depends on the inside address and the relationship between the sender and the receiver. Type the salutation two line spaces below the inside address. Salutations in business letters are usually followed by a colon. The following are examples of typical salutations:

Dear Mrs. Omli:

Dear Mr. Jones:

Dear Miss Jaskovak:

Dear Ms. Sandberg:

Dear Mr. Todd and Mr. Koestner:

Dear Messrs. Meehan, Rudman, and Jencon:

Dear Mmes. Schroeder, Moreman, Knudtson, and Chang:

Dear Mses. Karpel and Holm:

Dear Misses Grinton and McGrath:

Gentlemen: (*never* Dear Gentlemen)

Ladies: (*never* Dear Ladies)

Dear Mrs. Spaulding and Mrs. Folz:

Mesdames: (*never* Dear Mesdames)

Dear Personnel Director:

Dear Sir: (When name and title are unknown, *never* use Dear Sirs)

Dear LeRoy:

Dear Elsie:

Dear Dr. Roberts:

Dear Professor:

Ladies and Gentlemen:

Dear R. D. Dimitri:

As a result of the increasing number of women in business, modern usage is moving away from the use of the salutation, "Gentlemen," as the proper form of address for corporations. No acceptable substitute, however, has been found. We suggest that to avoid addressing business-women as "Gentlemen," you address your letter to either a specific person or a specific title (Personnel Director, Manager, Vice-President of Marketing). When you do not know to whom or to what office your letter should be addressed, you can avoid the salutation by using the simplified letter form shown on p. 26.

Subject Line

The subject line tells your reader what your message is about and serves as a guide for filing. Keep your subject line short; never make it more than one line. Regardless of the content of the letter, the subject line should be positive. The subject line is placed two line spaces after the salutation. Many styles are acceptable:

```
Subject: Expense Vouchers
SUBJECT: Vacation Schedule
Subject: Pay Increments
SUBJECT - POLICY 4503-2317
LETTER STYLES (omit the word subject)
```

Expressions such as *re, in re, in regard to, about, reference,* and *regarding* are becoming increasingly outdated.

Body

The body contains the essential information of the message. Single-space the body of the letter and double-space between paragraphs. Your letter will look better if you keep your paragraphs short. First and last paragraphs should be no longer than four lines. Middle paragraphs should be about eight lines. Be sure, however, to vary the paragraph length to keep your letter from having a choppy appearance.

Complimentary Close

The complimentary close is the conventional closing of the letter. It should agree with the formality of the salutation. When you omit the salutation in your letter, you should also omit the complimentary close. Type the complimentary close two line spaces below the last line of the body of the message. The most frequently used complimentary closes are the following:

```
Sincerely,                    Sincerely yours,
Cordially,                    Cordially yours,
Best regards,
```

The following complimentary closes are used less frequently:

```
Yours truly,                  Yours very truly,
Very truly yours
```

Company Signature

For legal reasons, some companies prefer to include the typewritten name of the company in the signature block. The first name appearing after the body of the letter assumes the legal responsibility for the contents. Because the company's name appears in the letterhead, most companies prefer to avoid the redundancy and to assume responsibility for letters in other ways.

When you include your company's name in the closing lines of the letter, type it in all capital letters two line spaces below the complimentary close.

```
Cordially yours,             Sincerely,

ZAPPO PRODUCTS INC.          B & B ENTERPRISES
```

Writer's Signature

Every letter must be signed. The writer of the letter signs his or her name in the space between the complimentary close (or company signature if one is used) and the typewritten signature.

Typewritten Signature and Title of the Writer

In informal situations the writer may choose to omit the typewritten signature. Most business letters, however, contain the typewritten signature and the title of the writer. This helps the reader decipher illegible signatures. The typewritten signature appears on the fourth line below the complimentary close (or company signature if one is used). The writer's title or department is typed on the line below the typewritten signature. If the writer's title is short, it may be typed on the same line as the typewritten signature with a comma separating the two.

Carmos Alveraz, Auditor
Accounting Department

Terrence Engelhardt Jr.
Service Manager

Benedict Beno, Dean

A. S. Zola, Bursar

Typewritten signature lines do not include the courtesy title "Mr." Typewritten signature lines of women may include the courtesy title to indicate how the women would prefer to be addressed, but it is not required.

Miss Ginger Prynn   Mrs. Cecilia Branch

Ms. Thomasine Kwarta   Doralee Wilmsen

Reference Initials

Usually, if the closing lines include the typewritten signature of the writer, his or her initials may be omitted in the reference initials. If the closing lines do not include the typewritten signature of the writer, his or her first and/or middle initials and last name precede the initials of the typist. The typist's initials, or the initial of the typist's last name only, are typed at the left margin one or two line spaces below the last line of the closing. If the initials of the writer are given, then a diagonal or a colon separates the typist's initials from the writer's initials. The following are acceptable:

```
CJJEFFERSON: tjk        ABK/mfd
sr                      k
ckd                     JPB:b
```

Enclosure Notation

If enclosures accompany the letter, a notation is typed one or two line spaces below the reference initials. The following are all acceptable:

```
Enclosure                 Enc. or enc
Check Enclosed            Enclosures (2)
2 Enclosures              Enclosures: 1. Check
                                      2. Contract
                                      3. Invoice
```

Copy Notations

To show that a copy of the letter is being sent to one or more persons, type a copy notation one or two line spaces below the reference initials (or enclosure notation if one is used). Because carbon paper is no longer the primary means of making copies of letters, the single letter "c" is now preferred to the older form, "cc." Here are a few examples:

```
C Miss Susan Zimmerman      C Jack Myrberg
CC: Accounting Department    C: Personnel Department
Copies to:  J. Kovacik       c Donna Jacquies
            A. Shutty
            L. Zajac
```

Blind Copy Notations

Some companies still send copies of letters to an individual other than the addressee without wanting the addressee to know that this is being done. Such copies are called "blind" copies because the addressee does not know that someone will receive a copy of the letter. The blind copy notation is typed on the copies of the letter but not on the original. It appears one or two line spaces below the copy notation.

```
bc Alex Sowa
BC: A. Zouganellis
bcc G. Peterson
```

Mailing or Addressee Notations

To indicate special mailing or addressee notations on the letter, type these notations in all capital letters or in initial capitals and lower-case either two line spaces above the inside address or two line spaces below the copy notation or whatever line was typed last.

```
CONFIDENTIAL             Special Delivery
Personal                 Please Forward
REGISTERED MAIL          CERTIFIED MAIL
```

Postscript

A postscript is an afterthought, and in formal letters it is usually a sign of poor planning. The postscript, however, has two legitimate functions:

1. To add a personal comment to a business letter.
2. To re-emphasize a reader benefit in sales letters.

The abbreviation "P.S." is not necessary to indicate a postscript. The position of the postscript tells the reader that it is one. The postscript is the last item in a letter, and it may be handwritten.

The Second Page

With the exception of sales letters, business letters are usually one page long, but sometimes a message is sufficiently complex to warrant two or more pages. When you have a second page, use one of the following second-page headings:

Horizontal Headings:

```
Mr. Gerald Vanderkoff      15 July 19_      2

The ABC Company      2      July 15, 19_
```

Vertical Headings:

```
Mrs. Mildred Goodwin        Cacaterra Company
Page 2                      January 16, 19_
August 15, 19_              Page 2
```

As we have already said, the second and succeeding pages of a letter are usually typed on plain stationery of the same quality, size, and color as the letterhead. Rather than use plain paper, however, some companies prefer to have an identifying mark, such as the company name, in small print across the bottom of the page, or a company slogan across the top of the sheet of the second page.

The date appearing on the second page is always the same date as is on the first, even though the second page of the letter may be typed on a different day.

The heading for the second page begins one inch from the top of the page. The second-page side margins are the same as the first-page side margins. Begin the message of the second page three line spaces after the heading. At least two lines of the body of the message must be carried over to the second page. The bottom margin is determined by the length of the letter.

PUNCTUATION STYLES

The two most common styles of punctuating the salutation and the complimentary close of the letter are as follows:

1. **Open Punctuation.** No punctuation appears after the salutation or the complimentary close.

```
Gentlemen                    Cordially yours

Dear Mr. Byers               Sincerely
```

2. **Mixed Punctuation.** A colon follows the salutation, and a comma follows the complimentary close.

```
Gentlemen:                   Cordially yours,

Dear Mrs. Beveridge:         Sincerely,
```

LETTER FORMATS

The usual formats for business letters include the following:

1. **Block.** In the full block letter format, all parts of the letter and all lines begin at the left margin. See Figure 2-3 for an illustration of the block format.
2. **Modified Block.** The modified block format has two versions. Modified block with blocked paragraphs has all lines beginning at the left margin except the date and the closing lines, which begin at the center of the page. Modified block with indented paragraphs is the same as the modified block except that the paragraphs are indented. See Figure 2-4 for an illustration of the modified block format.
3. **AMS Simplified.** In the Administrative Management Society's simplified letter format, all lines begin at the left margin. This format omits the salutation and the complimentary close. See Figure 2-5 for an illustration of the AMS simplified format.
4. **Personalized.** The personalized format is a combination of the block and the AMS formats. Like the AMS it omits the salutation and complimentary close, but it retains the traditional block appearance by providing personalized facsimiles of those two standard letter parts. See Figure 2-6 for an illustration of the personalized format.
5. **Memo.** For some business correspondence, memo format is more appropriate than letter format. Memos are used to exchange information within an organization, whereas letters are sent to persons

outside the organization. If, for example, you work for the Los Angeles branch of a New York company, your company may prefer that you use memo format when you correspond with the home office in New York. See pp. 31-32 for further explanation.

Vermont Manpower Center
202 W. Maple Street
Whitney, VT 02135


```
January 30, 19__


Dr. Patricia Marcum
Department of Business Education
  and Administrative Services
Illinois State University
Normal, IL 61761

Dear Doctor Marcum:

This letter is an example of a letter typed in block format
with mixed punctuation.  The block format is a more economical
format than modified block.

Notice that all lines begin at the left margin--the date,
inside address, saluation, body, and closing lines.  Observe,
too, that the spacing between letter parts is standard.

The block style is popular because it retains the traditional
appearance established by the modified block format while
providing a definite economic advantage.

Cordially,



W. I. Grogg
Manager, Education and Training

b
```

Figure 2-3. Block format, mixed punctuation.

Susan Rice • 14 Fulton Street • Ross, CA 94011

November 16, 19__

Ms. Louise Steele
Administrative Assistant
Business and Technical Writing
317b David Kinley Hall
University of Illinois
Urbana, IL 61801

Dear Ms. Steele

This letter is an example of a letter typed in modified block
format with blocked paragraphs and open punctuation.

Notice that all lines begin at the left margin except the date
and the closing lines, which begin at the center of the page.
The spacing between letter parts is standard.

Even though it is more expensive to use than the block format,
modified block is still used by many conservative American
businesses. It is the only letter format that gives the writer
the choice of indented paragraphs.

Sincerely yours

Susan Rice

Figure 2-4. Modified block format, blocked paragraphs, open punctuation.

Administrative Management Society
5211 Chagrin Blvd.
Cleveland, OH 44114

April 14, 19__

Mr. Lester P. Salisbury, Manager
Perry Manufacturing Company
3802 Karl Avenue
Nashville, TN 37203

AMS SIMPLIFIED FORM

This letter form, Mr. Salisbury, is typed in the simplified
format recommended by the Administrative Management Society.
To use this modern, time-saving format, follow these suggestions:

1. Use block format.

2. Omit salutation and complimentary close, but try to use the
   reader's name in the first sentence.

3. Use a subject line. Type it in ALL CAPS three line spaces
   below the inside address; triple-space from the subject
   line to the first line of the body.

4. Type enumerated items at the left margin; indent unnumbered
   listed items five spaces.

5. Type the writer's name and title in ALL CAPS at least four
   line spaces below the body of the letter.

6. Double-space closing notations--reference initial and
   enclosure and copy notations--after the writer's name.

AMS simplified letter format, Mr. Salisbury, is not only very
efficient but also quite attractive.

CHARLES POWERS, PERSONNEL DIRECTOR

m

c Thomas Goodwin
  Myles Murphy

Figure 2-5. AMS simplified format.

CONNECTICUT COLLEGE OF BUSINESS
_____

10002 Post Road
Fairfield, CT 06694

September 8, 19__

Dr. Henry McKeown
3150 Reynolds Road
Jackson, MI 49201

Yes, Henry,

standard letter formats are still correct, but many letter
writers are choosing to personalize messages with breezy,
"open" beginnings and closings in place of stilted, formal
salutations and complimentary closings.

These personal openings and closings have the advantage
of retaining the appearance of traditional formats while
substituting something useful for the dull salutation and
complimentary close.

Why say	Dear Mr. Dorsaneo:
	Here's a copy of the material you requested.
When you can say	Here, Mr. Dorsaneo,
	is a copy of the material you requested.
Why say	Dear Dr. Mascolini:
	The crushed velvet pantsuit you ordered is available in red, blue, black, and magenta.
When you can say	The crushed velvet pantsuit, Dr. Mascolini,
	is available in red, blue, black, and magenta.
Why say	Dear Bob:
	We enjoyed your visit and the lovely dinner at the Black Swan.
When you can say	Thanks, Bob,
	for the lovely dinner at the Black Swan. We thoroughly enjoyed your visit.

Why say   Sincerely yours,
                           Sincerely,
                           Cordially yours,

When you can say   When you're in town again...

                           Please call,

                           I'm so glad you got the job...

                           Congratulations,

                           Call me at (415) 989-9608...

                           When I can help again,

Dr. Henry McKeown   September 8, 19__   2

When you use the personal style, you show your reader that you
are a thoughtful letter writer and a person who can think for
himself.

Naturally, if you are writing to a very conservative company,
you would want to use a more traditional format to make sure
that you don't offend your reader. Your format, as well as
your language, should indicate your empathy for your reader.

We'll be glad to help again when you have questions...

Anytime,

Joel P. Bowman

Joel P. Bowman   *Bernadine P. Branchaw*

                                     Bernardine P. Branchaw

Figure 2-6. Personalized format.

ENVELOPES

The Return Address

The return address is generally printed in the upper-left corner of the envelope and matches the letterhead printing. If the envelope does not have a printed return address, type your return address in the upper-left corner, not on the back, of the envelope. Single-space the return address and use the block style. Addressee notations—*confidential, personal,* or *attention lines*—are typed three line spaces after the return address in all capital letters, capital and lower-case letters, or underscored.

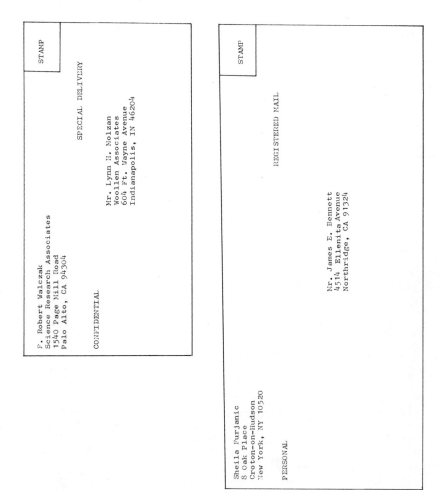

Figure 2-7. Large and small envelopes.

The Mailing Address

The mailing address is the same as the inside address. Type the mailing address about five spaces to the left of the center of the envelope and about halfway down from the top of the envelope. Single-space the lines of the mailing address and use the block style.

Mailing Notations

Mailing notations—*certified mail, registered mail,* or *special delivery*—are typed three line spaces after the stamp position in all capital letters, capital and lower-case letters, or underscored.

See Figure 2-7 for an illustration of the large (No. 10) envelope and the small (No. 6¾) envelope. Figure 2-8 illustrates the folding and inserting process.

```
Fold regular-size stationery (8½"x11") for insertion
into a small envelope (No. 6 3/4) as follows:
```

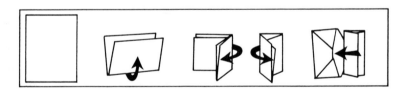

```
Fold regular-size stationery (8½"x11") for insertion
into a large envelope (No. 10) as follows:
```

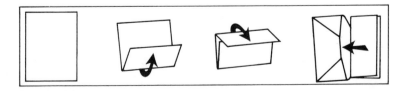

Figure 2-8. Folding and inserting process.

MEMORANDUMS

Although memorandums, commonly known as memos, are technically a short report form, they are worth considering here for two reasons: (1) they use the same basic organizational patterns, which we discuss in later chapters, to achieve the same kinds of objectives; and (2) like letters, they are usually brief, rarely being longer than a page.

```
15 August 19__


TO:       Gertrude Sonnevil, Office Manager

FROM:     John Mutchall, Personnel Director

SUBJECT:  Annual Review of Hazel Kramer


Please tell Hazel Kramer that her appointment for annual review
is Monday, 1 September, at 9 a.m.

Please complete the attached form and return it to me by
Thursday, 30 August.

Attachment
```

The purpose of the memorandum is to provide a rapid and convenient means of communication between employees within the same organization. Interoffice memorandums—or memos—are the company's major medium for internal written communication.

Because memos do not leave the organization, you need not be very concerned about public relations—you can use stationery that differs from letterhead stationery in color, printing, quality, and size. Use inexpensive wood-pulp paper rather than expensive rag-content paper. Sizes of memo stationery range from full sheets, 8½″ x 11″, to half sheets, 5½″ x 8½″. Some businesses prefer half sheets for economy; other companies choose full sheets for ease in filing.

Although most companies prefer white paper for their letters, they prefer using colored paper for memos to distinguish them from other business papers. Colors may designate particular departments.

Headings

Unlike letters, which use the formal inside address, salutation, complimentary close, and typed signature, memos require only informal headings. Normally, four informal printed headings appear on memo stationery: **To**, **From**, **Date**, and **Subject**. Although the arrangement and design may vary among companies, these four headings appear on most forms. Printing of the heading lines may be either vertical or horizontal.

Horizontal Headings:

```
   TO:                            DATE:

   FROM:                          SUBJECT:
```

Vertical Headings:

```
   DATE:

   TO:

   FROM:

   SUBJECT:
```

If your organization does not provide printed forms, you may omit the word *date* and simply type the date.

```
16 November 19_

TO:       All Employees

FROM:     Don DeLong, Personnel Department

SUBJECT:  Group Health Insurance


Mrs. Alice Flint, our representative from the Green Shield
Insurance Company, will be here on Monday, November 28, to
answer any questions you may have on our new medical coverage
insurance plan.

Mrs. Flint will meet with all interested employees at 9 a.m.
in Room 405. Should you wish an individual appointment to
discuss your personal needs, call me at Extension 22.
```

SUMMARY

A letter is a written message in a particular format—that is, the message is written in one of several standardized physical presentations which we generally take for granted. The first impression your reader will form of you, your company, and your message will be the result of your letter's appearance.

The appearance of your letter depends on five elements: (1) stationery, (2) letter layout, (3) parts of the letter, (4) punctuation style, and (5) the letter format itself.

When you select letterhead paper for your company, consider the quality, size, watermark, weight, and color. The parts of the letter are letterhead, date, inside address, attention line, salutation, subject line, body, complimentary close, company signature, writer's signature, typewritten signature and the title of the writer, reference initials, enclosure notations, copy notations, and postscript. The two most common styles of punctuating the salutation and the complimentary close are open punctuation and mixed punctuation.

The usual formats for business letters include the block, modified block, AMS simplified, and personalized. Each of these has certain advantages. Modified block is the most conservative. Block and personalized are more efficient than modified block and are usually considered more personal than the AMS simplified, which is the most efficient.

The memorandum is a short informal message that provides a rapid, convenient means of communication between employees within the same organization. Interoffice memorandums—or memos—are the company's principal written medium for internal communication.

EXERCISES

Review

1. What are the five elements that influence the appearance of a letter?

2. What are five features you should consider before purchasing paper for letterhead stationery?

3. Identify and explain the eight major parts of the letter.

4. What is meant by "picture framing" your letter?

5. About how long should the first and last paragraphs of a letter be? About how long should the middle paragraphs be?

Problems

1. Obtain at least three samples of business letters with letterheads and write a brief analysis of each letter's appearance.

2. What salutation would you use for the following:
   a. A letter addressed to a corporation?
   b. A letter addressed to Mr. Paul Barker and Mr. Daniel Kennedy?
   c. A letter addressed to Mrs. Matt Connor and Mrs. Robert Jackson?
   d. A letter addressed to the attention of the personnel director?

3. Type the following letter in
   a. Block format and address it to Dr. Herta Murphy, 408 Peck Drive, Seattle, WA 98105.
   b. Modified block format and address it to Mr. Anthony Bishop, Aero Space Equipment Company, 1919 South Fullerton Drive, Richmond, VA 23222.
   c. AMS Simplified format and address it to the attention of Mr. Dana Valverde, Schippers' Service Appliance Company, 3609 S. Tenth Avenue, Canyon, TX 79015.
   d. Personalized format and address it to Mrs. Jean Wilcox, President, Hanning Manufacturing Company, 187 Basset Boulevard, Miami, FL 33131.

```
You should receive the Stereo City clock radio you ordered by
Friday, 13 March. It will arrive prepaid by United Parcel Post.
The all-new digital clock radio was a good selection because it
comes complete with a five-year guarantee. You'll have many
years of trouble-free service. The light sensor automatically
dims the time display at night and brightens the display in day-
light. The 24-hour set-and-forget alarm wakes you up exactly the
same time every day. Be sure to read the manual packed with the
radio for complete operating instructions. The enclosed bro-
chure will acquaint you with Stereo City's other fine products.
The portable radio shown on page 6 is a fine companion for your
outdoor activities. Good listening.
```

4. Address large envelopes for the first two letters typed in Problem 3 and small envelopes for the last two letters. Correctly fold and insert the letters into the envelopes.

5. Type the following memo using the correct format. The memo is from Rick Franson, office manager, and it goes to the staff. Date the memo September 1.

```
     Please plan to attend the staff meeting at 9 a.m.
on Monday, September 14, in the conference room.

     Ms. Carolyn Spire, our IBM representative, will
demonstrate IBM's latest copier. Should you have any
material that you want photocopied, bring it along.

     The meeting should last about 45 minutes. Coffee
and rolls will be served.
```

3. The Communication Context

Objectives

After you have read this chapter, you should be able to

1. Identify and explain a reader's expectations and the five basic emotional needs.
2. Explain the difference between subject content and feeling content.
3. Identify the three specific business objectives of letters.
4. Identify the general structural principles of an immediate or a delayed message.
5. Analyze a reader's probable reaction to the subject content and feeling content of a letter.

All communication occurs in a context that includes the following:

1. A history of previous experiences.
2. A sender and a receiver.
3. A reason for communicating.
4. The sender's expectations.
5. The receiver's expectations.

To be successful, a letter writer needs to consider the various elements of the communication context before beginning the letter. By analyzing the audience and determining a letter's objectives, a writer is able to place a written message in its communication context.

AUDIENCE

The person or persons to whom you are writing should be a major influence on what you say in your letter and how you say it. After all, your reader frequently establishes the reason you are writing the letter: you want your reader to know or to do something. Whether your reader will understand your message and cooperate with you will depend on how well you are able to anticipate his or her expectations, attitudes, and needs. Obviously, if you know someone well, you will have a much better idea of what he or she will expect, want, and need in any given situation than if you don't know the person well.

Adaptation

Whenever you write a letter, you need to *adapt* your message and writing style to communicate successfully with your particular audience. When you are writing to friends and business acquaintances of long standing, you can—and should—be less formal than when you are writing to someone you don't know. Although most of the information we present in this book applies primarily to the letters you will write to people you don't know well, any letter you write will be more successful if you make an effort to analyze your audience's expectations, attitudes, and needs.

Your friends may forgive you if your letter is not as considerate as it might be, but they will certainly enjoy your letter more if you anticipate correctly how your message will affect them. When writing to your friends, you can visualize them and imagine yourself delivering the same message in person:

What would your greeting be?
Would you put business first and pleasure second?
Would you socialize a bit first and save business until later?
Would you use formal or informal language?
How would you convey good news? Bad news?
How would you ask for your friend's help?

Knowing what to say in a letter is much easier when you can visualize your reader and imagine his or her response to what you want to say. The more we know about a person, the easier it is to make accurate assumptions about that person's behavior. While no prediction that we may make about behavior—either our own or someone else's—can be absolutely certain, the more facts we have about our reader, the greater the certainty our assumptions will prove correct.

Even when we don't know our readers personally, we can usually make fairly accurate predictions about how they will react to our messages if we consider everything we do know before we write. The needs and expectations of people are basically similar:

1. We are all cheered by good news.
2. We are all disappointed by bad news.
3. We all tend to resist performing actions that will cost us either time or money.

Our intuition and previous experience with people help us predict how readers we don't know may react to a message. To increase the accuracy of our intuition, however, we should give careful consideration to the rather wide variety of expectations readers may have.

Reader's Expectations

People who are communicating by letter usually have expectations that may or may not be fully recognized. In Chapter Two, for example, we said that one of the principal reasons for using a standard format for business letters is that your reader expects to see a standard format. When you violate that expectation, you attract the reader's attention to the appearance of the letter, which may cause the reader to pay less attention to your content. Such a violation of expectation, however, may cause the reader to notice a letter that would otherwise be ignored.

Your readers' expectations will be influenced by several factors. To determine these, ask yourself the following questions:

1. What are my readers' previous relationships with me?
   a. Do they know who I am?
   b. How well do they know me?
   c. How well do they like me?
   d. Do they trust me?
2. Is my relationship with them primarily personal?
   a. Do I view them as friends?
   b. Which is more important to me—our mutual business or our friendship?
   c. Do we meet socially? Would I like to?
   d. Do I know anything about their lives away from the job?
3. Is my relationship with them primarily a business relationship?
   a. Have I ever communicated face-to-face with them?
   b. Do I ever correspond with them just for the fun of it?
   c. Do I ever exchange personal information in my letters to them?
   d. For what reasons do I correspond with them?
4. What kind of business relationship do I have with them?
   a. Are they businesspersons who understand business terminology and practices?
   b. Are they customers who work in nonbusiness jobs?
   c. Is our business relationship new or well established?
   d. Have I always been honest and fair with them?
   e. Have they always been honest and fair with me?
5. How important is the future of the relationship?
   a. Do I wish the relationship to continue?
   b. Do my readers wish the relationship to continue?
   c. Has the relationship been profitable?
   d. Has the relationship been enjoyable?

As you ask yourself the preceding questions in relation to a particular reader, you can determine whether that reader will welcome your letter and how he or she is likely to react to your message. When you are writing to someone for the first time, for example, you will have to be very careful with your explanation of why your are writing—your purpose will have to be stated clearly and explicitly. When you have a well-established relationship with a reader, the history of your communication with that reader will help place each new message in a meaningful context.

In addition to having certain expectations based on their previous experiences with you, whether face to face or through letters, your readers will also have certain emotional needs that will influence the way they respond to your message. The most important of these are the following:

1. **People are self-centered.** Your readers will always want to know what the message will do for them. They will expect your letter to have a specific point or purpose, and they will expect that purpose to benefit them. Your reader's first question will usually be, "How will this letter benefit me?" Successful letter writers answer that question by specifying the kind of satisfaction—material, emotional, psychological, or intellectual—the letter offers the reader.

2. **People are defensive.** Readers are frequently suspicious of promises made in messages. Readers also tend to perceive some kinds of messages as threatening. Constructive criticism may be perceived as a personal attack, and a careless choice of words in important correspondence may lead to an erroneous assumption.

3. **People aren't perfect.** Human error is a part of life, but no one—neither you nor your readers—enjoys having mistakes pointed out and criticized. We all like to consider ourselves a bit "more perfect" than the next person, and we all find it easier to discover and correct the errors of others. Your readers will respond more favorably to your letters if you concentrate on the positive aspects of a situation, de-emphasize mistakes, and focus on doing better in the future. Be especially careful to avoid directly accusing your readers of shortcomings. Accusations will cause them to become defensive and to resist your message.

4. **People need specific goals.** Most people do not feel comfortable with generalities, abstractions, and vague statements. Your letters will be more successful if you explicitly identify your own goals and help your readers establish clear, definite, and positive goals for themselves. Let your readers know what is going to happen next and who should take what action next.

5. **People do the best they can.** Even though your readers may have disappointed you and you may suspect that they are being less honest or less intelligent than they should be, grant them the benefit of the doubt as long as you possibly can. Assume that your

readers are acting honestly and intelligently in relation to *their* perception of the situation, even if *your* perception of the situation is different. If you can learn to see the situation from your readers' point of view, you will be in a better position to explain your own point of view to them.

Reader's Attitude and Knowledge

In addition to analyzing your relationship with your readers, you need also to consider the influence that each specific message will have on them. Each letter you write will have both a *subject content* and a *feeling content*. You will have certain ideas that you'll need to make clear to your reader, and you'll be expressing an attitude toward your reader. Unless you are careful, such feelings as anger, condescension, inferiority, or disappointment can interfere with the meaning of your message. Your reader will also be concerned with the subject content and feeling content of your letters. Successful communicators do their best to match the subject content of the letter with their readers' expectations. How will your reader *feel* about your message?

You can increase the accuracy with which you predict how your reader will interpret what you say by asking yourself the following questions:

1. What does my reader already know about the subject?
   a. Have we communicated about this subject before?
   b. Is my reader familiar with the specialized language of the subject?
   c. Is my reader familiar with basic business terminology?
   d. Will my reader require a full explanation of the subject, a simplified explanation, or no explanation at all?
2. What does my reader want to know about the subject?
   a. Is the subject already important to my reader?
   b. Can knowing about the subject benefit my reader?
   c. Does my subject have built-in reader interest, or must I create interest in some other way?
3. How does my reader feel about the subject?
   a. Does my reader have a positive, negative, or neutral view of the subject?
   b. What previous experience has my reader had with the subject that would influence his or her feelings about it?
   c. Are my feelings about the subject the same as my reader's?
4. How does my reader feel about me and my company?
   a. Does my reader have a positive, negative, or neutral view of me and my company?
   b. What previous experience has my reader had with me or my company that would influence his or her feelings?

    c. Are my feelings about my reader the same as his or her feelings about me and my company?

5. How does my reader feel about other people, business, and life in general?

    a. Is my reader optimistic or pessimistic?

    b. Does my reader tend to be accurate and precise in business dealings?

    c. Is my reader generally willing to grant the benefit of the doubt?

LETTER PURPOSE AND STRUCTURE

The audience to whom you will be sending your letter is one of the fixed aspects of your communication situation. The other aspect, the one you will usually begin with, is the purpose of your message—the reason you are writing. These two elements are usually interdependent—that is, you are writing to a particular reader or group of readers for a particular reason, and to alter either the audience or the purpose is to change the entire communication situation. The audience and the purpose of the message should be analyzed simultaneously.

While you are analyzing your readers according to the principles we discussed earlier, you should be determining the specific purposes or objectives of your letter and organizing the contents of the message to achieve those objectives.

The Letter's Objectives

Every letter you write will have two general objectives: a business objective and a human objective. The business objective establishes the subject content of the letter, and the human objective establishes the feeling content. To be successful, a letter must accomplish both objectives. The letter must make its purpose and any required action clear, and it must also make the purpose and action seem desirable. In addition to being clear, the letter must establish empathy between reader and writer.

Before you write a letter, you should establish its business objective by asking yourself the following questions:

1. Why am I writing this letter?
2. Who will receive the message?
3. Where and when (in what context) will the reader receive the letter?
4. What do I want the reader to know?
5. What do I want the reader to do?
6. When do I want the reader to do it?

7. How do I want the reader to do it?
8. How can I make it easier for my reader to do it?

Business objectives can be divided into three general categories: to inquire, to inform, and to persuade. A fourth possible objective of a message is to entertain, but while material designed to entertain a reader may help a writer achieve a business objective, entertainment is not of itself a practical objective.

1. **Letters to inquire.**   Inquiries include messages designed to obtain information, goods, or services: asking questions, placing orders, and making *simple* requests.
2. **Letters to inform.**   Informative messages can convey positive, neutral, or negative information. Information is positive if the reader will welcome it, neutral if the reader has no special interest in it, and negative if it will hurt the reader's feelings.
3. **Letters to persuade.**   Persuasive letters attempt to alter a reader's behavior.

Your business objective will naturally influence the way your reader will react to your message. To accomplish your purpose, you will need to consider your reader's probable reaction to this objective. Some messages will, of course, have more than one business objective. When you need to write such a letter, you should consider each objective separately to determine your reader's probable response.

It is only after you have established your business objectives that you can clarify the human objectives of your message by asking yourself the following questions:

1. **Will the message hurt my reader's feelings?**
2. **Is my reader likely to ignore or resist my message?**

The answers to these questions determine whether you can concentrate your attention on communicating the business objectives—the subject content—or whether you will need to concentrate your attention on your reader's feelings—the human objectives. Once you have determined the business and human objectives, you should structure the entire message to help you achieve the specific goals.

Message Structures

When your letter will neither hurt your reader's feelings nor cause your reader to resist your message, you should emphasize the subject content of your message. Letters that emphasize the subject content are called **immediate messages** because the most important aspect of the subject content is placed first, in the primary position. The main point of the letter is stated immediately.

When your letter will either hurt your reader's feelings or cause him or her to resist your message, you should emphasize the feeling content of the message. Letters that emphasize the feeling content are called **delayed messages** because they delay presentation of the subject content until the reader has been prepared emotionally. The writer delays presenting the business objective until the human objective has been accomplished.

In spite of their different objectives, both the immediate and delayed structures take advantage of the fact that readers pay closest attention to the beginning and the ending of a letter and tend to pay the least attention to the middle of a letter. All messages, whether they are immediate or delayed, follow the same general structural principles:

Primary Element: Information that the reader will consider positive or important. This element is usually one or two paragraphs long.

1. An important question
2. Good news
3. Important information
4. A statement of agreement
5. A statement complimenting the reader
6. Information that will benefit the reader

Secondary Elements: Information that the reader will consider negative or less important. This section may be several paragraphs long.

1. Explanations
2. Supporting, secondary details
3. Additional questions
4. Negative information
5. Reasons the reader should act

Closing Element: Information that the reader will consider positive or important. This element is usually one or two paragraphs long.

1. A clarification of who does what next
2. Information that will benefit the reader
3. Suggestions for specific, positive courses of future action

Immediate Messages

Several types of common business letters usually call for an immediate presentation because the subject content is more important than the feeling content. Letters of inquiry and letters that convey positive and neutral information, for example, are almost always immediate messages because the content of the message has built-in reader interest. These messages almost always begin with an explicit statement of—or question about—the letter's business objective.

> Please send me one dozen copies of <u>Understanding</u> <u>and</u> <u>Using</u>
> <u>Communication</u> <u>in</u> <u>Business</u> by Bowman and Branchaw.
>
> Would the Grand Hotel be able to accommodate the 300 persons
> attending the American Business Communication Association
> annual convention from 29 to 31 December?
>
> Yes, Mr. Bach, Motown Records would be glad to consider your
> concertos for publication.
>
> Beginning 15 February, George, order all replacement parts
> by part number <u>and</u> and factory number.

When you begin a letter with the subject content of the message, you are giving primary emphasis to the business objective. The human objectives are secondary in these messages, not because they are unimportant, but because the positive nature of the business objectives helps the reader and writer establish the empathy required for good communication.

Delayed Messages

When the reader is likely to find the subject content of the letter unpleasant, either because it will hurt his or her feelings or because it requires the reader to expend time or money, the situation calls for a delayed message. The subject content is delayed until the writer has prepared the reader for it psychologically. Letters that convey negative information and letters that persuade a reader to act require delayed structures.

Bad news and persuasive messages both require the writer to pay special attention to the feeling content of the letter. The human objective of the letter is still to establish empathy between the reader and writer—to convince the reader to agree with the writer. The subject content of such letters, however, is likely to anger, offend, or bore the reader.

When the subject of a letter is a point of disagreement, delay the disagreement by finding something you can agree with.

> You're certainly right about the kind of management
> problems facing modern businesspersons.

When the subject of a letter is that you can't—or won't—participate in something, delay the negative aspect by finding a compliment you can pay the reader.

```
Your idea for a fund-raising pancake breakfast is a good one.

Your clients would undoubtedly benefit from the communication
seminar you are planning, Ms. Schumacker.
```

When you're asking the reader to spend either time or money on something that will benefit you, give the reader a reason to act. Begin the letter by promising something that will benefit the reader more than the time or money you are going to ask for.

```
Are you tired of the same old daily grind?

Why throw money down the drain?

Could you use an extra four hours a day?
```

Delayed messages always begin with something to create empathy between reader and writer. The how, why, and what of the message are presented after the reader feels that the message contains something of value.

LETTERS WITH MORE THAN ONE PURPOSE

Many business letters have just one clear-cut objective. But many do not. When your objectives are completely unrelated, you are usually better off writing two separate letters, each with its own specific goal. When your objectives are related, however, you should combine them into a *mixed message*—a single letter containing two or more objectives.

In some cases the writer must select from two or more possible objectives the one that seems most important. For example, you may need to decide whether you should *inform* your readers that you are offering a new product or service, or whether you should *persuade* them to purchase the product or service. You may need to decide whether you should *inform* your readers of a delay in shipment, or whether you should *persuade* them to wait to purchase until you can fill the order.

In such cases, honesty usually dictates that you clarify the situation well enough to enable the reader to make the proper decision. When your reader has a choice, be sure to indicate what that choice is. Honesty, however, does not preclude your constructing your letter to emphasize the objectives that will be best for you. Take advantage of the extra attention your reader will pay to the beginning and ending of your letter to stress positive human elements and the business objectives you would like to achieve. Place negative information and the alternatives you wish to discourage in the middle of the letter.

In some mixed messages, both of your business objectives may be equally important, but the two objectives require different treatment because of the way your readers would react to the associated feeling content.

Your subject content may, for example, contain both positive and negative information. You may need to tell a reader both that you are sending part of his or her order and that the reader failed to provide sufficient information for you to complete the order.

Or your subject content may contain both negative and persuasive information. For example, you may need to inform your employees of a new method of submitting reports that will require more work of them and to persuade them to accept the new method because it will ultimately save the company a great deal of money.

Whenever you must combine objectives into a single message, put the emphasis on the aspects of the message that the reader will consider positive by placing them in the beginning and closing positions in the letter. Use the positive or persuasive aspects of the subject content to help you establish and maintain empathy with the reader in spite of the negative information that will be included.

Successful Messages

Successful messages achieve both business objectives and human objectives. Achieving these objectives requires planning. As tempting as it may be sometimes, business letters should not be written to accuse people of shortcomings, to argue, or to blow off steam. Business letters should be written to improve business—to help sell products and services—and to build goodwill between reader and writer.

Once the specific objectives are set, the letter should be planned to maximize the chances of the writer's achieving them. And regardless of the nature of the objective, the same general principles apply:

1. A letter is successful only if it accomplishes both the business objectives and the human objectives.
2. Material the reader will react to positively belongs at the beginning and the closing of the letter, where it will receive the most attention.
3. Material that the reader is likely to resist or find unpleasant belongs in the middle of the letter, where it will receive less attention.

SUMMARY

All communication occurs in a context that includes a history of previous experiences, a sender and a receiver, a reason for communicating, the sender's expectations, and the receiver's expectations.

Your audience should be a major influence on what you say in your letter and how you say it. Whether your audience will understand your message and cooperate with you will depend on how well you are able to anticipate your audience's expectations, attitudes, and needs.

Whenever you write a letter, you will need to adapt your message and writing style to communicate successfully with your particular reader. Knowing what to say in a letter is much easier when you can visualize the person to whom you are writing. Your readers' expectations will be based on their previous experiences with you and with letter writing. Your readers will also have emotional needs which will influence the way they respond to your message: (1) people are self-centered, (2) people are defensive, (3) people aren't perfect, (4) people need specific goals, and (5) people do the best they can.

You also need to consider the influence that each specific message will have on your readers. Each letter you write will have both a subject content and a feeling content. Successful communicators do their best to match the subject content and feeling content of the letter with their readers' expectations.

Every letter you write will have two general objectives: a business objective and a human objective. The business objective establishes the subject content of the letter, and the human objective establishes the feeling content.

Business objectives can be divided into three general categories: to inquire, to inform, and to persuade. These objectives will influence the way your reader will react to your message; to accomplish your purpose, you will need to consider your reader's probable reaction to these objectives.

When your letter will neither hurt your reader's feelings nor cause your reader to resist your message, you should emphasize the subject content of your letters. Letters that emphasize the subject content are called immediate messages. When your letter will either hurt your reader's feelings or cause him or her to resist your message, you should emphasize the feeling content of the message. Letters that emphasize the feeling content are called delayed messages.

Many business letters have just one objective, but many do not. When your objectives are unrelated, write two separate letters. When your objectives are related, however, you should combine them into a mixed message, containing two or more objectives.

Once the specific objectives are set, the letter should be planned to maximize the chances of the writer's achieving them.

EXERCISES

Review

1. What factors influence a reader's expectations, and how are these expectations influenced by the five basic emotional needs?

2. What is the difference between subject content and feeling content?

3. What are the three specific business objectives of letters?

4. What are the general structural principles of immediate and delayed messages?

5. What makes a mixed message different from a message with only one objective?

Problems

Analyze the reader's probable reaction to the subject content and the feeling content in the following letters:

1. We have received your letter in which you claim that five of the 14 Model 12 portable color televisions arrived in a non-functional condition.

   We are at a loss to explain how this unlikely event could have occurred because each television is tested thoroughly before it is crated in a specially designed, damage-proof carton. We suspect that faulty handling in your store is responsible for the trouble.

   Since you have been a good customer of ours, however, we are willing to send you five more Model 12 televisions, and we will do so as soon as you return the televisions which you claim are defective.

2. Your letter has been forwarded to this office for reply. I'm very sorry that five of the 14 Model 12 portable color televisions arrived in unsatisfactory condition, and I apologize for the inconvenience this has caused you.

   Since you have been a good customer of ours, we are sending you five additional Model 12 televisions, assuming, of course, that you will return the five which were probably damaged in shipment.

   Again, I apologize for all the trouble this has caused you, and I assure you that in the future, all television sets will be examined thoroughly so an event of this magnitude will never occur again.

3. You will receive replacements for the five Model 12 portable color televisions by Tuesday, 15 December.

    When the carriers arrive, simply give them the original color televisions. We will examine the sets thoroughly to see what caused the trouble, and as soon as we know the cause, we'll let you know. Thank you for bringing the matter to our attention so quickly. Your promptness will help us give you better service.

    The enclosed brochure on the Model 12 television is new. I'm sending you 100 along with the new Model 12 televisions for free distribution to your customers. Should you need more before your next order, call me collect at (415) 967-4419.

4. I'm sorry to have to tell you, but your application for employment at Universal Products has been turned down.

    Of all the people I interviewed, I thought that your qualifications were best. It seems, however, that our personnel people preferred some of the other candidates. I can't understand why you weren't selected.

    I certainly hope that you'll find success elsewhere and that you'll continue to purchase our fine merchandise. If you have any questions about this matter, do not hesitate to contact me at your earliest convenience.

5. Your application reveals many fine qualities, Mr. Knapper. Your resume shows you to be a well-organized, experienced person.

    As you'll recall from our interview, the job of Manager, Education and Training, for Universal Products is one that requires extensive knowledge of communication and media presentations. Because your education and experience are both primarily in personnel management, we have narrowed our final choice to three other candidates.

    I did enjoy meeting you and discussing our needs and your goals. Universal will automatically keep your application on file for six months. Please write before 1 April should you wish us to keep your application in our active file.

4. Elements of Effective Letters

Objectives

After you have read this chapter, you should be able to

1. Identify and explain the six elements of effective letters.
2. Explain how to achieve these six elements in your writing.
3. Define and illustrate you-attitude and positive tone.
4. Control emphasis and subordination in your letters.
5. Use the six elements of effective letters in your writing.

After you have analyzed your audience, determined your purpose, and adapted the subject content and the feeling content to achieve your objectives, you are ready to consider the actual communication process. You are ready to begin selecting the words and forming the sentences that will make your ideas clear and desirable to your reader. Unlike interpersonal situations, in which the sender and receiver can use means other than language to help establish the empathy necessary for effective communication, written communication must establish empathy through the use of language alone.

In written communication, *how* something is said is frequently as important as *what* is said. The *how* controls the feeling content of the message, while the *what* controls the subject content. The elements of written communication that help us achieve both the how and what are frequently called the "Cs":

1. Clarity
2. Courtesy
3. Conciseness
4. Confidence
5. Correctness
6. Conversational tone

CLARITY

Which would you choose?

1. The choice of exogenous variables in relation to multi-collinearity is contingent upon the derivations of certain multiple correlation

coefficients.
2. Supply determines demand.

Clarity, the transfer of a writer's thoughts to a reader without mis-understanding, is the single most important factor in written communication. A misunderstood message is worse than no message at all. The foregoing example is an illustration of what can happen when an expert in a subject forgets that the audience may not have the same expertise.

One classic and often quoted illustration of miscommunication be-cause of lack of clarity involves a plumber and the National Bureau of Standards. The plumber had written to the Bureau to say that hydro-chloric acid was effective for cleaning out clogged drains. Someone at the Bureau replied in typical bureaucratic language.

```
The efficacy of hydrochloric acid is indisputable, but the
corrosive residue is incompatible with metallic permanence.
```

The plumber wrote back, thanking the Bureau for *agreeing* with him. Another member of the Bureau tried to straighten the plumber out with the following message:

```
We cannot assume responsibility for the production of toxic
and noxious residue with hydrochloric acid and suggest you
use an alternative procedure.
```

The plumber thanked the Bureau a second time, saying that he was getting fine results and that the Bureau should suggest the use of hydro-chloric acid to other people. Finally, the problem got passed to the de-partment head, who wrote:

```
Don't use hydrochloric acid. It eats the hell out of the pipes.
```

The first two bureaucrats did not analyze their audience well enough to communicate a clear message. They selected words that were clear enough to them without thinking about whether the plumber would also know the words. The department head saw the communication problem from the plumber's point of view and selected words that would be effective in that particular context.

Because a message that is not clear to a reader cannot possibly com-municate the writer's intentions, clarity is the writer's first responsibility. Only after the writer is absolutely certain that the message—especially the subject content of the message—will be clear to the intended receiver, should the writer begin to analyze the reader's probable reaction to the message and adjust the feeling content accordingly. The first—and most important—task of a writer is to be understood. Clarity depends essentially on the right word in the right place at the right time.

The Right Word

As the plumber story illustrates, certain words will be unfamiliar to some people. In general, short, familiar, everyday words communicate more effectively than longer, less well-known words. It's true, of course, that a well-educated audience will have a better-developed vocabulary than a poorly educated audience, but even the best-educated audience will not appreciate having to struggle with your vocabulary. Choose the short, simple word rather than the long, complicated word.

Complicated word	Simple word
ameliorate	improve
interrogate	ask
cognizant	aware
consummate	complete

In addition to examining your writing to eliminate words that may be unfamiliar to your audience, you should check to make sure that the words you have selected will mean the same thing to your audience as they do to you. Words have both denotations (dictionary meanings) and connotations (associated, personal meanings). The words *inexpensive* and *cheap* can both denote the same thing, but their connotations are decidedly different.

For most people, *inexpensive* simply means low in cost while *cheap* means poorly made or a poor value. Many words have connotations that are fairly well agreed upon. The neutral word *smell*, for example, has synonyms with both positive and negative connotations. Compare *odor*, *stink*, and *stench* with *aroma*, *fragrance*, and *bouquet*. Many words, however, have associated meanings that vary greatly from person to person. For example, depending on family background and income, *inexpensive* could mean anything from $1 to well over $1,000.

The word *friend* may mean an intimate companion to one reader, a casual acquaintance to another, and a Quaker to yet a third. In fact, it may have all three meanings for the same reader depending on the context in which the word is used. That the writer means a particular thing by a particular word is not a guarantee that the reader will also attach the same meaning to that word.

While it is impossible for a writer to preclude a reader's private interpretations and associated meanings for words, a writer should attempt to select words that will result in a correct interpretation of the message as a whole when they are considered together in a particular context. By selecting the right word, the writer reduces the number of possible interpretations; and by placing that word in the right context, the writer further reduces the possibility of miscommunication.

Because nouns and verbs carry the essential information in your sentences, pay particular attention to the words you have selected to serve as subjects and objects and to show action. These words should be concrete and specific rather than abstract and general. Being specific—specificity—is an important aid to clarity because specific language enables the reader to visualize the action of your letter, and it also creates believability.

General: This television set is high quality.

Specific: All components in this television meet or exceed government specifications for use in manned satellites.

Always give exact facts, figures, details, explanations, and examples. Use specific words rather than general ones.

General	Specific
soon	15 March, tomorrow
number	nine
city	Atlanta
contact	call, write, visit
somebody	Dr. Kitty Locker
dog	Fido
high profits	a 42 percent markup
our product	The Norton Blender
a magazine	*Woman's Day*

Abstract	Concrete
Consideration was given	I considered
Prior to the termination of your policy	Before your policy ends
My analysis of your situation	I think that
The electrical potential may be injurious	Danger. High Voltage.

The Right Place

The kinds of sentences you put your words in are also an important consideration in achieving clarity. The easiest sentences to read and to understand are short, simple sentences using active voice in the past, present, or future tense, and making an explicit statement. While it's true that to avoid monotony, sentence length should be varied (see page 72), short sentences are easier to read and are therefore usually clearer than long sentences. Use short sentences for your main ideas, and place supporting information in the longer sentences.

The simple tenses—past, present, and future—are also clearer than the compound tenses: present progressive, past progressive, future progressive, present perfect, past perfect, and future perfect. When possible, use the simple tenses in your letters. Naturally, some ideas require the compound tenses, and you'll need to use them to express your idea accurately. When you are using a compound tense, make sure that your tense progression is logical and clear so that your reader will know when each event takes place. Figure 4-1 illustrates the verb tenses.

TENSE	USES	EXAMPLE
Present	action occurring now	I go
Present progressive	action ongoing in present	I am going
Past	action completed in the past	I went
Past progressive	action ongoing in the past	I was going
Future	action that will take place in the future	I will go
Future progressive	action that will be taking place	I will be going
Present perfect	action completed at the present	I have gone
Past perfect	action completed before another past time	I had gone
Future perfect	action that will be completed in the future before a certain time in the future	I will have gone

Figure 4-1. Verb tenses.

Active voice also aids clarity by simplifying the description of the events taking place in your letter. Because active voice is more direct and focuses on people in action, it is easier to read and to understand than passive voice.

Active: You will receive the items listed on the enclosed invoice by 7 April.

Passive: The items listed on the enclosed invoice will be received by you by 7 April.

Your message will also be clearer if you state it explicitly rather than implicitly. That is, your message should be definite and straightforward, leaving nothing implied or assumed. Using specific and concrete words, as we discussed previously, will help you make explicit statements.

Implicit: The items you ordered will be arriving soon.

Explicit: You will receive the Minolta SRT-101 and POW-27 electronic flash attachment in about 10 days. I shipped them by United Parcel this morning.

An explicit statement, however, not only includes the *who, what, when,* and *where* of the events described in your letter but also answers the important question *why.*

Implicit: It will be to your advantage to order now.

Explicit: By ordering now, you will receive two issues absolutely free.

A message should be implicit rather than explicit only when the explicit statement would be unnecessarily negative or offensive.

Explicit: You forgot to specify the color and size of the shirt you ordered.

Implicit: The shirt you ordered is available in several colors and sizes. Please use the enclosed card to indicate your choice of color and size.

In the foregoing example, the explicit statement is unnecessarily negative because it accuses the reader of being forgetful. The implicit statement is clear because it asks for a specific action, yet it avoids a direct accusation.

Explicit: Spring is coming. You'll need to replenish your stock of Lawnamatic Power Mowers now.

Implicit: Because spring is coming, the demand for Lawnamatic Power Mowers will soon be increasing. To ensure beating the spring rush, use the enclosed order blank to replenish your stock.

In this example, the explicit statement offends the reader by focusing on something that is obvious to the reader (spring is coming) and by giving the reader instructions for managing his or her business. The implicit statement subordinates the obvious (*because* spring is coming) and emphasizes *why* rather than *how* the reader should act.

The Right Time

Clear writing depends on logical structure. A clear message requires a definite beginning, middle, and end. While the general structure of a letter will be either *immediate* or *delayed* depending on the reader's probable reaction to the content of the message, the reader still needs to feel that the message begins at the beginning, has a definite direction, and concludes at the end.

To provide this kind of structure, the beginning needs to place the message in a particular communication context. In old-fashioned business letters, writers would say, "I have received your letter of the 12th," or "In reference to your letter of the 5th instant," to place the communication in context. Modern business communicators try to place their letters in context without being so stilted or obvious.

```
Here, Clyde, is the information you requested. Model Y, which
you asked about, offers many advantages.

You're right to expect many years of trouble-free service from
Guardsman surveillance equipment.
```

Once the message as a whole is placed in a specific context, each of the elements within the message should also be placed in its own specific context. The basic structures for immediate and delayed messages discussed on pages 41-44 help a writer provide a logical presentation for messages in general. In addition to providing a logical structure, however, a writer also needs to provide the reader with a unified message that moves clearly from point to point.

A unified message has continuity of thought and singleness of purpose. Unity, like structure, requires planning. You should group related ideas together and then arrange the groups into a logical sequence. Eliminate ideas that do not pertain to either your subject content or your feeling content. So that your reader will always know where your message has been and where it is going as you move from idea to idea, provide your reader with a clear, specific reference to the preceding idea or anticipate your next idea with an explicit statement of direction. The four principal ways of establishing the **unity**, **coherence**, and **transition** required for clarity are

1. **Repetition.** As you move from sentence to sentence, repeat key words or ideas or use pronouns to stand for key words and concepts.

```
You're right to expect many years of trouble-free service from
Guardsman surveillance equipment. Our equipment provides. . . .

Congratulations on your upcoming graduation. To celebrate this
joyous occasion. . . .
```

   Repetition of sentence structure can also be used to give added emphasis to the ideas put into parallel structure.

```
First, examine everything you've written for clarity.
Second, examine everything you've written for proper tone.
Third, examine everything you've written for proper emphasis.
Finally, examine everything you've written for completeness.
```

2. **Cause and effect.** A second way of establishing unity, coherence, and transition is by showing a cause and effect relationship between two or more events. Words, such as *thus, therefore, due to,* and *because* indicate that one event is the cause of another. (Although some writers use the word *since* to indicate cause and effect, it is best used to indicate the passage of time.)

Because Fran bought 42 shares of American Business stock, Arno
purchased 45.

Because you said that I should take whatever steps were necessary to save the money, I assumed that I had the authority to
close the plant in Pontiac.

> Writers need to take special care with cause-and-effect statements.
> Whenever you use this method to establish transition, make sure
> that the one event is the cause of the other. The following statement
> may or may not be true:

The low morale on the assembly line is due to the antiquated
equipment.

> Until the writer knows for certain that the antiquated equipment is
> the direct and only cause of the low morale, the sentence should be
> less absolute.

The low morale on the assembly line is at least partly due to
the antiquated equipment.

The low morale on the assembly line may be due to the antiquated
equipment.

3. Comparison/contrast.   You can also establish unity, coherence,
and transition by pointing out the similarities and differences between two concepts or events.

Douglas McGregor and Rensis Likert have both developed
methods of analyzing managerial characteristics. McGregor
calls the basic styles of management Theory X and Theory Y,
and Likert calls them Job-centered and Employee-centered.

The difference between a university and a trade school is that
the university is more concerned with the why than the how,
while the trade school is concerned more with the how than with
the why.

Business communication is more complicated than other kinds of
communication because the communicators must not only worry about
communicating, but they must also worry about the cost.

Foreign cars offer better gas mileage than American cars, but
American cars offer more options.

4. Time and place.   Because our thinking ability depends so heavily
on chronological order, it is very important for a reader to know
when and where the events you refer to in your letter are taking
place.

You should receive the marble faun Tuesday, 17 November. I
shipped it by United Parcel this morning.

By making your references to time and place as specific as you can, you are establishing a logical order for events that will be clear to your reader.

```
Before deciding which car to purchase, I looked at Pintos,
Vegas, VW Rabbits, and Hondas. After driving the cars, I
narrowed the possibilities to either the Pinto or the Rabbit,
and I made my final decision on the basis of the Rabbit's
better gas mileage.
```

Time and place transitions are best indicated by steps 1, 2, 3, or points 1, 2, 3. Frequently you can use a *numbered list* to show that the steps or points are related parts of a larger whole.

As is true for all communication situations, the *timing* of letters is very important. It is timing that places a letter in a particular communication context, and it is timing that makes immediate or delayed presentation more effective in a particular situation. When you tell your reader a particular fact is important, your message and its parts should be timed for greatest success.

But providing the right word in the right place at the right time involves more than timing. It also involves the guarantee of timeliness that results from the writer's providing information that is both in time and complete. The reader should know what is happening, when it is happening, and who is to do what next.

Because business letters are always written for a specific purpose, it is important that they be written in time for the reader to take whatever action is necessary. As a general rule, **you should answer any letter you receive within 48 hours** even if you can't provide a complete answer and will need to write again later. When you are initiating the correspondence, be sure to allow your reader plenty of time to complete any action you are requesting. To make it easy for your reader to reply, consider dividing complex tasks into a series of simpler items so the reader can reply to each item separately.

Readability

A clear message is also a readable message. Readability is a broad term, and most of the suggestions we have offered thus far are concerned with the readability of your letters. Using short paragraphs (see pp. 18-19), placing key ideas in short sentences (see pp. 52-53), and using specific language (see pp. 52-54) all contribute to the readability of a letter.

To increase the readability of your letters, remember that no one likes to work at understanding a message. Readers appreciate receiving letters that they can read quickly, easily, and without misunderstanding. Keep your message as simple, straightforward, and uncluttered as you can without talking down to your reader. If you can't read your message quickly and easily, your reader probably won't be able to either. Obviously, you'll have to spend a little extra time and put forth an extra effort to ensure a readable letter. But the time you invest in achieving a clear, readable letter will provide a much better return than the time you would spend in writing a second letter to clarify the first.

COURTESY

A courteous message takes its reader's feelings and point of view into consideration. A courteous message, like a courteous person, is polite, considerate, and emphatic. Courtesy is extended primarily through the feeling content of your letter, though the subject content may well be influenced by your consideration for your reader. The basic assumption of a courteous message is that writer and reader are both reasonable people with good intentions who can solve problems, make decisions, and understand each other without resorting to any form of psychological or physical force. Courtesy depends on the writer's understanding the reader's viewpoint and on the assumption that the writer and reader are able to cooperate as equals.

The You-Attitude

The questions we listed in Chapter Three (see pp. 37-40) are designed to help you see a business communication situation from your reader's point of view. Empathy is only possible when you can see a situation from the other person's perspective. A courteous message has empathy; it takes the reader's thoughts, feelings, and point of view into account. It anticipates the emotional response a reader might have to a message and takes the steps necessary to help the reader feel good about the message. It anticipates the reader's needs and questions and offers explanations and answers before the reader is even aware that they are necessary.

The basic message structures are designed to help you establish empathy with your reader even when your message will be unpleasant for your reader. Remember that your letters will be more successful if you **put your readers and their problems first**. Your readers will expect you to have legitimate interests and concerns, and it is courteous for you to specify where your own interests lie. Your readers, however, will appreciate your showing them, by emphasizing the ways in which they will benefit, that you do understand their needs.

One measure of the you-attitude is to count the *you's* and compare that number to the number of *I's* and *we's*. When you can, make the reader or the reader's company or product the subject or object of your sentences. While this will not automatically guarantee the you-attitude, such an attitude is impossible to achieve without using second-person pronouns.

Writer viewpoint: We are happy to have your order. We shipped it this morning.

Reader viewpoint: You will receive your solid walnut desk by Tuesday, 23 October.

Writer viewpoint: We have been making Model 12 radios for over ten years.

Reader viewpoint: Your new Model 12 radio is backed by ten years of testing and improvements.

Writer viewpoint: I have ten years' experience in management.

Reader viewpoint: My ten years' experience in management would enable me to make an effective contribution to your planning board.

Writer viewpoint: We regret that you've had so much trouble with your Soob automobile, and we apologize for not solving your problem sooner.

Reader viewpoint: You were right to ask me about the troubles you've been having with your new Soob. Thank you for giving me this opportunity to answer your questions.

When the statement is accusatory, however, the you-attitude is better served by omitting the you. In such cases passive voice and implied statements show more empathy.

Writer viewpoint: You neglected to take care of the requirements of Form 123.

Reader viewpoint: To enjoy the full benefits of your new ABC, you should follow the procedures on Form 123.

Writer viewpoint: You failed to tell us the color of the dress you ordered.

Reader viewpoint: The dress you ordered comes in seven brilliant colors. Please indicate your choice on the enclosed card.

Writer viewpoint: Your conclusion is incorrect because our contract clearly states that. . . .

Reader viewpoint: Paragraph 7 of our contract seems to state
that. . . . Do you agree?

Writer viewpoint: You forgot to check the color coordinator
adjustment on the 24" television sets.

Reader viewpoint: The color coordinator adjustment on the 24"
television sets should be checked before
final assembly.

Each part of the letter presents certain hazards for the writer who
wishes to achieve the you-attitude. In the opening of the letter, writers
are frequently tempted to begin with a statement of what they have done
or why they have done it. Always attempt to use the word *you* early in
your first sentence. Avoid the *I* and *we* beginnings.

Writer viewpoint: I have approved your request to substitute
Coorson fire extinguishers for the
Lablatts extinguishers.

Reader viewpoint: Yes, you may substitute Coorson for the
Lablatts extinguishers.

Because the middle of the letter usually contains some kind of explanation, the writer is tempted to focus on the explanation and neglect the
way the reader is affected, which is naturally the thing of interest to the
reader. Remember to keep your reader in the picture by referring to him
or her—as the subject or the object of the sentence when possible—or
by referring to the reader's company or product.

Writer viewpoint: Lewis and Clark has been in the expedition
business for more than 100 years. We've
guided successful tours of Asia, Africa,
Europe, and the Louisiana Territory. We make
every effort to cover all the points of
interest, and we always offer first-class
accommodations.

Reader viewpoint: With Lewis and Clark, you will receive a
guarantee backed by more than 100 years of
successful expeditions. Whether you wish to
see Asia, Africa, Europe, or the Louisiana
Territory, Lewis and Clark is able to provide first-class accommodations close to
all the points of interest.

The ending of the letter presents problems because the writer is tempted to focus on his or her own needs rather than focusing on how the
action, information, or decision will influence the reader.

Writer viewpoint: I need this information by March 12 to make
a decision about where we should have our
convention.

Reader viewpoint: Your answer by March 12 will enable me to
consider your hotel as a possible conven-
tion site.

Writer viewpoint: I will be glad to receive your future orders
and look forward to doing more business
with you.

Reader viewpoint: Thank you for your order. When we can serve
you again, call our toll-free number (800)
432-3295.

Cooperation of Equals

Correspondents should usually consider each other—and treat each
other—as equals. Business relationships are interdependent: sellers can't
exist without buyers; buyers can't exist without sellers; manufacturers
can't exist without distributors; distributors can't exist without manufacturers. And regardless of the goods or services being offered, one of
the parties in any business transaction can always do without these
goods or services or can go elsewhere. Any letter you write should demonstrate your knowledge that the reader is doing business with you
because he or she has *chosen* to do business with you at that particular
time.

Anything that interferes with the one-to-one relationship of equals is
usually detrimental to the success of a letter. Even when you are writing
the same letter to many people—as with direct mail advertising and
some insurance correspondence—you can still write to one person at a
time. Use a form letter to reduce the expense of writing, printing, and
mailing the letters, but use *you singular* rather than *you plural*.

Poor: Dear Stockholder:

This letter is to inform you of an important
change in our policy concerning dividends.

Better: Because you own stock. . .

in Gibson Guitars, we're writing to let you
know about an important policy change.

The reader will still recognize your letter as a form letter and will
understand that it is going to a number of other people, but your letter
will be more effective because each of your readers will see that you
took the time to consider him or her as an individual rather than as a
member of a particular group.

In writing to one reader at a time, you show all your readers that you
respect them as individuals. It's also important that your language demonstrate respect for your readers and your expectation of mutual respect.

Your choice of words and phrasing reveals your attitude toward your reader, and expressed feelings of either superiority or inferiority will interfere with the success of your letters. The following negative emotions are the principal offenders:

1. **Indignation.** Do not let your emotions interfere with your ability to achieve a particular objective with your letter. Do not accuse the reader of a deliberate shortcoming or show resentment at having to write or explain a situation. The seemingly harmless statement "Your letter has been referred to this office for a reply" may imply that the writer resents having to answer the letter.

2. **Mistrust.** When you have a reason to doubt your reader, give your reason explicitly. When you are unsure of something, ask a question. Never use language that implies mistrust. The statement "You claim that five ceramic figurines were damaged in shipment" implies that the reader was lying about how the figurines got damaged.

3. **Paternalism.** Do not grant favors, give orders, or lecture your reader. The statement "We are pleased to grant you permission" places the writer in a superior position. The statement "You must complete the enclosed application and return it by Wednesday" implies that the reader is not free to choose an alternate course of action. The statement "You will need to stock more than one dozen Kingly Electric Blankets because they sell so quickly" implies that you know more about the reader's business than he or she does.

4. **Humility.** Do not place yourself in a position inferior to that of the reader. Remember that business relationships are interdependent, and your reader usually needs you just as much as you need your reader. The statement "I hate to bother somebody as important as you are with this little problem of mine" implies that the problem—and the writer—are not worth the reader's attention.

5. **Flattery.** No one likes a sycophant. Legitimate praise for a job well done is one thing, but do not try to win your reader with flattery. Give your reader credit for knowing how much praise is appropriate for a particular accomplishment, and give your reader credit for being able to recognize self-seeking motivation hiding behind unearned praise. The statement "You are *the only person in the United States who knows enough about television to . . .* " attributes a uniqueness to the reader that a reader with intelligence (and knowledge of other experts in television) would recognize as false.

CONCISENESS

In many ways, conciseness is an extension of the first two elements, clarity and courtesy. We are concise primarily to help make our message clear and to show consideration for our reader's time. A concise letter, however, is not necessarily a short letter. A concise letter is one that does not waste words. Make sure that each word and each sentence accomplish something for you. But in your effort to trim the fat from the meat of your message, do not forget that each letter has two objectives: a business objective and a human objective.

A letter cannot successfully accomplish its business objective without meeting the reader's human needs. Your readers do not want to wade through three or four pages when one will do, but neither do they want to feel as though you could hardly wait to get their letters out of the way.

Three Examples

Compare the following letters:

Wordy:

We're so glad that you've written your letter of the 12th to ask about our Jetliner service to Japan. I have your letter before me in which you ask whether we offer such a service and how much the cost would be for a party of two adults and three children for the Jetliner service to Japan.

Our Jetliner flights leave from San Francisco International airport at 12:00 noon every day, seven days a week. The flight time is about 16 hours, and the flight is nonstop from San Francisco to Japan. The airplane will land in Tokyo, and the cost for two adults and three children is only $3,700 for ten days.

You may reserve a reservation on our Jetliner service to Japan by completing the enclosed reservation card. We'll be glad to process your application when we receive a ten percent deposit of $370.

Too Brief:

The Jetliner service you asked about leaves San Francisco International airport every day at noon. The cost for two adults and three children is $3,700 for ten days. The flight to Tokyo takes 16 hours. Please complete the enclosed application and return it with your 10 percent deposit.

Concise:

The Jetliner service you asked about leaves San Francisco International airport every day at noon. The 16-hour flight is nonstop, and the airfare includes two dinners, a breakfast, and a lunch.

```
The cost of round-trip airfare, seven days in Tokyo, and the
extended tour of Honshu, including overnight stays in Yokohama,
Osaka, and Sakata, is $3,700 for two adults and three children.

Complete the enclosed application and return it with your deposit
of $370 to ensure reservations for the tour in June. Should you
have questions about the Jetliner service, about Japan, or about
your passport, just write. I'll be glad to help.
```

Wordy Expressions

As you can see from the foregoing examples, the wordy letter uses more words than necessary. It contains many redundancies—that is, the letter says the same thing two or three times. In the case of "reserving a reservation," the repetition is obvious. But many of the redundancies that make letters wordy have worked their way into the language in such a way that we use them unconsciously. The following are among the more common:

Wordy	Concise
the month of April	April
at the present writing	now
in the amount of	for
effect an improvement	improve
in the neighborhood of	about
new innovation	innovation
assembled together	assembled
exact replica	replica
true facts	facts
widow of the late	widow of
postponed until later	postponed
qualified expert	expert
entirely complete	complete
square in shape	square
basic fundamentals	fundamentals
the color red	red
a bad disaster	a disaster
the most unique	unique
first of all	first
in order to purchase	to purchase
needless to say	(omit)
it goes without saying	(omit)
there is, there are, it is	(omit)

Completeness

A concise letter is still complete. Examine your letters to make sure that you have covered everything you intended to cover and that you have provided sufficient detail for your reader to know what you expect of him or her. **Make sure the reader knows who is to do what next.** Ask yourself the following questions:

1. Have I answered all my reader's questions?
2. Have I anticipated questions my reader may have but forgot to ask?
3. Have I provided all the information necessary for my reader to make a logical decision?
4. Have I explicitly asked the reader to perform an action?
5. Is the subject content sufficiently clear to accomplish the business objective?
6. Is the feeling content suitable to accomplish the human objective?

CONFIDENCE

Your letters will be more successful when you show confidence in yourself, confidence in your reader, and confidence in your message. Optimistic letters do not neglect problems or negative factors; rather, they approach problems as solvable when reader and writer work together. Confidence is frequently called **positive tone**.

Confidence in Yourself

Confidence in yourself can only result from the feeling that you have made the best business decision possible. When you have faith in the fairness of your decisions and actions, it's easier to explain them without becoming defensive or apologetic. Show your reader that you are a decisive, positive, straightforward businessperson. Present your message with self-confidence so that your reader will understand and accept what you have to say. Structure your letter and select your words and phrases to emphasize the positive aspects of your message. Subordinate negative ideas as much as you can without sacrificing clarity.

Negative: We cannot comply with Part II of your request.

Positive: We agree completely with Parts I, III, and IV of your request. Because our delivery schedule is already established for the next fiscal year, implementation of Part II will begin next January.

Negative: I regret that you were caused such a terrible
inconvenience and hope that the enclosed
refund will restore your faith in Goldsmith
products.

Positive: You're right, Mr. Schneider. We inadvert-
ently overcharged you. The enclosed check
doesn't show it, but our face is red.

Your choice of words can indicate to your reader how you really feel
about yourself and your ability to get a job done. People with a negative
outlook on life frequently use negative words, such as the following:

can't	unfortunately	difficult	trouble
impossible	won't	misfortune	unable
unwilling	problem	regret	apologize
bad	inferior	damaged	no

People with confidence in their abilities to do a job and to do it correctly focus on *what* they can do and *when* they can do it. Realism dictates that problems and limitations receive the attention they deserve,
but confidence in yourself dictates that you look through the problems
and limitations and provide your reader with solutions and alternatives.

Confidence in Your Reader

As you assume the best from yourself, you should also assume the best
from your reader. Assume that your reader will do what is right until you
have absolute proof that he or she won't, and assume that your reader is
capable of overcoming obstacles. Naturally, confidence in your reader
does not include an automatic granting, without question or clarification,
of every request a reader might make. You should, however, always give
the reader the benefit of the doubt.

Don't say "no" when you can legitimately say "maybe."

Remember that your reader's perception of your situation and of the
communication context will not be the same as yours. Before you make
a decision that will affect your relationship with the reader, you should
try to see the situation from the reader's point of view. Be especially
careful to avoid words and phrases that imply that you doubt your
reader's truthfulness or ability to get the job done correctly.

You claim (state, imply, suggest) that . . .
If what you say is true . . .
We are at a loss to understand . . .
It's unlikely that your explanation is . . .
You forgot (failed, neglected) to . . .
You must (should, ought, need) to . . .

In addition to your expressing doubt, threats and bribes will also be offensive to your reader. Expressions that attempt to exert psychological force, grant undeserved favors in return for something, or appeal to the reader's worst motives will usually backfire.

```
This is done with the understanding that you will . . .
What would your neighbors think if you . . .
You will certainly regret. . .
Because you have been a good customer of ours, we are willing . . .
Even though you don't meet all of our requirements, we will . . .
How much would it be worth to you . . .
Great wealth can be yours . . .
Imagine everyone falling at your feet, willing to do whatever
     you ask . . .
```

Confidence in Your Message

You should also show confidence in your message. Spend the time necessary to ensure that your message accomplishes its business objectives *and* its human objectives, and avoid expressions which indicate that you don't believe that your message is clear or that your reader will accept it. **I hope**, **I trust**, **if**, and **why not** imply that your message has not done everything it should.

```
I hope that this letter answers all your questions.
Why not send in your order today?
I trust that this will prove satisfactory.
If you want to order, complete the order blank at the back
     of the brochure.
If you have further questions, do not hesitate to contact me.
```

Confident messages eliminate the implication of doubt.

```
I'm glad to have been of help.
To order, simply mark your choice and drop the enclosed card
     in the mail.
Call me again when I can help.
```

Overconfidence

While you are working to be confident, however, remember that overconfidence leads to presumptuousness, which is a violation of courtesy. Do not *presume* that your readers will act or think in a particular way just because you want them to. When your readers have a choice, make sure that you don't take that choice away from them. Acknowledge the choice, and make it sufficiently clear that the reader *can* choose.

Presumptuous: You must complete your application today.

Positive and courteous: By completing your application today, you will be assured a reservation for June 20.

Presumptuous: `Your inventory is not complete without one`
`dozen bottles of Flash perfume, so order`
`some now.`

Positive and courteous: `The combination of 42 percent markup and a`
`fast turnover would make Flash perfume a`
`profitable addition to your stock.`

CORRECTNESS

As an element of effective letter writing, correctness is an extremely broad term. On one level it refers to correct facts and figures, accurate statements, and explicit identification of assumptions and opinions. On another level it refers to correct spelling, grammar, letter mechanics, and language usage. It's obvious that without correct facts, figures, and statements, accurate communication is impossible. Businesspersons very early get in the habit of double-checking facts, figures, and statements.

The need for grammatical correctness, however, is not quite so obvious. Does it make a difference if you misspell a word or two and write run-on sentences as long as the rest of your letter is correct?

Yes, it does. Even though most readers will be primarily concerned with the content of your letters, they will expect grammatical correctness. Misspelled words, faulty punctuation, and awkward constructions will be barriers to communication. Your ability to use language correctly and to write a letter free from superficial errors is a nonverbal message that tells your readers that you are an intelligent, careful person who cares enough about them to pay attention to the details of your letter. Because your letters provide a lasting record of your abilities to think, write, and communicate about business matters, you should take the time to ensure correctness. Communication errors will undermine your business effectiveness.

That does not mean that you need to become a grammarian to communicate effectively. Unlike your high school and college instructors, business readers will not be making a deliberate search for mistakes. Concentrate on the basics:

1. **Spelling.** Misspelled words are the single most common error in business letters. We have found that our students frequently misspell the following words:

accommodate	benefit
business	congratulate
convenience	definite
embarrass	February
its (it's)	morale
opportunity	personnel (personal)

receive	recommend
separate	sincerely
sophomore	to (too, two)
writing	written

2. **Punctuation.** Review the rules for using commas, semicolons, and quotation marks.
3. **Subject-verb agreement.** Subjects and verbs must agree in number and in person.

```
The manager (singular) is (singular) quite young.
The managers (plural) are (plural) going to meet on Tuesday.
```

4. **Pronoun-antecedent agreement.** Pronouns and their antecedents must agree in person, number, and gender.

```
John (singular, masculine, third person) is pushing his
(singular, masculine, third person) product.

Susan (singular, feminine, third person) is pushing her
(singular, feminine, third person) product.

The company (singular, neuter, third person) is pushing
its (singular, neuter, third person) product.

The dealers (plural, common, third person) loved the new
displays we sent them (plural, common, third person).
```

5. **Tense progression.** Review the uses of the eight verb tenses (see Figure 4-1, p. 53). Use the simple tenses (past, present, and future) whenever possible. Make sure that the verbs used for each event referred to in your letter accurately depict the time appropriate for that event.
6. **Parallel construction.** Like ideas should be expressed in like grammatical structures. Pay particular attention to series, lists, appositives, and ideas preceded by correlative conjunctions (either . . . or, neither . . . nor, not only . . . but also).

Faulty Parallelism: Either he should quit his job or learn to operate the machine.

Parallel: He should either quit his job or learn to operate the machine.

7. **Correct placement of modifiers.** To avoid misplaced and dangling modifiers, place modifiers close to the word or idea that they modify.

Dangling: By working hard, the report will be finished soon.

Correct: By working hard, I will finish the report
               soon.

Dangling: I know a man who sells filing cabinets
              named Smith.

Correct: I know a man named Smith who sells filing
               cabinets.

Remember to proofread your letters. When correspondence has your name on it, it represents the best work you are able to do. If your secretary can't type a decent letter, that is still your responsibility, and your business associates will judge you—rather than your secretary—by the letters you sign.

CONVERSATIONAL TONE

Your writing style should be an extension of your personality, and your letters should read much the same way you would talk to your reader were you communicating face-to-face rather than by mail. Even though one of the main advantages of written communication is its ability to convey complex information better than oral communication, the best writing sounds comfortable and natural to the ear.

Inconspicuous Style

Your letter-writing style should be natural, conversational, unpretentious, and inconspicuous. Although your purpose for writing is to achieve specific goals, your writing style can be lively and interesting without detracting from the content of your message. Business letters are not scholarly dissertations, and your readers will be more impressed with your abilities as a communicator if they understand what you are saying than if you attempt to sway them with your vocabulary. Be especially careful to avoid legalese and business jargon.

Say this	Rather than this
tell	beg to advise
before, after	prior to, subsequent to
know	cognizant of
the enclosed booklet	please find enclosed
to use	in order to utilize
read	peruse
pay	remunerate

I would appreciate	thanking you in advance
try	endeavor
ask	interrogate
library	educational resource center
then	in that time frame
a possibility	a viable alternative
we, the company	the subject company
of, about	as to
about	in regards to
by parcel post	under separate cover
send it back	return same to this office
(omit)	this will acknowledge receipt
(omit)	please be advised that
finally	in the final analysis

In addition to the common phrases of legal and business language that too frequently are passed from generation to generation of letter writers, business jargon includes its own list of "in" words that can be every bit as offensive to some readers as teen-age slang is to those over 30. Such word usage is popular because it lets people sound knowledgeable without requiring them to be specific. Many words that fit into this category are perfectly good technical words that have been ill-adapted to nontechnical situations. Others have been created by writers to suit their own needs. The following are examples:

parameters	formalize
conceptualize	prioritize
systematized	contact (in place of write or call)
logistical	profitwise
consequate	employee-type
finalize	time-oriented
interface	impact (as a verb)

Words of this variety go in and out of fashion so rapidly that a current, definitive (authoritative and complete) list would be impossible. If you are tempted to use a word that you cannot define quickly and easily, you should suspect that the word may not mean to your readers what it seems to mean to you. Check the words in the foregoing list in the dictionary. How many can you find? How many mean what you thought they did?

Your writing will be both less conspicuous and more interesting if you find new expressions to replace common clichés. The following are only a few of the trite phrasings you should avoid.

bolt out of the blue	lock, stock, and barrel
hook, line, and sinker	fast as lightening

clear as crystal	hard as nails
pretty as a picture	good as gold
last but not least	sly as a fox
nose to the grindstone	shoulder to the wheel
green with envy	burn the midnight oil
first and foremost	father time
crack of dawn	sober as a judge
home sweet home	man about town
his true colors	generous to a fault

The trouble with such expressions is that they have been worn out with overuse, and now they have no real meaning. As is the case with legalese and business jargon, readers skip over trite figures of speech without paying attention to what you are trying to say. To prevent your style from creating a barrier to communication, say what you have to say simply, using fresh terminology.

Variety

Conversational tone, however, requires more than the elimination of jargon and pompous language. It also requires the same kind of variation and emphasis you provide naturally in oral communication. As you write, vary your words, sentence structure, and paragraph length to keep your message from becoming monotonous.

1. Rather than repeat the same word over and over, find acceptable synonyms, use pronouns, or restructure the sentence to avoid unnecessary repetition.
2. Most of your sentences should be short and direct, but if all your sentences are short, your writing will be choppy and your readers will think either that you're a simpleton or that you're talking down to them. Your sentences should average about 17 words.
3. The standard order for sentences in English is subject-verb-object. Use modifiers, subordinate clauses, and a mixture of sentence types to achieve variation.
4. Your first and last paragraphs should be about four lines long. Your middle paragraphs should be about eight lines. Paragraph length, however, should be varied—letters written entirely in four-line paragraphs would have a choppy appearance, and letters written entirely in eight-line paragraphs would appear heavy and uninviting.

Emphasis

Oral communication allows you to emphasize the ideas you wish to stress by raising your voice, gesturing, and soliciting feedback from your audience to confirm the importance of a point. The means of controlling emphasis in written communication are the following:

1. **Placement.** As we've already mentioned (see p. 42), *where* you place an idea in a letter influences the amount of attention a reader will pay to it. The opening and closing paragraphs usually receive the most attention.
2. **Proportion.** How much space you give an idea indicates your degree of concern. Take extra time—and space—to explain the ideas that are most important to you and to your reader.
3. **Language.** Sentences are most emphatic when they are about people doing things. They are less emphatic when they have ideas as subjects. Nouns should be concrete and specific, and verbs should be in the active voice for greater emphasis. Remember that some ideas should be subordinated rather than emphasized. If the reader will find part of your message accusatory or negative, you should subordinate that part by using abstract, general words and passive voice.
4. **Mechanics.** You can also emphasize important ideas by underscoring, using capital letters, using color, putting key ideas in a numbered list, and surrounding main points with extra white space.

YOU ARE WHAT YOU WRITE

Even though the contents of your letters are more important to your readers than your manner of expression, your letters should show that they have been written by a warm, breathing, feeling human being. All readers appreciate a personal, individualized touch. In today's mechanized, synthesized, computerized society, it is especially important that letter writing be human rather than technological communication.

Use letter writing as a means of establishing a human relationship. See your readers first as people and second as customers, dealers, or manufacturers. We are all people first, and our roles in society are merely superimposed on our basic, common humanity. Help when you can, and when you can't, be nice about it. We are not suggesting that you should let the feeling content of the letter detract from the subject content, but we guarantee that your letters will be more successful if they are obviously written from one human to another rather than from one machine to another.

Do not let our suggestions—or those of anyone else—for effective letters become formulas or law. Do not let your old letters—or anyone else's—become models for all future correspondence. Learn the basic principles well enough to apply them automatically in your own business communication, but retain enough flexibility and independent thinking to be able to adapt to situations which may require a unique approach.

SUMMARY

In written communication, how something is said is frequently as important as what is said. The *how* controls the feeling content of the message, while the *what* controls the subject content. The elements of written communication that help us achieve both the *how* and the *what* are frequently called the Cs: clarity, courtesy, conciseness, confidence, correctness, and conversational tone.

Clarity, the transfer of a writer's thoughts to a reader without misunderstanding, is the single most important factor in written communication. Because a misunderstood message is worse than no message at all, use the short, simple word rather than the long, complicated word. Ask yourself whether the words you have selected will mean the same thing to your reader as they do to you. Choose concrete and specific words rather than abstract and general words. The easiest sentences to read and to understand are short, simple sentences using active voice in the past, present, or future tense. Clear messages require a definite beginning, middle, and end. Four principal ways of establishing the unity, coherence, and transition required for clarity are repetition, cause and effect, comparison/contrast, and time and place.

A courteous message takes its reader's feelings and point of view into consideration. A courteous message, like a courteous person, is polite, considerate, and empathetic. Empathy is only possible when you can see a situation from the other person's perspective. Your letters will be more successful if you put your readers and their problems first. It's also important that your language demonstrate respect for your readers and your expectation of mutual respect. Your choice of words and phrasing reveals your attitude toward your reader, and expressed feelings of either superiority or inferiority will interfere with the success of your letters. The following negative emotions are the principal offenders: indignation, mistrust, paternalism, humility, and flattery.

Conciseness is an extension of the first two elements, clarity and courtesy. A concise letter is one that does not waste words. Make sure that each word and each sentence accomplish something for you.

Your letters will be more successful when you show confidence in yourself, confidence in your reader, and confidence in your message. Present your message with self-confidence so that your reader will understand and accept what you have to say. Structure your letter and select your words and phrases to emphasize the positive aspects of your message. Subordinate negative ideas as much as you can without sacrificing clarity. Assume the best of your reader. Assume that your reader will do what is right until you have absolute proof that he or she won't, and assume that your reader is capable of overcoming obstacles. Also show confidence in your message. Spend the time necessary for your message to accomplish its business objectives and its human objectives. While you are working to be confident, however, remember that over-confidence leads to presumptuousness, which is a violation of courtesy.

Correctness refers not only to correct facts and figures, accurate statements, and explicit identification of assumptions and opinions, but it also refers to correct spelling, grammar, letter mechanics, and language usage. Concentrate on spelling, punctuation, subject-verb agreement, pronoun-antecedent agreement, tense progression, parallel construction, and correct placement of modifiers.

Your writing should be an extension of your personality, and your letters should read much the same way you would talk to your reader were you communicating face-to-face rather than by mail. Your letter-writing style should be natural, conversational, unpretentious, and inconspicuous. Your style can be lively and interesting without detracting from the content of your message. Be especially careful to avoid legalese, business jargon, and clichés. Your letters should show that they have been written by a warm, breathing, feeling human being. All readers appreciate a personal, individualized touch. Use letter writing as a means of establishing a human relationship. See your readers first as people and second as customers.

EXERCISES

Review

1. Define the six elements of effective letters.

2. What is you-attitude? Positive tone?

3. What are the four principal means of establishing unity, coherence, and transition?

4. How do you control emphasis in written communication?

5. Why do readers appreciate letters that demonstrate a personal touch?

Problems

Revise the following sentences to eliminate the negative elements.

1. You failed to tell us which model desk you wanted.
2. We are sorry, but we cannot ship your order until August 2.
3. There will be a delay of four weeks before we can fill your order.
4. I cannot be a speaker at your annual sales meeting because I will be out of town that day.
5. If you have any further questions, please do not hesitate to contact us.
6. You neglected to use the oil specified in the operator's manual, so we can't give you a refund.
7. We regret that you have had trouble with our machinery. Did you follow the directions in the operator's manual?
8. Because you don't have a steady job, we can't give you credit.
9. Your lamps were damaged in shipment because your truck driver drove the truck too fast and jarred the boxes.
10. You forgot to send your check with the order. When you send it to us, we'll ship your order, but not until then.

Rewrite the following sentences so that they emphasize the you-attitude instead of the we-attitude.

1. To help us fill your order, please send us the size for the sweaters you ordered.
2. We are happy to announce our grand opening, and we would like you to come and register for door prizes.
3. We shall ship your order as soon as we hear from you.
4. We permit a 2 percent discount for cash payments.
5. We have enclosed an envelope for your convenience.
6. We welcome you as our client. If we can be of further help, please do not hesitate to call us.
7. We want to hear from our customers. Write to us and tell us how much you enjoy our products.
8. We have the finest merchandise in town; stop in and see us soon.
9. We want to congratulate you on the opening of your new plant.
10. We are glad to have your order for six Model 438 steel saws.

Rewrite the following messages to improve clarity, courtesy, conciseness, confidence, correctness, and conversational tone. Remember that you may need to change the basic structure to make the message effective.

1. The items which were ordered by you are going to be shipped sometime soon. They all have many fine features which you are sure to enjoy, and their efficacy is indisputable. If you have any questions about their use, do not hesitate to contact me at your earliest convenience.

2. We have received your letter in which you claim that the crystal wine glasses you ordered from the House of Glass arrived broken.

   We are at a loss to understand how this unlikely event could have happened. The House of Glass has over 100 years of packing and shipping experience, and we have never had a complaint. We always use great care in packing and shipping.

   You also state that the glasses had been packed without adequate packing material, which we find hard to believe because all our packing material--we now use a special polystyrene plastic of our own manufacture--is added by hand.

   Since you have been a good customer of ours, however, we are willing to take back the wine glasses which you claim are damaged and replace them.

3. I know it's a terrible imposition of me to ask a person as important as you to do this, and I apologize for bothering you.

   Again, I regret very much having to ask, but if you could please do us the inestimable honor of speaking at our annual conference, we would be forever in your debt.

   Won't you, therefore, write me and say yes? I apologize again for any inconvenience this may have caused you, and I hope you'll forgive me for it. If you have any questions, do not hesitate to contact me.

4. I have your letter before me and I'm happy to answer it for you. You asked me about our company policy on preparing checks written by our company.

   Effective July 1st and thereafter, because of the request by our company president and the company's Board of Directors, checks written in the amount of over one thousand dollars must be co-signed by the controller of our company in addition to the signature of the head of the accounts payable department.

   We take this necessary precaution so that in order to prevent misuse of our company checks and funds we have two signatures which would help to alleviate this misuse of company funds and checks.

   If you have any further questions you would like to ask us, do not hesitate to contact us.

For each of the following clichés, substitute an original expression.

better late than never

burn the midnight oil

bit off more than they can chew

the last straw

bright as brass

clear as crystal

fair and square

shake a leg

in the final analysis

by hook or by crook

Find an easier, more direct way to state the following:

"The emotional intensity factors of my cognitive areas have been evaluated; and the resultant data suggest the conclusion that my conceptualization of the factors of your personality structure, and its continued proximity to my own, are of significant quantitative value to my sustained happiness level rate."

5. Getting Ready to Write

Objectives

After you have read this chapter, you should be able to

1. Solve a written communication problem by achieving both the business objective and the human objective.
2. Analyze a letter-writing situation according to the letter's purpose, the reader's point of view, and the elements of effective letters.
3. Coordinate the purpose, plan, and content when writing business letters.

In Chapters Three and Four we discussed several of the preliminary steps you need to take in solving written communication problems in business. Stated simply, you need to

1. Know the specific purpose or purposes of your letter.
2. Understand your reader's point of view.
3. Use the elements of effective letter writing as they apply to your purpose and reader.

When you are faced with a specific business communication problem, answering these questions may not be easy at first. The following procedure and examples will show you how to apply the steps we've outlined thus far in analyzing and solving business communication problems.

PROBLEM SOLVING

Because a business communication "problem" is not solved unless the communicator achieves both the business objective and the human objective of the situation, both objectives require specific attention. And frequently the situation is more complex—and requires more attention—than is first obvious. For example, place yourself in the following communication context:

You have been having trouble starting your new, imported car in cold weather. The dealer has been very helpful in trying to solve this problem but hasn't been successful. The dealer has written and telephoned the U.S. distributor to find out what the factory recommends but so far hasn't been able to get anything specific. The dealer thinks that a letter from you would help get a faster response from the distributor. Because you are eager to have the problems corrected, you write to the distributor and send a copy of the letter to the dealer.

How do you determine what points to include in your letter, and how do you determine how to arrange those points for greatest effectiveness? First, you analyze the communication context by asking yourself the following questions:

1. What is the letter's purpose?
2. What is my reader's point of view?
3. What is necessary to achieve the six elements of effective letters?

The Letter's Purpose.   As you'll recall from our discussion in Chapter Three, each letter has two categories of purposes: business objectives and human objectives. You need to consider both.

1. Your business objective is to obtain the information that will help your dealer help you.
2. Your human objective is to establish empathy with the distributor so that the spirit of cooperation will prevail.

Your Reader's Point of View.   To your reader, your problem—and your dealer's—is just one among many. It is probably being considered by someone, but it may not be a high-priority problem. Your dealer has already written and telephoned about it, so the distributor may feel a little resentful that you are writing. But it is in the distributor's interest to help solve your problem, and you can probably help speed up the process by reminding the distributor that the problem is sufficiently important to receive immediate attention.

The Elements of Effective Letters.   After you have analyzed the communication context, ask yourself what information, language, and organizational pattern are required to achieve the six elements of effective written communication.

1. **Clarity.**   What information do you need to include to be clear? Exactly what do you expect your reader to do? What is the specific problem? What language and vocabulary should you use?

2. **Courtesy.** Get the distributor's name from the dealer, and use it. Take your reader's point of view into account. Remember that the reader is not responsible for your problems, but that it is in the reader's interest to help you. Express yourself using "reader viewpoint" language (see pp. 58-61). Avoid accusing the reader of not working quickly enough, and avoid expressing negative emotions (see p. 62). Do you give the dealer proper credit?

3. **Conciseness.** Your reader will not have time for a long letter. Don't include extraneous material. Focus on the problem and what should be done about it rather than on how frustrated or angry you are. In your desire to be brief, however, do not overlook the need for achieving the human objective. Make sure you have provided all the information your reader will need to provide a solution to your problem. Be complete.

4. **Confidence.** Assume that your reader is willing to do whatever is necessary to help you solve your problem. Use positive language throughout, but avoid giving orders.

5. **Correctness.** Do you have specific dates and an accurate record of what the dealer has already tried?

6. **Conversational Tone.** Does your finished letter read naturally, as though you were holding a friendly conversation with the distributor about your problem? Have you arranged your message to provide reader interest and proper emphasis?

After you've considered each of the foregoing steps, you'll end up with a letter something like this:

Dear Mr. McCarty:

The subject line identifies the problem.

SUBJECT: Starting a 19_ Renabbitt in Cold Weather

The "name" opening places the letter in a specific context and shows that you and the dealer are cooperating rather than arguing.

My Renabbitt dealer, Hermann Bussmann of Bussmann's Renabbitt in Joplin, Missouri, suggested that I write to you about the problems I've been having starting my 19_ Renabbitt in cold weather.

Provide the necessary explanation in the secondary position. The distributor may know most of this already.	When I first purchased the Renabbitt in October, the car started quickly and easily every time. When the weather turned colder in late November, however, starting the car in the mornings has become nearly impossible. The critical temperature seems to be about 20 degrees. Once the car has been started and has warmed up, restarting is no problem.
Provide the specific details so that the reader knows what has already been done.	Since the starting problem developed, Bussmann's has replaced the battery, tuned the car twice, and replaced the fuel pump. Nothing has helped. Mr. Bussmann thought that you might be able to provide some pertinent information.
Close by letting the reader know who is to do what next.	I would certainly appreciate it if you would investigate the starting problem and suggest possible causes and cures.

The preceding letter is simple, straightforward, courteous, and concise. It should result in an answer that will either help or promise to help. Many problems, however, are more complex. Your first letter, for example, might not get results. Your second letter might have to be more complex. Some problems of business communication require both a more complex analysis and a more complex solution. Place yourself in the following communication context:

You own a small ceramics business specializing in high-quality dinnerware. Some of your dinnerware is sold by a few quality stores across the country, but most of your products are made to order and sold directly to customers who appreciate fine craftsmanship. You have received a letter from a new, very wealthy and influential customer stating that her shipment—a $3,500 order for a handmade 5-piece place setting for 12—was completely ruined in transit. She has requested replacement in six weeks so that she can use the dinnerware for an important party where the guests would all be potential customers for your quality ceramics.

The shipment was insured for $500, and because of the care you take with packing, you question whether the entire shipment could possibly have been damaged. Until now, you've never lost more than a few pieces of any one shipment in your 15 years of doing business. Your carrier, however, inspected the damage and reported that the packing crates were "in bad shape" and has agreed to pay you the $500.

You can't possibly duplicate the entire shipment in six weeks because each piece must be hand turned on a wheel (and you must produce at least 25 to end up with 12 that are close matches), given time to dry, individually glazed, and kiln fired twice before you can crate and ship them.

Obviously, this is a rather nasty problem; fortunately, most letter-writing problems aren't this complex. But all problems in business correspondence are solvable with the same kind of analysis.

The Letter's Purpose.   This letter actually has several purposes. (It is a *mixed message*. See pp. 44-45.)

1. You must inform the reader that you will replace the entire shipment. The carrier said the shipment was a total loss, so you have no choice.
2. You must inform the reader that you are unable to replace the entire shipment in six weeks.
3. You must inform the reader how much of the shipment you can replace in six weeks and when you can replace the remainder.
4. You must retain the reader's goodwill even though you suspect that she is being less than fully honest with you.
5. You need to find out whether she has sufficient good pieces from the first shipment for you to provide enough replacements for use at the dinner party.

Some of these purposes are strictly business objectives. Some are human objectives in that they are likely to evoke an emotional response in the reader. The reader, for example, will be disappointed that you can't replace the entire shipment in six weeks, and she would be angry if you accused her of having some good pieces left. You need to consider which objectives are strictly business and which have sufficient feeling content to deserve special treatment.

Your Reader's Point of View.   Your reader probably doesn't have a good idea of how time consuming it is to produce ceramic dinnerware. She undoubtedly thinks that six weeks is ample time for you to complete the order. If the reader does possess some good pieces from the first shipment, she probably feels entitled to keep them without paying for them because of the irritation she has been caused. Your reader would undoubtedly like to have the special dinnerware for use at the party and might be willing to cooperate by telling you which pieces are absolutely essential and which can wait—if you can ask her without implying that she has good pieces from the first shipment and is trying to cheat you.

The Elements of Effective Letters.   Because of the complexity of this problem, it is going to be more difficult for you to achieve clarity, courtesy, conciseness, confidence, correctness, and conversational tone. Your reader will need to know something about how ceramic dinnerware is made if she is to understand why you can't replace the entire shipment in six weeks. But she is more interested in her problem than in yours and won't want to hear too much about turning, glazing, and double firing. Note the elements in the following example:

Dear Senator Jones:

The beginning con-centrates on feeling content rather than on subject content.	Thank you for writing so promptly about your dinnerware. We have already begun duplicating your order and will work as quickly as we can without sacrificing quality.
The explanation is given before the subject content and is connected to a reader benefit.	As you may know, our handcrafted dinner-ware and other specialty cermaic products must receive careful, individual atten-tion at each stage of their production from artisans who care about quality workmanship. The kind of quality you ex-pect requires us to produce more than twice the pieces actually purchased so that we may sell you only those pieces that are truly perfect.
Clarify what you can do. Stress the reader benefit as-sociated with the delay.	In the next six weeks we will be able to manufacture and ship duplicates of about half the pieces in your original order without sacrificing quality. It will take us another six weeks to produce the re-mainder. Because you would like to use the dinnerware for the party you are having, we will concentrate on producing those pieces that will enable you to set your table with elegance.
Clarify what you are doing. Try to talk the reader into cooperating.	We have begun work with the dinner plates and will have all 12 finished in plenty of time. Please use the enclosed card to indicate your priority for completion. Because each piece is individually pro-duced, we do not have to work in lots of 12. Should 6 or 8 of one item be enough for the purposes of your party, we could produce 6 or 8 now and the remainder later.
Assure the reader that she will receive a complete dupli-cate set. Remind her to complete and return the card.	We will, Senator Jones, work as quickly as fine craftsmanship permits, and you'll receive a complete set of the dinnerware you ordered. When we receive your instruc-tions, we'll do everything possible to finish the essential items in time for your party.

COMBINING PURPOSE, PLAN, AND CONTENT

All business letter writing situations can be analyzed according to the foregoing method. And, as infinitely varied as the possibilities are, all business letters should answer the same general questions and contain the same basic elements. Check every letter you write for answers to the following questions:

1. Is the letter structured to emphasize its main purpose?
   a. What is its business purpose?
   b. What is its human purpose?
2. Does the letter have secondary purposes?
3. Does the letter take the reader's point of view into account?
   a. What does the reader already know?
   b. What does the reader want to know?
   c. What is the reader hoping to hear?
4. Does the letter contain enough information to be clear?
5. Does the letter maintain a courteous tone throughout?
6. Is the letter concise?
7. Is the letter grammatically, mechanically, and factually correct?
8. Does the letter express confidence in the reader and the message without being overconfident?
9. Does the letter have a pleasant, conversational tone?
10. Have you specified how your reader will benefit from your message?

It may seem as though checking each letter you write against these objectives would be a terribly time-consuming process—one that will rob your letters of creativity and naturalness. Actually, the reverse is true. Having specific questions to answer will greatly reduce the time it will take you to write effective letters. And, by making sure that you have answered each of the questions in a letter, you will frequently avoid having to write a second, follow-up letter to clarify points you may have neglected in your first letter.

As a writer of business letters, you owe it to your reader to write interesting, conversational letters. You need to remember, however, that most business letters do not require creativity to be interesting. The content and purpose of your letter should receive the reader's attention. You do not write business letters to entertain. You write them to convey information to your reader quickly, clearly, and pleasantly. Your letters will be successful and interesting when you concentrate on achieving the business and human objectives inherent in the communication context.

SUMMARY

To determine what points to include in your letter, and to determine how to arrange those points for greatest effectiveness, you need to analyze the communication context by asking yourself what is the letter's purpose, what is your reader's point of view, and what is necessary to achieve the six elements of effective letters. All business letters should answer the same general questions and contain the same basic elements. By making sure that you have answered all the questions in a letter, you will frequently avoid having to write a second, follow-up letter to clarify points you may have neglected in your first letter.

You owe it to your reader to write interesting, conversational letters. The content and purpose of your letter should receive the reader's attention. Your letters will be successful and interesting when you concentrate on achieving the business and human objectives inherent in the communication context.

EXERCISES

Review

1. How do you determine what points should be included in your letter?

2. What must you consider to coordinate the purpose, plan, and content when writing business letters?

Problems

Analyze the following communication situations according to (a) the letter's purpose, (b) the reader's point of view, and (c) the elements of effective letters.

1. I like to fish. I usually go up North every summer to fish. There are some lovely lakes there and these lakes have some lovely fish in them that I would like to catch in the summer when I go up North. Because I like to fish up North every summer, I need a three-room cabin where I can sleep at night. I heard you had some nice cabins to rent that are near the lake. How much are they? I want to stay for one week. Usually I like to stay for one week the first week of August. Do you have a cabin available the first week of August?

2. We're sorry we cannot give you a refund. The shirt you purchased from us was new when you bought it from us. We can't help it that you found a hole in the pocket of the shirt. You should have looked at the merchandise before you bought it. Next time you come to our store, look at our well-made slacks. I bet you could find a pair that would match that shirt of yours that has a hole in the pocket.

3. I am president of the Altrusa Club in Goshen, IN. This is a
   professional women's service club. We do many good things for
   the city of Goshen in the state of Indiana. We meet the first
   Monday of every month. Sometimes we meet twice a month. Sometimes we meet at noon. Most of the time we meet at six for
   dinner at some restaurant in Goshen. We usually have a social
   hour before the dinner hour if we meet for dinner. After the
   dinner, we have a speaker. We get our speakers from all over--
   anyone who will give us a talk. Could you give us a talk? You
   can talk on any subject you like. Since we don't have any funds
   to pay you, would you mind if we just served you the dinner free.
   Can you give us a talk the first Monday in June. If you come before 6 p.m., we'll buy you a drink before dinner. You can talk
   for about 45 minutes. We might have some questions after the talk.
   If you have any questions, feel free to contact us. We sure would
   like for you to be our speaker. Thanks a whole bunch.

4. I would like to take this opportunity to introduce myself. I am
   a 1975 graduate of Central Michigan University. I am currently
   enrolled in the department of Counseling and Personnel here at
   Western Kentucky University. It gives me great pleasure to
   assume the responsibilities of Coordinator of Campus Visits in
   the Undergraduate Admissions Office.

   I am a native of Dearborn, Michigan, and a graduate of Fordson
   High School. After graduating from Central Michigan, I was an
   elementary school teacher before beginning graduate school in
   January, 1977.

   I would like to take this opportunity to reacquaint you with
   our campus visits program. The Undergraduate Admissions Office
   will again be providing regularly scheduled campus tours orig-
   inating from the office reception area on Monday, Wednesday,
   and Friday at 10:00 a.m. and 2:00 p.m. for prospective students
   and/or visiting dignitaries. If this time is inconvenient, a
   special tour may be arranged upon seven days' prior notice.
   We hope that you will utilize our campus tour program, whenever
   you have occasion to entertain campus visitors. If I can be of
   further assistance, please do not hesitate to call me at the
   office.

PART TWO
Specific
Message Types

6. Requesting Information, Goods, or Services

Objectives

After you have read this chapter, you should be able to

1. Apply the general structure for all inquiries to orders, direct requests, invitations, and direct claims.
2. Write a letter ordering items.
3. Write a letter requesting information.
4. Write a letter of invitation.
5. Write a letter requesting a refund, a replacement, or an adjustment.

Letters that request goods, services, or information are known as *inquiries*. Most inquiries are letters your readers will welcome because your request will give them the opportunity to sell goods or services, build goodwill, or share information about something of common concern. Because inquiries are almost always well received, you should use an immediate structure, placing an important business objective in the opening sentence.

The writer's main problem with letters of inquiry is providing the specific details necessary for the reader to perform the requested action. You must make the opening question or request absolutely clear; you must include all the information your reader needs to help you; and you must also clarify who is to do what next.

GENERAL STRUCTURE AND CHECKLIST

The general structure for all inquiries is as follows:

1. **Immediate Beginning.** Begin the letter with a specific request for what you want or with your most important question. Your request places your message in a specific communication context.

2. **Explanation.** Explanations always belong in the secondary position. Your reader needs to know the purpose of the letter *before* reading about who you are and why you want something. As you explain, be sure to keep your reader in the picture by referring to the reader and the reader's product, company, or service.

3. **Secondary Matters.** Other questions or specifications should follow the explanation. Using a numbered list for secondary matters will help focus the reader's attention on each item separately. When each question requires its own explanation, however, do not use a numbered list. Instead, put each question and its explanation in a separate paragraph.

4. **End Dating.** Many inquiries should conclude with an end date or deadline which lets the reader know when you need the information or goods. Be polite and give a reason to justify the deadline. When end dating is inappropriate, be sure to let your reader know who is to do what next.

ORDERS

Buying and selling by mail is big business. Sears, Penneys, Marshall Fields, Montgomery Wards and many other retailers use catalogs and the mail to sell their goods and services to those customers who do not have direct access to their stores. Also, publications ranging from the *International Yellow Pages* to *The Whole Earth Catalog* to the classified sections in popular magazines encourage ordering by mail. Most of the companies that sell by mail provide customers with well-designed catalogs, order blanks, and reply envelopes.

When an order blank is not available, you need to make sure that you include all the specific information your reader will need to fill your order quickly and easily. Remember that your offer to buy will constitute a contractual agreement, so it is important that it be accurate and complete. Check for the following:

1. Have you specified that your letter is an *order* and not a request for information? The best beginning for an order is "Please send me . . . ."

2. Have you specified the goods completely? In addition to the quantity, catalog number or issue, name of the product, and price, you need to specify all the details appropriate for each particular item, including color, size, grade, machine or part number, pattern, finish, style, or weight. Omission of these details will delay your order.

3. Have you specified how you intend to pay? When you enclose a check or money order, be sure to say that the enclosed check is in payment for the goods. When you request credit, make sure that you provide the appropriate credit information with the order.
4. Have you specified where, when, and how you want the goods shipped? Each year retailers receive hundreds of orders complete with money orders (and sometimes even cash) which do not provide either a shipping or a return address.

Note the way the following letter illustrates the foregoing points:

```
Please send me the following items listed in your spring/summer
19_ catalog:

1 Large 41 K 48537 F Navy Creslan acrylic sweatshirt
       with zipper                                          $ 6.99
1 Large 41 K 47241 F Faded blue hooded sweatshirt             8.99
1 Medium 41 K 45161 F Navy sport trunks                       6.99
4 51 K 12335 F 32 x 32 Blue denim bib overalls,
       $11.97 ea.                                            47.88
                                                            ───────
                              Tax                             3.54
                                                            ───────
                              Total                         $74.39

The enclosed check for $76.39 includes shipment by parcel post.
I would appreciate receiving the merchandise by 27 June because
I will be leaving on vacation on that date.
```

When no catalog or parts list is available, you need to take special care in supplying the reader with the specific information necessary to determine your particular needs. In some cases you may have to order a catalog or parts list before you can order the item you need. You can't expect your reader to know exactly what you want unless you can specify exactly what you want. Even in the most complicated case, however, you can expect your reader to be helpful; if you provide sufficient information for the reader to help at all, you'll eventually receive what you need.

DIRECT REQUESTS

Companies welcome letters asking about their goods, services, operations, and (usually) personnel. Such letters offer businesses an opportunity to make a sale or to build goodwill. Individuals welcome letters asking about matters of common concern, especially when they have particular expertise in the area asked about. Direct requests are immediate messages because the reader is already motivated to reply. Because the human objective is not a problem, the business objective receives the main emphasis.

The business objective in direct requests, as it was with orders, is letting the reader know what you want in a way that will permit a quick and easy reply. Direct requests should always begin with your most important question.

```
What are the differences between the 16-foot Hydrofoil and the
16-foot Hydroplane sailboats? I saw your ad in the December Sail.

How much experience does a hobbyist need to assemble a Heathkit
GR-101 color television set?
```

Your opening question should always be specific. Whenever possible, you should include some reference to let the reader know what you already know by mentioning where you saw the ad or heard about the product, service, or subject. Vague questions and requests result in vague answers. For example, were you to ask, "Please send me any information you have about the GR-101 television set," your reader might not provide an answer to the question about how much experience was required for assembly. A general request for additional information should only *follow* all your specific questions and explanation:

```
In addition to answering the foregoing questions, please send me
any other information you think I would find helpful.
```

The only way to ensure that you will receive the information you want is to ask for it, and the information you want most should be specified in your opening sentence—the sentence that will receive your reader's closest attention. What if you don't know exactly what information you want? Guess. Ask the question you think will *most likely* give you the information you want. Keep in mind that the most important question is almost never cost. When you are tempted to use cost as your lead question, ask a question related to *value* instead.

```
What is the guarantee covering the Autolectric Zig-Zag sewing
machine you advertised in the July issue of Family Circle?
```

Ask about cost later in the letter.

After you have asked your most important question, provide the reader with the explanation required for a complete answer. Your opening question will place your letter in a specific communication context, and your explanation, in the secondary position, will not only make sense, but also serve as transition to your other questions. Use a numbered list for your questions when your questions require no explanation or when they can be made specific and clear by a single, inclusive explanation following your opening question. If each question requires a separate explanation, a numbered list will lose its impact. When possible, arrange your letter so that you can use a numbered list.

By asking specific questions and emphasizing each one separately, you greatly increase your chances of receiving specific answers to each question. You will also increase your chances of receiving the information you want when you want it by setting and justifying an end date—or deadline—for your reader's response.

Of course, if you have no need for the information by a specific date, you should not manufacture an end date and justifying reason. Show confidence in your reader's willingness to respond promptly.

You should also assume that the reader will be well acquainted with the benefits of a cordial response, so you don't need to draw special attention to those benefits. Also, do not thank the reader "in advance" for cooperating. If the reader's reply warrants a word of thanks, send it *after* you have received the reply. Thanking in advance is discourteous because it shows that the writer assumes that the reader will respond in a particular way.

Compare the following examples:

Ask the main question. Tell your reader how you learned about the product, service, or idea.	What are the differences between your Model L-100 and Model M-101 word processing centers? One of these models, advertised in the July issue of Business Education Forum, may be the answer to my problem.
Explain your situation fully, but keep the reader in the picture.	I own a small direct-mail advertising company, employing five copywriters, a business manager, and three secretaries. Because all of our work must be carefully done, one of your word processing centers may provide the solution to our extensive editing problems. Currently all the written work produced by the copywriters and the business manager is dictated to one of the secretaries. The material is transcribed in draft form and may undergo more than ten revisions before it receives approval. We have reached the point where we may need to hire an additional secretary to keep up. Would either the Model L-100 or M-101 help us reduce the time we spend revising?
Put the secondary questions in a numbered list.	Answers to the following questions would help me decide about purchasing one of your machines: 1. How much of an increase in efficiency can we expect with a word processing center? 2. What is the total cost--including tax, shipping, and service contract--for each model? 3. How much training is required for dictating and transcribing with the machines?

4. Are both models compatible with
   IBM Mag Card II and Memory Typewriters?

5. Which machine would you recommend
   for my office?

Ask for other infor-
mation **after** you've
asked specific
questions.
Set and justify an
end date. DO NOT
THANK THE READER
IN ADVANCE.

In addition to answering these questions, please send me any other information you think might help me. As our
busiest season begins in August and I
will need to decide whether to hire
additional help by 1 July, I would
appreciate receiving your reply by
15 June.

Ask a main question
first.
Tell the reader how
you know about
the product.

How much experience does a hobbyist
need to assemble a Heathkit GR-101
color television set? A friend of
mine owns a GR-101, and I'm very impressed by its performance.

Explain the
situation,
subordinating
elements the reader
already knows.

Although your catalog states that only
experienced kit builders should attempt
to build Heath color televisions, my
friend thought that I would be able to
do a satisfactory job by taking my time
and paying close attention to your directions.

Explain each
question
separately.

Admittedly, my kit building experience
is limited. Nearly 20 years ago I built
a Heath hi-fi, and almost as long ago I
built a Heath portable radio. I can
still make a decent solder joint. Do
you think that I should attempt a GR-
101?

If you think that I should practice kit
building first, will you recommend
Heathkit projects that will prepare me
for building one of your color televisions?

Would reading a book on electronics
help? Can you recommend a book that
would be useful?

Encourage a
prompt response
even when you
don't need the in-
formation by a
specific date.

May I have your answers to these questions soon? I'm eager to begin.

Requests for information about people present special hazards for letter writers because of the so-called "sunshine" laws. Information that formerly could be kept confidential is now available to the person asked about and, in some cases, to other interested parties as well. The most common requests for information about people are concerned with employment, school applications, and credit. In each case the person asking for the information should be asking only because he or she has a legitimate interest to protect, and the person asking should also be prepared to keep the information received as confidential as the law will permit. Whenever you inquire about somebody, you should protect yourself and your reader as much as possible by observing the following precautions:

1. State whether the person being inquired about authorized your request for information.
2. State whether the person being inquired about has waived right of access to the reply.
3. State whether you will keep the information confidential.
4. Show your reader that you are asking for the information because you have a legitimate interest to protect.

The following example illustrates these points:

Please use the space below to give us your opinion of Linda M. Mishall's chances of succeeding in graduate school. She listed you as a reference on her application for admission and has waived right of access to your apply.

When Linda was your student, did she demonstrate superior academic skills?

Did she do her work promptly?

How would you rate her in comparison with the other students you have taught: upper 5 percent, upper 10 percent, upper 25 percent, upper 50 percent?

Would what you predict are her chances for success in graduate school?

Please use the reverse of this form to give us any other information you think will help us decide about Linda's admission to our graduate program. We will keep your reply strictly confidential.

INVITATIONS

Most invitations are a special category of direct requests because it will be primarily to the reader's advantage to attend or participate in the event you are planning. When it is primarily to your advantage—as when you invite a "name" speaker to appear before your group—you will need to write a persuasive request according to the principles presented on pp. 152-57. When invitations are special goodwill messages involving no persuasion, they use an immediate presentation. State the main idea, the invitation, first. Explanations and a request for confirmation (when necessary) follow. Most invitations are fairly short because the advantages for the reader are obvious.

The invitation, including purpose, place, and time.	Please be our special guests at the grand opening of the Houston Renaissance Center on Saturday, 14 November, from 10:00 a.m. until 2:00 p.m.
Explanation and details.	Celebrate our opening with us by enjoying a champagne brunch and tours of the 67 stores and specialty shops in the Center.
	The enclosed SPECIAL GUEST identification tags will admit you and your family to the Houston Renaissance Center and the champagne brunch free of charge.
Request for confirmation is last.	Come celebrate with us. To help us prepare for you, please call 789-6000 and let us know whether you plan to attend.

DIRECT CLAIMS

Requests for refunds, replacements, and adjustments on goods and services are usually immediate messages because companies know that the only way they can stay in business is by satisfying their customers. Reasonable requests are granted automatically as long as the letter writer is careful to communicate the reasonableness of the request. Only when your reader has demonstrated an unwillingness to respond to reason or when your request is based on your emotions rather than logic should you write a persuasive request. Persuasive requests are discussed on pp. 152-57.

When you make a claim, your basic assumption should be one of confidence in your reader. You should assume that your reader will do the right thing if you explain the situation accurately. Remember that your reader is *not* personally responsible for the trouble you have had with the company's product or service, and remember that your reader—and the reader's company—will most likely be glad to receive information that will permit an improvement in goods and services.

Always make your claim as specific and as definite as you can. When you know what the problem is and what is required to correct it, state the problem explicitly—giving all the details—and ask for the specific correction. When you do not know exactly what is wrong, explain the situation as best you can. The sample letter shown on pp. 81-82 is an example of a direct claim when the writer does not know what specific action will solve the problem. The following example shows you the basic technique for writing a direct claim letter when you know exactly what you want.

Begin with a straightforward, positive description of the problem. Assume that your reader wants to help.	The Ranger pocket calculator in the attached package does not compute problems containing the number 8 correctly. I purchased the calculator at K-Mart two weeks ago, and the store manager thought that I would receive faster service by sending the calculator to you.
Give as complete an explanation of the problem as possible.	While it always solves other problems correctly, even simple problems containing 8 result in a wrong answer. A simple problem like 2 x 8, for example, can result in an answer as low as 9 or as high as 108.
Close by asking for what you want. If you need it by a certain date, say so.	As I am an engineer and need a reliable calculator every day on my job, I would appreciate a prompt replacement.

SUMMARY

Letters that request goods, services, or information are known as inquiries. Inquiries are well received by the reader because they give the reader an opportunity to sell goods or services, build goodwill, or share information about something of common concern. The writer's main problem with all letters of inquiry is to provide the specific details necessary for the reader to perform the requested action.

The general structure for all inquiries is (1) immediate beginning, (2) explanation, (3) secondary matters, and (4) a justified end date.

When ordering by mail, be sure to (1) specify that your letter is an order, (2) describe the goods completely, (3) state how you intend to pay, and (4) specify where, when, and how you want the goods shipped.

Direct requests—letters asking about goods, services, operations, and personnel—are immediate messages because the reader is already motivated to reply. Begin direct requests with your most important question. After you have asked your most important question, provide the reader with the explanation required for a complete answer. Use a numbered list for your questions when they require no explanation or when your questions can be made specific and clear by a single, inclusive explanation following your opening question. To increase your chances of receiving the information you want when you want it, end date and justify your request.

Most invitations are a special category of direct requests. When invitations are special goodwill messages involving no persuasion, they use an immediate presentation. State the main idea—the invitation—first, and follow it with the explanation and a request for confirmation.

Requests for refunds, replacements, and adjustments on goods and services are usually immediate messages because companies know that the only way they can stay in business is by satisfying their customers. When you make a claim, explain the situation accurately. Make your claim as specific and as definite as you can. State the problem explicitly— giving all the details—and ask for the specific correction or an investigation.

EXERCISES

Review

1. What is a letter of inquiry? Give four examples.

2. What type of structure—immediate or delayed—does a letter of inquiry have? Why?

3. State the general structure for all inquiries.

4. When ordering by mail, you should check your letter for four specific points. What are they?

5. Why do requests for information about people present special hazards? What precautions should you observe?

Problems

1. You and your family are planning a one-week vacation and would like a two-bedroom cabin with kitchen, living room, and bath facilities. Because the prices listed in the brochure you received are reasonable, write to Scott's Ranch, 1457 Trail Lane, Estes Park, CO 80517, and make reservations. Ask for a confirmation.

2. Order for your firm, Flair Electric Company, 1204 Milham Road, Hayden, AZ 85235, three Model 239 executive desks, three Model 485 swivel chairs, and one Model 7896 conference table from Bon Office Furniture, 126 Peekstok Road, Phoenix, AZ 85000. The desks are walnut and sell for $675 each. The chairs sell for $110 each. The 12-foot conference table sells for $789. Have the items shipped COD by Ready Truck Lines.

3. Look over the advertisements in a trade publication or a discount catalog and write a letter ordering four or five items. Be sure to supply all the necessary information. Send a check for the items and specify how you want the items shipped.

4. As purchasing agent for Arco Chemical Company, 324 Second Avenue, Midland, MI 48640, order five tons of used paper from Ferlinsky Paper Company, 2450 Hillcrest Street, Midland, MI 48640. You want a ton delivered each Monday for five consecutive weeks. You ask for the 5 percent discount for ordering five tons or more.

5. Write to the personal shopper at Marshall Fields, One State Street, Chicago, IL 60610, and order three pairs of white Isotone (one size fits all) gloves for Christmas gifts for your friends. Items are to be sent three weeks before Christmas, gift wrapped, and accompanied with a greeting card. Your charge plate number is 460-14-649. Names and addresses of your friends are

Mrs. Agnes Daly, 4514 Ellenita Avenue, Tarzana, CA 91356

Mrs. Lorraine Blaha, 1521 Merriman Drive, Glendale, CA 91202

Mrs. Joann Reiter, 815 Valley Lane, Lockport, IL 60441

6. You're the program chairperson for the American Business Communication Association's annual convention to be held December 27-30. Write the Hilton Inn, 301 Park Avenue, New York, NY 10022, and request information about convention facilities. Because you expect about 500 conventioneers, ask if the Inn would be able to accommodate a group this size. What's the seating capacity of each of the conference rooms? Does the Inn have facilities for serving a banquet? What recreational facilities are available? What is the cost for a single room? double? suite?

7. As president of the Alpha Kappa Psi Fraternity, 735 Fraternity Village Row, Bloomington, IN 47401, write an inquiry to Nicholas Brothers, 1012 Avondale Drive, Louisville, KY 66450, asking about trophies. Ask for descriptions, sizes, and prices. You need to have all the trophies in time for your awards banquet. Is there a special charge for engraving?

8. You are the office manager of Kiep Associates. You've been looking over your various office forms and realize that they are inefficient. You decide to write a letter to Tripleday Brothers, 222 Douglas Avenue, Marietta, OH 45740, asking for prices and possible delivery dates for the following forms: petty cash disbursements, expense report sheets, requisition slips, interoffice memorandums, and telephone message pads. Ask if the forms come in various colors? Sizes?

9. You're interested in certificates of deposit. You've heard that the First National Bank in Los Angeles, CA 90242, offers them at interest rates from 8 percent to 9 percent. Write the bank and ask what the minimum deposit is and the number of years the certificates must be held. Is there a penalty for early withdrawal of the money?

10. As Ms. Quinta Mandez, real estate agent, write a letter inviting a prospective home owner to an open house on Sunday, May 5, at two o'clock. The house is at 2317 Outlook Street, Pittsburgh, PA 15202.

11. Sandra Kasan, 1409 Morrow Lane, Jud, ND 58454, ordered three $6.50 red cotton T-shirts for her nieces as follows: one size small with the printed name Judi; one size medium with the printed name Becki; and one size large with the printed name Kathy. When Sandra opened the package from the Teen Tee-Shirt Shop, Box 12144, Atlanta, GA 30319, she found one size small with the printed name Becky, one size medium with the printed name Kathi, and one size large with the printed name Judy. Write the shop and ask for replacement of the shirts with the correct sizes to correspond with the correct spelling of the names. Also ask the shop what you are to do with the three shirts that are unacceptable because of improper sizes and incorrect spelling of names.

12. Paul Apson purchased an 8-oz. package of dried apricots for $1.59 from a local supermarket. When he arrived home and opened the package, he found black "specks" that resembled dead insects. Rather than return the package to the local supermarket, Paul asked you to help him write to the distributor, Foodco Products, 1494 Riverview Drive, Cincinnati, OH 45200, and ask for an explanation and a refund. Write the letter for Paul and return the empty cellophane package with the price marked on it.

13. Sheila Rae Thompson, 411 Whitney Avenue, Louisville, KY 40200, received her monthly statement along with duplicate copies of gasoline and oil purchases from Stancrest Oil Company, 9034 Broadway, Centerville, NE 68724. After checking her copies with the duplicates, Sheila found a copy dated March 19 for $9.58 that she couldn't match with her receipts. On the copy she noticed the name Sheila Mae Thompson, 902 Roseland Street, Louisville, OH 44641. Return a copy of the duplicate to Stancrest and ask for an adjustment on your next statement.

14. Perhaps you (or someone you know or heard about) have been dissatisfied with a recent purchase. Write a claim letter to the company explaining the situation and requesting action.

15. Write the Foline Linen Company, 200 Spring Street, Dayton, OH 45401. You recently purchased a 52″ × 70″ red and white checkered

polyester kitchen tablecloth. After the first washing (you followed the washing instructions explicitly), the colors ran together. You want a replacement. Return the original tablecloth to them.

16. Using the information in Problem 15, write to Foline Line Company and request a refund.

17. Write a letter to a college, university, or graduate school of your choice and ask for information about a specific course of study. Ask about the cost of a school catalog and about the method for ordering one.

18. As personnel director of Rimco Manufacturing Company, 3311 Douglas Avenue, Memphis, TN 38118, write to Professor Jamie Summers, Department of Business and Technical Writing, Rensselaer Polytechnic Institute, Troy, NY 12181, and ask about Mark Goodwin, a graduate of Rensselaer, who listed Dr. Summers as a reference. You not only want to know what kind of student Mark was, but you'd also like to know how well Dr. Summers knows Mark, how well Mark gets along with others, and something about Mark's attitude toward school and work.

7. Conveying Positive Information

Objectives

After you have read this chapter, you should be able to

1. Apply the general structure for all positive messages.
2. Provide positive information clearly, concisely, and completely.
3. Write positive acknowledgments of orders and requests.
4. Write business announcements and special goodwill letters.
5. Write a letter of apology.
6. Write a letter of transmittal.

Letters conveying information, often called **informational messages**, are either reader initiated (your reader wrote to you first and asked for something) or writer initiated (you are writing first and your reader does not expect your letter). In either case, when your message contains information to which the reader will respond in a positive way, you should use an immediate structure and present the business objective first. Human objectives are not critical in positive messages because the reader will welcome the information.

As is true for inquiries, the writer's main problem in writing letters containing positive information is conveying the information clearly, concisely, and completely. The opening should be direct, placing the letter in a specific communication context, and positive. The letter needs to answer all of the questions the reader may have asked and should anticipate questions that may occur to the reader after the letter is received. The closing of the letter should either make clear who should do what next or help establish a better business relationship.

GENERAL STRUCTURE AND CHECKLIST

The general structure for all positive messages is as follows:

1. **Immediate Beginning.** Begin the letter either with a positive answer to a reader's question or with your most important item of

information. The first sentence should place the letter in a specific communication context.

2. **Explanation.**   When an explanation is called for, it should follow the important opening statement.

3. **Secondary Matters.**   Answer any questions your reader may have. In addition to specifically answering those questions your reader has asked, you should anticipate questions your reader may have, and you should provide answers for those questions your reader should have asked but didn't. Complete, thoughtful answers show your courtesy and willingness to cooperate. Your explanation and secondary matters should be arranged in a logical sequence, with explicit transition from point to point. Enumerated lists help in the same way they do in inquiries (see pp. 91-92).

4. **Positive Close.**   After reading your letter, the reader should know who is going to do what next. When no further specific action is required, you may either stop or use the closing element of the letter to improve the future of the business relationship. When it's appropriate, you should resell the product or service the reader has already purchased or sell the reader a new product or service.

ACKNOWLEDGMENTS

Acknowledgments are reader-initiated letters. In all acknowledgments, you are providing information about products, services, personnel, or some other item of mutual concern because your reader has asked you to provide that information. When a reader sends you an inquiry, you can respond in one of three ways: you can say yes, no, or maybe. When you decide to say yes, use an immediate structure to convey the positive answer. Even when you are not fully satisfied with your positive decision, take advantage of the situation—and your decision—to build a better business relationship. When you can't give an immediate positive answer, your acknowledgment is a negative message, which we will discuss in Chapter Eight.

When you can give a positive acknowledgment, your reader will obviously welcome your letter. Because the human objective is not a problem, place the main emphasis on the business objective of supplying the information, goods, or services the reader has asked about.

Acknowledging Orders

Readers expect prompt, courteous replies to their requests for goods and services, and by fulfilling that expectation, you can increase the positive feelings your readers have for you and your company. Acknowledgments of orders are either directed toward dealers or consumers, and—as is true for all business letters—the writer needs to adapt the letter to the particular needs of the audience. The writer also needs to consider the relative costs of the acknowledgments and the goods or services ordered. It makes no sense to send a $9 personalized acknowledgment for a $2 order. On the other hand, a customer who places a $200 order deserves a well-written, personal reply. Most orders should be acknowledged with a carefully prepared form letter that

1. Lets the reader know that the correct merchandise is on its way by specifying the items shipped and the method of shipment.
2. Expresses appreciation for the reader's business.
3. Suggests possibilities for future business transactions.

While printed forms, along with a specific invoice, can be used effectively, computerized letters and letters composed from standard paragraphs stored magnetically (as with IBM's Mag Card II typewriter) offer the possibility of greater personalization.

Whether you use one of the form replies or a personal letter, be sure to include as much you-attitude as possible. Resale material, which stresses the benefits of the goods or services already purchased, will help convince the reader that he or she made the correct decision. Sales material, which suggests that the reader would do well to purchase something else from you, helps reinforce the idea that the business relationship will continue.

Note the way the following examples adapt the general structure to meet the needs of different readers with orders of different sizes.

Printed Form:

Specify the merchandise and method of shipment.	You should receive the merchandise listed on the enclosed invoice in about ten days. We are sending your order by parcel post.
Express appreciation for the order. Stress reader benefits.	Thank you for your order. We're glad to provide the Mail Shopper service for you.
Resell the product, service, or your business in general.	In addition to the convenience of home deliveries, Mail Shopper gives you an absolute ten-day guarantee on all merchandise ordered through us. We want you to be fully satisfied.

Suggest possible future business. Sell a new product.	Next month, Mail Shopper's summer white sale will offer you the opportunity to stock up on sheets, pillow cases, and towels. All linens and towels listed in our winter catalog will be reduced 50 percent beginning June 1.
Suggest a specific and positive course of action.	Use the enclosed special "red flag" order blank to order the sale merchandise.

Individual Reply:

Specify the merchandise and method of shipment.	You should receive four dozen reams of the Royal Papers specified on the enclosed invoice early next week. As you requested, I sent them by United Parcel Service.
Explain the financial details.	Your total bill was $288, and the enclosed check for $22 is your refund. Because you paid in advance, you received our 3 percent cash discount, and we paid for shipping and handling.
Express appreciation for the order. Adapt the letter to the interests of your specific reader —dealer or consumer. Resell the product.	Thank you for your order. Royal Papers is glad to add you to its list of dealers. You'll find that the combination of a quality product and national advertising will make Royal Papers a profitable line for you.
Sell a new product.	Another product which should do well in your store is Royal's new line of color-coded memo forms. To receive your samples, complete the enclosed reply card and drop it in the mail.
Stress reader benefits.	Along with your shipment of Royal Papers, you will receive 500 copies of a colorful brochure announcing Royal products for distribution to your business friends. The brochure cover carries the embossed name, address, and phone number of your store.
Suggest possible future business.	Should you wish to take advantage of our regular terms of 3/10, n/60, complete and return the enclosed credit application. Mr. William McPherson, our sales representative in your area, will be in to see you in about two weeks. He will be glad to help you with store displays and will explain our volume discount to you.

Acknowledging Requests

Positive acknowledgments of requests fall into two general categories: those that give you the opportunity to sell your goods or services to your reader and those that should contain no sales material. Obviously, if you are in a business that exists by selling products or services, you will want to use every opportunity to increase your chances of making a sale. Before you answer any request for information about your products or services, ask yourself whether you should concentrate on the objective of supplying the information or the objective of selling the product or service.

The two objectives call for different treatments. A letter concentrating on supplying the information is an immediate message because its true business objective can be stated in the opening sentence. A letter concentrating on selling the product or service is a delayed message because its business objective is delayed until the reader is prepared psychologically for your request for action. Because they are persuasive messages, replies with sales opportunities are discussed in Chapter Nine, pp. 157-60.

When you have determined that the communication situation does not offer you the opportunity to persuade the reader to make a purchase, you should still use your acknowledgment of your reader's request to build goodwill. When you can do or provide what the reader has requested, you should say so in the opening sentence. A positive answer to a reader's question will place the message in a specific communication context and will be of more interest to the reader than statements of receipt or appreciation.

Poor: We have received your request for a copy
               of our manual, "How to Assert Yourself on
               the Job Without Being Fired."

Improved: Here is your copy of "How to Assert Your-
               self on the Job Without Being Fired."

Poor: Thank you for asking me to speak at the
               monthly meeting of the Marshall Hospitality
               Chapter of the National Secretaries
               Association.

Improved: I'll be glad to speak at the monthly meet-
               ing of the Marshall Hospitality Chapter of
               the National Secretaries Association next
               April.

Be sure to answer all of your reader's questions, including those questions asked explicitly, those implied, and those which should have been asked but weren't. Be specific in supplying information, and interpret any facts and figures which may not be absolutely clear to your reader. Should some of your information be negative, de-emphasize it by placing it in the middle of the letter. Your closing should be forward-looking and positive. Avoid clichés and statements which show a lack of confidence.

Poor: If I can be of further service, do not
               hesitate to contact me.

Poor: Feel free to call on me again.

Improved: Call on me again when I can help.

Poor: I hope that this letter answers your
               questions.

Improved: I'm glad to have been of help.

Avoid these	Use these
I hope	We're glad
We trust	I'll be glad to
Do not hesitate	Write me
If you have any questions	When you're in town
Why not call	Visit our showrooms
Thank you again	You've been a big help

Most acknowledgments without sales opportunities are fairly straight-forward—you simply agree to do or provide what your reader has requested. Positive replies to requests for adjustments and replies to requests for credit require more thoughtful treatment because the reader's ego is more involved in the situation. When the reader has requested an adjustment or credit, he or she has a strong interest in the action you take on the request. Even though your positive reply to the reader's request makes it a direct message, such letters present important human objectives to consider.

The business objective of a positive reply to a claim is to grant the requested adjustment, but the human objective of restoring the reader's confidence in your company, product, and service is equally important. Positive replies to claims should contain resale and some new sales material to demonstrate your confidence in your products and the future of the business relationship. Because the reader is more concerned with the fair and complete resolution of the complaint, too much sales material would be offensive. The following example illustrates the basic pattern for a positive acknowledgment of a request.

| Immediate beginning. Make the adjustment. | You will receive a replacement for your Moonbeam Blender 23 in two or three days. It will arrive by United Parcel Service. |

| Some resale here, but avoid the specific topic of the complaint. A word of thanks helps build goodwill. | Each Moonbeam product is fully guaranteed, and we're glad to make this adjustment for you. Thank you for writing so promptly. |

| Get the problems out of the way early in the letter. Make required action easy. | When your new Blender 23 arrives, please send us the original blender (Note—avoid the word "defective" when writing to consumers.) so we can determine the exact cause of the difficulty. While we need to inspect the original blender to be absolutely sure about what caused the problem, your description leads me to believe that there is a break in one of the motor windings. |

| When possible, give a full, honest explanation for the problem. | One of the ways Moonbeam is able to achieve 23-speed flexibility in the blender you purchased is by using a special motor-winding technique. While the technique is more complex and delicate than that usually found in blenders, it results in superior performance. |

| Resell the product by stressing its features and the benefits the reader will receive. | The Blender 23 is the best Moonbeam makes, and its versatility is unmatched. It is the only blender on the market that can whip cream without turning it to butter. It is also the only blender that can make peanut butter without requiring additional oil and fluff egg whites. Your new Blender 23 will make cooking a pleasure for you for many years to come. |

| Your closing should look forward rather than backward. New sales material shows confidence in the future of the business relationship. | Along with your new Blender 23, we're sending a brochure of other Moonbeam products. Each Moonbeam product carries an absolute five-year warranty. The Deluxe Food Chopper shown on p. 23 of the brochure would be a perfect kitchen companion for your blender. |

Acknowledgments of requests for information about people and credit are usually a matter of completing the forms supplied by the company making the request. Occasionally, however, you will need to write a letter—either because the requester did not supply a form or because the circumstances are sufficiently unusual to make a standard form inadequate.

Positive replies to requests for information about people are frequently called letters of recommendation because the writer is asked whether the person should be admitted to college, be offered a scholarship or job, be granted credit, and so on.

When you can make a positive recommendation, your recommendation should be first. Negative material, as always, should be placed in the middle of the letter and stated in a positive way. Honesty, however, dictates that negative information that would influence the reader's decision be presented fairly and clearly. Replies to requests about people should acknowledge that the information is confidential (see p. 97) and that it was requested.

Begin with the recommendation or other positive statements.	I'm glad to recommend Ms. Carmen Montagano for the job of secretary to the President of Sprinkle Equipment Company.
Tell the reader how you know what you know.	When Carmen (Note—use first or last name depending on how well you know the person.) was my student in a one-semester business communication course, she consistently demonstrated superior ability, willingness to work, and a positive attitude. She always did her work on time and was always willing and eager to learn. Her happy, energetic nature made her a joy to have in class. Carmen demonstrated her ability to write a variety of business letters in a clear, concise manner and earned an A for the semester.
Subordinate negative elements.	Because of her eagerness to complete tasks, Carmen occasionally did less than accurate work, and she had not yet fully developed her proofreading skills. She did want to do a job right, however, and was fully capable of absolute accuracy if its importance was stressed.
Provide additional information that your reader will find useful.	Since the completion of the course, I have had the opportunity to know Carmen on a more personal basis. She continues to be the same cheerful person who brightened my class.
Your closing should be positive.	I'm certain that Carmen would brighten the offices of Sprinkle Equipment Company, too.

Another kind of acknowledgment is a reply for a request for credit. When you have determined that your reader deserves an extension of credit, it is because your reader's character, ability to pay, and business conditions all indicate his or her willingness and ability to handle credit transactions honestly. Your reply approving the request for credit should acknowledge the reader's having earned the privilege of doing business by credit. When the credit approval is accompanied by the shipment of goods, you should begin the letter by saying that you have sent the merchandise. Sending the merchandise implies the extension of credit, and except for the credit information, a credit approval letter is similar to an order acknowledgment (see p. 105). When writing to consumers, you should always clarify your credit terms and the procedure for paying. When you are writing to dealers, adapt your language to avoid an explicit explanation of terms the dealer probably already knows.

Send the merchandise.	You should receive the items listed on the enclosed invoice in time for your Saturday morning sale. We've shipped them by Air Express.
Welcome the reader and make clear that credit is earned, not granted.	The charges for the cosmetics and air freight total $460, which we've billed to your new account. Because of your excellent record of prompt payment, we're glad to have you as a credit customer.
Explain the terms, but subordinate all details the reader should know. Be explicit about discount savings.	Under our usual credit terms of 3/10, n/60, you can save $13.80 by paying the discount price by the date specified on the invoice. The full amount is due 60 days after the invoice date.

After the explanation of credit terms, provide resale and new sales material as for an order acknowledgment (see p. 107).

Letters to individual consumers are essentially the same. The credit terminology will be different because an individual consumer usually receives a charge card and a "revolving" account which extends limited credit ($300, $500, $1,000 limits are typical) based on the person's character, ability to pay, and needs. Letters approving personal credit accounts need to explain the use of the charge card, the method of billing (usually once a month with an end date and minimum amount due), and the finance charges (usually 1½ percent a month on the unpaid balance). Because these messages are often form letters, resale and new sales material are limited to service, the advantages of credit purchasing, and seasonal sales information.

ANNOUNCEMENTS

Messages that announce sales, special events (such as conferences, meetings, formal parties, or other celebrations), and special awards are immediate messages because readers will welcome receiving them. When the reader will respond favorably to them, messages that announce changes in policy, procedure, or responsibilities are also immediate messages.

Because many announcements imply an invitation, they are written in much the same way as invitations (see pp. 97-98). The difference between them is that an invitation always contains an explicit "please attend" or "your presence is requested" whereas an announcement merely announces the event and suggests that you should attend because of the benefits you will receive.

Most business announcements are printed or photocopied and are sent to regular charge customers with the objective of building goodwill.

Use a simulated inside address to avoid a mailing-list salutation.	Because you are One of Gilmore's Special customers...
Specify the who, what, when, where, and how. Write to one reader at a time.	We're glad to give you a head start on our annual Spring Sale. Tuesday, February 25, from 6:00 p.m. until midnight, you and a few other select customers may take advantage of our "by invitation only" evening at our downtown store. Simply present this letter at the door when you arrive.
Provide necessary explanation, details, and sales material.	As a regular credit customer of Gilmore's, you're entitled to something special. This invitation gives you the opportunity to shop at leisure, have first pick of the sale items, and receive discounts up to 75 percent on nearly everything in stock.
Make the action as easy and as attractive as possible.	To make your shopping even easier, we'll provide a free-parking pass for you, free babysitting service while you shop, and free coffee and cookies. Because you're special... This sale is for you.

Announcements sent within the company to co-workers follow the same basic pattern. Common uses for these messages are to announce retirements, parties, staff meetings, promotions, special achievements (board appointments, publications, sales awards, and project completions), policy statements, procedures, new products and services, and changes in benefits. The announcement will go to the entire company or a specific department. Some of these situations call for personal letters as well.

Unfortunately, many business people receive so many announcements that they do not read them all. The problem of too many messages is known as *message overload*. To help ensure that *your* announcements are read: (1) announce only those events that are truly important, (2) color code your announcements for instant recognition, and (3) don't send too many.

While the communication context will, of course, govern the tone and formality of these announcements, they are all immediate messages in which the positive, important information is stated first. Explanations and secondary details belong in the middle of the message, and the closing should specify who is to do what next, making the suggested action as easy as possible. These messages frequently use the memo format.

```
12 March 19_


TO:      Production Department

FROM:    Thomas Carlyle

SUBJECT: Vacation Schedule


Here is the summer vacation schedule. This year (for a change)
everyone got his or her first choice.


    NAME                 DATES              SIGNATURE

    L. Burry             Jun 19-24          ———————————————
    A. Calhoun           Jul 11-15          ———————————————
    D. Dowling           Aug  8-12          ———————————————
    S. Mazade            Jul  4- 8          ———————————————
    C. Welborn           Aug 22-26          ———————————————
    M. Wheeler           Jul 18-22          ———————————————

Please confirm your schedule by signing your name next to your
dates, and return this sheet to my office by 26 March.
```

Because announcements go to groups of people, they are prepared as a form. Very formal announcements (some wedding invitations and new business partnerships) are engraved. Other announcements, depending on formality, are printed, photocopied, or mimeographed. Very informal announcements are reproduced inexpensively by a ditto machine. Very formal announcements are more a matter of etiquette than of business communication and usually use old-fashioned, stylized English. For information about these announcements, consult a printer or books on etiquette.

SPECIAL GOODWILL LETTERS

Letters that do not have a particular business objective are known as special goodwill letters because their only purpose is to improve the relationship between writer and reader. They are letters that are especially meaningful to readers because they weren't required. To include sales material or to conduct business of any sort in these letters would defeat their special goodwill. The following are typical categories of special goodwill letters:

1. **Letters of congratulations.** Significant accomplishments, such as promotion, retirement, election to an office, winning a competition, or marriage, deserve special letters of recognition and praise.

2. **Letters of appreciation.** Whenever someone does you a favor, you owe that person a word of thanks. When the favor is large enough, the person deserves a letter. Many businesses send routine thank-you letters to customers for prompt payment, patronage, or for recommendations to others. These letters are most effective when they conduct no business.

3. **Letters conveying season's greetings.** Special business relationships merit an exchange of greetings at appropriate times of the year. Most businesses limit season's greetings to specially prepared cards.

4. **Letters of welcome.** Businesses use letters of welcome to make new customers, prospective customers, and new employees feel at home. Letters of welcome should emphasize useful information and a willingness to help the newcomer.

5. **Letters of sympathy.** Letters extending condolences are difficult to write, but your business friends will appreciate your having cared enough to express your sympathetic feelings. Even though the subject is melancholy and seems negative, letters of sympathy are immediate messages. Your reader will already know of the misfortune, so your opening should acknowledge the unhappy event and place your message in the proper communication context. When writing a letter of sympathy, take special care to match your vocabulary to the situation. For example, "greatly distressed" is more appropriate for a death than a broken toe.

Except for season's greetings, each of these letters requires specific, personal details to be convincing. Letters of congratulation and appreciation should focus on the reader's accomplishment or efforts. Letters of welcome should provide helpful information, and letters of sympathy

should mention the deceased person's fine qualities to show your aware-
ness that the relationship was human as well as business in nature.

APOLOGIES

When apologies are called for, they are positive, immediate messages.
In most cases, however, apologies are unnecessary because the reader
will be more concerned with whether you have corrected the error than
with how sorry you are it happened in the first place. When you can correct the difficulty, you should begin the letter with your statement
correcting the problem.

Poor: I'm sorry that you were inconvenienced by
            having to return your Astrosonic clock
            radio for repairs.

Improved: You'll receive your fully repaired Astro-
            sonic clock radio in just a few days. I've
            sent it by United Parcel Service. When our
            technicians examined the radio, they dis-
            covered. . . . (Give a full explanation, provide resale,
            and add some new sales material.)

Apologies are required when you, your company, or a company representative has made a mistake that can't be corrected. Having caused
an inconvenience is not in itself a reason to apologize. People in business and the general public expect things to go wrong once in a while.
Nothing—and nobody—is perfect. Faulty products and mistakes are
bound to occur. Apologies for solvable problems usually serve no purpose and are perceived as insincere. When you can solve the problem,
solve it. When you can't solve the problem, apologize.
  Apologies are required in the following circumstances:

1. You've taken too long to answer a letter.
2. You tried to solve the reader's problem once and failed; the reader
   had to ask a second time.
3. A defect in your product injured a customer. (For legal reasons
   you should avoid admitting guilt. Let your lawyer see your letter
   before you mail it.)
4. A representative of your company was rude to someone.
5. A defect in your product was of such a nature that the customer
   won't be interested in a correction. (A cockroach in a jar of peanut
   butter; a dead mouse in a bottle of beer.)
6. A problem in your business operations has cost someone else time,
   money, and exasperation.

When your reader deserves an apology, put it first in the letter. Never
try to subordinate an apology by placing it in the middle of a letter,

and—even more important—*never* apologize at the end of a letter. The secondary elements in a letter of apology should include a full, positive explanation of the problem, and the closing element should look forward to a positive, continuing business relationship.

Apologize first. Let the reader know that you care.	I was sorry to hear, Mrs. O'Brien, that Mr. Roger Malanchuk, a Standard Brush salesperson was rude to you. Thank you for bringing this matter to my attention. Your letter will help us improve our service.
Do what you can to make things better.	I will have the field manager talk to the salesperson about his behavior. While I can't explain his rudeness, I can assure you that Standard Brush sets high standards for courtesy and expects every salesperson to meet those standards.
When appropriate, do something nice to make the reader feel better.	Because you were nice enough to take the time to write, I'm sending you a complimentary set of Standard brushes. You'll receive them in about two weeks.

TRANSMITTALS

Letters of transmittal are used to transmit something else—a report, a resume, or some other enclosure—to a reader. A message is a letter of transmittal when the item transmitted provides the principal reason for the letter. In most cases, the letter of transmittal begins with a reference to the item transmitted, which places the communication in the proper context.

```
Here is the report you requested.

Here are the brochures you asked for.

The enclosed schedule, Mr. Swados, shows you
what I propose for the summer scouting pro-
gram.
```

Sales letters transmitting enclosures and letters transmitting resumes are the exceptions. They are delayed rather than immediate messages and do not refer to the enclosure until late in the letter (see p. 152 and 157-59).

The secondary elements of a typical transmittal letter explain or summarize the contents of the item transmitted, and the closing element specifies who is to do what next.

Immediate beginning.	The enclosed schedule, Mr. Swados, shows you what I propose for the summer scouting program.
Explanation and summary of highlights.	The three weekend outings—11-12 June, 9-10 July, and 30-31 July—will prepare the boys and girls for the week-long Jamboree scheduled for 13 to 20 August.
	As the schedule shows, on each of the weekends and during the Jamboree nearly all of the scouts' time will be structured and supervised.
Specify who should do what next.	When I receive your approval and suggested changes, I will have the schedule printed and distributed to area leaders.
	Let me know what else I can do to help.

SUMMARY

Letters conveying information, often called informational messages, are either reader initiated or writer initiated. When your message contains information to which the reader will respond in a positive way, you should use an immediate structure and present the business objective first. Human objectives are not critical in positive messages because the reader will welcome the information. The general structure for all positive messages is (1) immediate beginning, (2) explanation, (3) secondary matters, and (4) positive close.

Acknowledgments are reader-initiated letters. In all acknowledgments, you are providing information about products, services, personnel, or some other item of mutual concern because your reader has asked you to provide the information. When a reader sends you an inquiry, you can say yes, no, or maybe. When you decide to say yes, use an immediate structure to convey the positive answer. When you can't give an immediate, positive answer, your acknowledgment is a negative message.

Readers expect prompt, courteous replies to their requests for goods and services, and by fulfilling that expectation, you can increase the positive feelings your readers have for you and your company. Most orders should be acknowledged with a carefully prepared form letter that (1) lets the reader know that the merchandise is on its way, specifying the items shipped and the method of shipment, (2) expresses appreciation for the reader's business, and (3) suggests possibilities for future business transactions.

Positive acknowledgments of requests fall into two general categories: those that give you the opportunity to sell your goods or services to your reader and those that should contain no sales material. A letter concentrating on supplying the information is an immediate message because its true business objective can be stated in the opening sentence. A letter concentrating on selling the product or service is a delayed message because its business objective is delayed until the reader is prepared psychologically for your request for action.

Acknowledgments of requests for information about people and credit are usually a matter of completing forms supplied by the company making the request. When you make a positive recommendation, your recommendation should be first. Place negative material in the middle of the letter and state it in a positive way.

A letter approving a request for credit should acknowledge the reader's having earned the privilege of doing business by credit. When the credit approval is accompanied by the shipment of goods, you should begin the letter by saying that you have sent the merchandise. Sending the merchandise implies an extension of credit.

Messages announcing sales, special events, and special awards are immediate messages because readers will welcome receiving them.

Letters that do not have a particular business objective are known as special goodwill letters because their only purpose is to improve the relationship between writer and reader. They are letters that are specially meaningful to readers because they weren't required.

When apologies are called for, they are positive, immediate messages. When you can correct the difficulty, you should begin the letter with your statement correcting the problem. When you can't, apologize first and go on to more positive, forward-looking things.

Letters of transmittal are used to transmit something—a report, a resume, or some other enclosure—to a reader. A message is a letter of transmittal when the item transmitted provides the principal reason for the letter.

EXERCISES

Review

1. What is the general structure for all positive messages?

2. What information should be included in letters acknowledging orders?

3. In acknowledging requests, when do you use the immediate beginning? the delayed beginning?

4. Name the various categories of special goodwill letters. What is the purpose of these letters?

5. When are letters of apology required?

6. When do you use a transmittal letter? Are letters of transmittal immediate or delayed messages? Why?

Problems

1. Mr. Frank Busey, owner of Central Hardware, 980 Landau Avenue, Hattiesburg, MS 39401, has ordered $800 worth of 10-gauge electrical wire from you (Williams Die Casting and Wire Company, Bainbridge, GA 31717) and has requested rush shipment. You called Busey's credit references, who confirm that he always pays his bills on time. Busey needs the rush shipment because a new Crunchy Cereal factory is being constructed in Hattiesburg, and the construction will require a great deal of electrical wiring. Send the wire air express and extend Busey a $1,500 line of credit with terms of 2/10, n/30. Tell Busey that you also make high quality 12- and 14-gauge electrical wire, and encourage his future business.

2. Mrs. Sylvester Balboa, 1927 Highland Avenue, Durango, CO 81301, applied for a revolving charge account with a $1,000 line of credit with your store, Crepe's of Chicago, 7500 S. Pulaski Road, Chicago, IL 60652. Your credit check reveals that Mrs. Balboa is sometimes a little slow to pay, but she always pays eventually. You decide to grant her credit, but limit her to $500. You also want to remind her that the finance charge on revolving accounts is high (1½ percent on the unpaid balance every month, or 18 percent a year). Encourage prompt payment. You will also include some standard paragraphs describing your personal service, exclusive merchandise (everything a woman could want), and your custom-made jewelry.

3. Because of your expertise in business communication, you have been asked to speak to the English classes at your local high school. Although accepting the invitation means that you would be responsible for speaking for about 40 minutes (and a 10-minute question and answer period) to five English classes beginning at 9:00 a.m. and ending at 3:00 p.m., you are willing to take the time because of the importance of the topic. The dates you've been offered, however, are not convenient. You were given a choice of 14, 15, or 16 November, and you have important appointments on these days. You would be glad to visit the classes on 17 or 18 November. Write your letter of acceptance to Mr. William Atkins, English Coordinator, Houston High School, 7722 Braesview, Houston, TX 77071.

4. Mr. Atkins (see preceding problem) has again asked a favor. This time he would like to borrow several issues of *The Journal of Business Communication* to show his students. You agree to lend him five issues. You'd like them back in about three weeks so your own students can use them to research their term projects. Write the letter and send the journals separately by parcel post.

5. As owner of the Wilkins Real Estate Agency, 498 Kilbourn Avenue, Provo, UT 84602, you decide to write a letter of welcome to all new-

comers to your home town. For a fee, the Chamber of Commerce furnishes you with a list of newcomers. Because you receive a limited number of names, you will compose a form letter but type each letter individually. You want your letters to be of real service (so that the readers will remember you and your firm when they decide to look for a home), so you will provide the most useful information about your community. You will also enclose a map of your home town provided by the Chamber of Commerce. Write a letter of welcome to Mr. and Mrs. Charles Cowan, 451 Grandview Drive, Kirkland, WA 98033.

6. Your company, J & J Ballbearings, 410 East River Drive, Ames, IA 50011, has grown large enough that you have purchased group health insurance for your 35 employees. The new policy provides coverage for all hospitalization and doctor's office calls up to $10,000 for each off-the-job accident or illness. (On-the-job accidents are covered by your Worker's Compensation policy.) In addition the policy pays for 80 percent of all prescribed medication costs. To qualify for the benefits, your employees will need to complete a medical expense form (a sample of which you will enclose with your letter) for each accident of illness. Your employees will also need to send the *original* bill for medical treatment or the *original* copy of their receipt for prescription drugs. You should remind them to keep a copy of any bills and receipts for their own records. Write a form letter.

7. As Louise Fritzler, Manager of Customer Relations for World Insurance Inc., you receive several inquiries a day requesting information about your various insurance packages for health, auto, life, and home. Even though your national advertising instructs people to call or visit their local World agent, they write to you because they are afraid that your agent's will pressure them into buying insurance that they don't really want. Prepare a letter that will explain that

   a. you have forwarded their inquiry to a local agent (give a specific name and address),
   b. the agent is in a better position to help them because he or she can better determine their individual needs, and
   c. World agents do not use high-pressure techniques but are genuinely concerned with providing the kind of coverage that will ensure lasting satisfaction.

While the letter will be prepared as a form letter, each person will receive an individually typed, personal copy. Send a sample letter to Victor Giffin, 369 Indian Mound, Cincinnati, OH 45212. Enclose a brochure describing World Insurance package coverage.

8. You're Ms. Tonile Levy, Manager, Consumer Relations, Kool Kola Company, 286 Greencrest Drive, Wilmington, NC 28401. You've been making Kool Kola for more than 20 years, and while you've received a few letters of complaint, the one you received today is the nastiest you've ever read. Using unrepeatable language, your customer informed you that he discovered a partially smoked cigar in a bottle of Kool Kola. Chemical analysis of the cigar (which the customer enclosed, telling you what you could do with it) revealed that the cigar indeed had been extinguished in the bottle of Kool Kola before the bottle was capped. You suspect that one of the workers you had to lay off because of a business downturn about three months ago was responsible. Write a letter to Mr. John Pauley, 307 W. Brooks, Norman, OK 73069, and explain the situation in a way that will help re-establish his good feelings about Kool Kola.

9. You are Richard LaMere, Personnel Manager of Micro-Electronics, 6321 Natural Bridge Road, St. Louis, MO 63121. You and the other managers decide that you could improve company morale and reduce personnel turnover by writing letters commending employees on their noteworthy community accomplishments. The company has two employees who deserve special recognition. Write letters to them.

   a. Ms. Lora Williams, 1107 Darton Avenue, St. Louis MO 63121, who works in your word-processing center, just completed her college degree by taking courses at night. She's demonstrated a lot of initiative and perserverance and is now eligible for a promotion. She should come see you and fill out the proper forms so she can be considered for a job as administrative assistant or secretarial supervisor.

   b. Mr. Richard Ryan, 601 South Union Street, St. Louis, MO 63121, who supervises circuit board assembly, was recently credited with saving the lives of a St. Louis family. He was on his way home from the company bowling tournament when he spotted smoke coming out of a house. He immediately stopped, turned in the fire alarm, and with disregard for his own personal safety, broke the bedroom windows and helped to safety the residents who were overcome by the smoke.

10. When you applied for a part-time writing and editing job to help pay for your college expenses, you listed one of your professors, Dr. Francis W. Weeks, Chairman, Division of Business and Technical Writing, University of Illinois, Urbana, IL 61801, as a reference. Upon being hired for the job, you learned that Dr. Weeks had written an excellent letter of recommendation for you, which was the main reason you were hired. Write a thank-you letter to Dr. Weeks.

11. In your job as Dean, College of Business, Western Kentucky University, Bowling Green, KY 42101, you are frequently asked to write letters recommending students for employment. While each letter must be individually written to be effective, you would like to standardize the letters enough so that composing each one would be relatively easy. For each of the students, you need to discuss academic achievement, participation in Alpha Kappa Psi (the business fraternity), participation in other paraprofessional activities (Marketing Club, Administrative Management Society, Finance Fraternity, Women in Business, and Pi Omega Pi), and personal qualities. Write a letter recommending Ms. Susan Rice for a job as administrative assistant, Gibson Guitar Company, 225 Parson Street, Kalamazoo, MI 49001. Her qualifications are a straight A average in her major, administrative services, and an A− average in her minor, general business. Her all-university average is B+. She has an admirable list of extracurricular activities, including associate membership in Alpha Kappa Psi, and served as president, vice president, and treasurer of Pi Omega Pi. In addition, during the four years she was in college, she worked part-time as a secretary in your office to finance her education. She is personable and well qualified for the administrative assistant's job. Write your letter for Susan in such a way that you can adapt the letter for other recommendations.

12. As P. K. Dresser, owner of Johnson Moving and Storage Company, 442 Brodway Street, Lincoln, NE 68516, you receive the following letter:

> I believe that I'm entitled to a partial refund on the moving job Johnson Moving and Storage did for me Friday, 23 August 19_.
>
> As you can see from the enclosed copy of the bill, I was charged for 5 hours, and I should have been charged for 3 hours and 45 minutes. The bill shows that the driver left your warehouse at 7:00 a.m., but he didn't arrive at my house until 8:15, even though my house is less than one mile from your warehouse. I don't mind paying for the driver, his assistant, and the truck while they were working to move me, but I strongly object to paying for the time the driver and his assistant took to have a leisurely breakfast before they began work.
>
> Please send my refund of $55 to my new address: 1127 Rabling Road, Lincoln, NE 68516.

You agree that the customer, Mr. Earl Halvas, deserves a refund. The refund, however, will be $45 for the unnecessary hour. You are going to charge him at your usual rate ($25 an hour) and include a reasonable amount of transportation time. You investigate and discover that the reason for the delay in your driver's reaching Mr. Halvas' home was that the moving van broke down, and it took the company mechanics nearly an hour to fix it. Mr. Halvas should not have been charged for that time, and you're glad that he's given you the opportunity to correct the error.

13. It's your job as sales manager for Tot Toy Shop, 6437 Pierce Street, Albia, IA 52531, to acknowledge the order received from Mrs. Arlene Dahl, 2311 Curtis Court, Benton, KY 42025, for the following items: two model FX 1186 Fox Super Sport Trainers, one Tonka Mighty Grader, and three 12″ Musical Lullabye Baby Dolls. Tell Mrs. Dahl that she'll have the items in time for Christmas.

14. Assume that you are an assistant to the sales manager of the Oaks Pharmaceutical Company, 150 Spring Street, Euclid, OH 44717. You just received a request from Wyer's Pharmacy, 9714 Washington Avenue, Providence, RI 02911, for a gross of 2-oz. bottles of desiccated liver pills, 12 tubes of O-P medicated shaving cream, and 24 8-oz. bottles of O-P cough syrup. Acknowledge the order. Tell how and when shipment will be made.

15. Write a letter to Mrs. Wilson Tarkinson, Tarkinson Clothiers, 408 Henderson Avenue, Boston, MA 02109, telling her that you'll be shipping her order for the following:

    1 doz Style 33 K391 100% Quiana nylon, panel pattern tie, blue and rose.

    1 doz Style 33 K392 100% Quiana nylon, panel pattern tie, green and rust.

    1 doz Style 33 K393 100% Quiana nylon, panel pattern tie, silver and brown.

    Tell how and when you plan to ship the items.

16. As Ms. Alice Harris, Manager, Consumer Relations, Natural Foods Inc., 1906 Cheshire Lane, Greeley, CO 80631, write a letter of apology to Mr. Herman Grotzinger, who found a (dead) cockroach packed in a box of your 100 percent whole grain cereal.

17. Your secretary has just brought you a letter more than six months old. How the letter got lost and where it has been are a mystery. It's from a new and important customer, Mr. Curtis Matthews, General Manager, Rollin Manufacturing Incorporated, 4242 Western Avenue, Superior, WI 54880. In the letter Matthews says that if he can have immediate written confirmation that your company, Williams Tool and Die, Main and Race Streets, Emporia, KS 66801, can supply the required machine parts, Rollin Manufacturing will be eligible for a large government contract. Matthews clearly states that he wants your letter—and not a phone call—in seven days. If he doesn't have

your letter by then, he'll have to take the business to a local firm. Write a letter to Mr. Matthews, apologizing for your late response, and try to win his future business.

18. As sales manager for Natural Foods Inc., 8450 Ravine Road, Battle Creek, MI 49000, you receive a letter from Mrs. Agnes Richards, 1133 Benjamin Road, St. Louis, MO 63122, who enjoys your natural cereals but says she doesn't understand why the boxes of this cereal are only ¾ full when she opens them. Write Mrs. Richards and explain to her that each box of cereal you produce does contain the weight specified on the box and are full when they leave the plant, but because of the settling of the cereal flakes during shipment and handling, some of the boxes may appear to be not quite full.

19. As head of Payroll, you have the task of computing sick leave and vacation days accrued by each person in your firm. Because you've recently switched computer systems, you want to double-check the figures entered for all employees. Prepare a memo to send to department heads, which they should then route to each employee in their departments so that each person can check his or her own record. If both sick leave and vacation time are correct, the employee should sign in the space provided. If either sick leave or vacation time is incorrect, the employee should make an appointment with Al Smith, your assistant.

20. As the head of the Marketing Department, Olsen Graphics Company, 711 Suffolk Place, Streamwood, IL 60103, you conduct year-end performance appraisal interviews with each of your 12 staff members. The past year you have had a high turnover in staff, and your seven new staff members might feel threatened by the upcoming interviews. Write a memo to your staff that, in addition to setting up specific times for the interviews, will help convince the new staff members that the interviews are designed to help them by answering questions, establishing goals, and identifying problems.

8. Conveying Negative Information

Objectives

After you have read this chapter, you should be able to

1. Apply the general structure used for all messages conveying negative information.
2. Present negative information in a way that will help your reader accept it.
3. Write letters delaying or declining orders.
4. Write negative replies to requests for favors, adjustments, and credit.
5. Write letters announcing negative information.

Letters conveying negative information, often called negative informational messages, contain a business objective to which the reader will respond in a negative way. Even though a message may contain a "no" or other negative information, it is not a negative message unless the reader's feelings will be hurt by the content. The reader's response determines whether the informational message is negative. When your message will hurt, anger, or upset the reader, you should use a delayed structure. In negative informational messages, the human objective is critical; you need to emphasize the feeling content of the letter to achieve the human objective, which will increase the chances that you will achieve your business objective.

The writer's main problem in conveying negative information is presenting the negative aspect in a way that will help the reader preserve a positive self-image and maintain the reader's positive attitude toward the writer and the writer's company. The use of the delayed structure helps prepare the reader for the negative aspect of the message by placing the emphasis on the reasons for the negative decision and on the positive alternatives to the original course of action. A delayed presentation allows you to place greater emphasis on the feeling content of the message than on the subject content.

It's very important for you to present negative messages with confidence. Because you should send a negative message only when you are fully convinced that you've made the correct decision, you should explain your decision with confidence. Your assumption should be that your reader will understand and accept your point of view if you explain it adequately. Do not apologize for your decision, and do not say that you wish you could have done otherwise ("I really wish I could, but"). Focus instead on the rightness of your decision and the other courses of action available to the reader.

GENERAL STRUCTURE AND CHECKLIST

The general structure for all negative informational messages is as follows:

1. **Delayed Beginning.** Deal first with the human objective— retaining the reader's goodwill. Delay your presentation of the business objective—the negative message. Begin with something the reader will respond to positively, but be sure to place the message in its specific communication context. Find something to agree with, pay the reader an honest compliment, give a positive answer to one of the reader's questions, or—as a last resort—thank the reader for having written to you. You should not mislead the reader into thinking that the letter will contain positive information, nor should you give the negative aspect away too soon. Especially avoid "however," "but," "although," and "even though" in your opening sentences. A delayed opening is frequently called a **buffer beginning** because it "buffers" the negative business objective which follows.

2. **Explanation.**   Give good, logical reasons in a positive way, and— when possible—connect the reasons to a long-term reader benefit (for example, keeping prices low, providing better service to all customers, receiving the exact item of choice, or avoiding credit difficulties). Be sure to give *real* reasons rather than hiding behind company policy or the small print in your warranty. When giving more than one reason for the negative message, you must provide some rational transition from reason to reason. But don't practice overkill. If *one* of your reasons is an *absolute*, you don't need a list of all the other reasons you have for your decision.

3. **Subordinated Refusal.** Subordinate the refusal as much as possible without sacrificing clarity (recall the plumber on page 50). Make sure that at least one good reason precedes the refusal, and use positive language in making the refusal itself. To avoid

accusing the reader, you may need to use passive voice. When you can do so, make the refusal by implication—give your reasons and suggest alternatives but omit the refusal itself.

4. **Positive Close.**   Whenever you can, suggest ways in which your reader can achieve the stated objective. When there is no way for the reader to achieve that objective, offer positive alternatives, resale, or goodwill. Always show your intention to maintain a positive business relationship. Frequently new sales material will demonstrate your confidence in the future of the relationship. When further action is required, specify who should do what next.

NEGATIVE ACKNOWLEDGMENTS

A negative acknowledgment of a reader's request for goods, service, an adjustment, or credit is bound to upset the reader. Because your reader will expect to have the request granted, your negative reply will come as a disappointing surprise. When you decide that the negative reply is the only one possible under the circumstances, you need to make the best of the situation by

1. Working to maintain a positive human and business relationship.
2. Making certain that the reader understands the reasons for your decision and knows what other courses of action are possible.

Delaying or Declining Orders

Delays in filling orders and refusing orders are caused by a variety of circumstances, some of which are the reader's fault and some of which are the writer's fault (or the fault of the writer's company). When the reader has been at fault by not supplying complete order information, the writer's principal task is to obtain the information required to complete the order without accusing the reader of having written an inadequate order ("You forgot to specify . . ."). When the writer or writer's company is responsible for the delay or refusal, the writer's principal task is to persuade the reader to wait until the order can be filled or to order elsewhere without making the reader lose faith in the writer's company or its products.

Delays in shipment for which the reader is at fault require (1) careful, positive handling of the request for the missing information, (2) resale material, and (3) a request for specific, prompt action on the part of the reader.

Use a delayed beginning, but place the message in a specific communication context. When possible, send part of the order. Do **not** thank the reader for the order or say that you're glad to have it.	You will receive the Moonbeam Model 14 electric can opener you ordered in just a few days. We shipped it by United Parcel Service.
	The Model 14 is the best can opener Moonbeam makes, and it is well known for its rugged dependability. All of Moonbeam's blenders have the same kind of rugged construction, and one of our blenders is sure to be right for your needs.
Keep the reader's interest in your product by using resale material and focusing on the reader's choice rather than the mistake.	To meet the variety of kitchen demands, Moonbeam makes six different models of blender, each of which comes in four vibrant colors.
	The enclosed brochure fully describes the models, their uses, and some of their unique features. So you may receive the blender that best meets your needs, please review the brochure and complete the order card on the last page. (**Not** "*You neglected* to tell us which model . . . ." and **not** "*We need* to know which model . . . .")
	The Model 14 and all of Moonbeam's blenders come with an absolute five-year warranty for your added assurance of quality.
The amount of resale (and the length of the letter) should be appropriate for the product or service involved.	We designed Moonbeam electric kitchen aids to make all your kitchen duties a pleasure. The Model 14 electric can opener will handle any size can regardless of shape. It's also completely submersible for easy cleaning. Whichever Moonbeam blender you select, you will receive a highly versatile product which will cut in half the time required to scramble eggs, make pancakes or waffles, and crush ice.
Close by telling the reader exactly what to do and by encouraging prompt action.	As soon as we receive the card indicating your choice of blender, we'll send it to you by UPS. By returning the card now, you can be enjoying the speed and convenience of automatically mixed, chopped, and pureed foods in about ten days.

Delays in filling orders caused by problems at the writer's company also have the objective of keeping the order in spite of the negative aspect. When the writer's company is responsible for the delay, the writer needs to explain the reason for the delay, let the reader know how long the delay will be, and persuade the reader to wait. When the delay is going to be a long one (and what constitutes "long" will vary depending on the nature of the product or service involved), you should acknowledge the reader's right to make the decision about waiting. When the delay will not be long, you should assume—with confidence—that your decision to complete the order later will meet with the reader's approval.

When you can't send part of the order, find a positive opening with which the reader will agree.

Your order for a Guardsman 10-horse-power, 40-inch, electric-start Lawn Tractor shows your concern with quality. The Guardsman exceeds the American National Safety Institute's standards and offers the ruggedness and durability of solid steel construction.

Begin your explanation fairly soon. Your reader will want to know why you haven't said, "Your order is on its way."

We usually try to fill orders for Guardsman Lawn Tractors in about two weeks, and we can understand your desire to have your Guardsman when the grass begins its spring spurt in April. Because of the steel workers' strike and an unprecedent demand for Lawn Tractors this season, it will take us six to eight weeks to fill your order.

Use resale material to discourage the reader from buying elsewhere.

You'll find the Guardsman 10 worth the wait. The electric-start, 350-cubic-inch, 10-horsepower engine has plenty of reserve power for tackling the toughest of home-mowing needs. The engine governor automatically increases gas feed to maintain blade speed in tall grass and weeds—even on steep hills.

In addition to the many features designed to make the Guardsman 10 the most versatile home lawn tractor on the market, any family member old enough to drive it can use it with complete confidence. The Guardman 10 comes with a safety interlock which permits the engine to start only with the mower in neutral and the blades disengaged. Another safety feature you'll appreciate is the automatic cut off that disengages the blades and kills the engine should the driver leave the tractor seat while the tractor is in gear. Guradsman is the only lawn tractor available with this important feature.

Because the delay is a long one, you should make clear that you know the reader has a choice. You should also encourage the decision you want the reader to make.

Please use the enclosed card to let us know your decision. We will continue with our evaluation of your application for credit but will hold your deposit until we hear from you.

Now that the steel workers' strike is over, we're building Guardsman 10 Lawn Tractors as fast as possible without sacrificing the famous Guardsman quality. Because we want you to be fully satisfied with your Guardsman, we

```
                        assemble each one carefully so the
                        Guardsman you receive will work flaw-
                        lessly—and look as good as it works.
```

Specify who is to do   By returning your card today, you can
what next. The last   receive your Guardsman 10 before 15
sentence should   June—in plenty of time to help you
mention a reader   with those midsummer and early fall
benefit.   chores.

When you must decline an order because business conditions make it impossible for you to supply the goods or service (or a reasonable alternative), you need to explain the situation in a straightforward way. Your reader will appreciate it if you supply information about where and how the requested goods or services can be obtained. You should offer resale or new sales material when such material would be appropriate for your reader.

It's more usual, however, that you will need to decline customer orders because you market your products through a system of established dealers. When you need to refuse a customer who has ordered directly through the mail, your business objective is to persuade the reader to visit a local dealer. The human objective is to retain the reader's goodwill in spite of the disappointment that your negative reply will create. Both objectives call for a delayed structure.

1. **Delayed Opening.**   Find a positive opening that will place the message in its communication context.

2. **Explanation.**   Your explanation must clearly indicate the reader benefits associated with your system of dealers (such as direct, personal service; free installation; or the need to examine products before purchase).

3. **Resale.**   Be sure to include the same kind of resale material as you would in delaying an order. Resale material will help retain your reader's interest in your product.

4. **Positive Close.**   Conclude by telling the reader exactly what to do and where to go to complete the purchase.

Should you need to decline an order from a dealer, it will be for one of the following reasons:

1. **The dealer has not established sufficient credit.**   Because in this case your business objective is to retain the order on a cash basis, this type of letter is a credit refusal and *not* an order refusal. We discuss credit refusals on pp. 136-37.

2. **You already have an exclusive dealer in the area.**   In this case, your explanation of the arrangement you have with the existing dealer will justify your declining the order. Your positive close should be limited to simple goodwill and should avoid resale, new sales, and positive alternatives (don't send your readers to the competition—they'll get there on their own).

3. **The dealer doesn't meet your requirements.**   This is a broad category, covering financial matters (the dealer insists on a larger markup than you offer) and character (the dealer has a reputation for not providing the high-quality customer service you expect from your dealers). You must base your letter of refusal on the particular circumstances and your analysis of the communication context (see pp. 35-41).

Negative Replies to Requests

Most people only make requests and claims when they feel that they truly deserve a positive reply. Anytime you must refuse a request or claim, the human objective—retaining your reader's goodwill—should receive the emphasis. You should delay the presentation of the business objective—the refusal—until you've prepared the reader by stating your reasons. In a negative reply, the refusal itself should always be subordinated as much as possible without sacrificing clarity. In the following example note the way the writer says *maybe* rather than *no* while making absolutely clear that he or she is unable to comply with the reader's request.

The beginning must place the message in its context without suggesting approval or refusal of the request. Provide a clear transition to the reasons that follow.	Every professional realtor should benefit from the session titled "The After Market Created by the Selling of Land Contracts in the Second Mortgage Money Exchange" at the upcoming convention of the National Association of Realtors.
Keep expressions of apprecication short and simple. They may mislead the reader or sound vain, but they can help establish empathy if focused on the reader.	Most members of our association would be honored to head a session of such importance. I am no exception. Your idea for the session is a good one. Through continued association with the major banks and lending institutions, Woodhaven (the writer's company) has confirmed that the "after-market" is ignored by a great number of realtors.

Make sure the refusal is clear. Note the use of specific dates in this example.	Woodhaven usually supports attendance at professional conventions, and I have already submitted my request for travel funds. My employer will determine the amount of my support as soon as all requests are submitted. Because Woodhaven has not yet assigned me funds for attending the convention and because of schedule conflicts arising from the convention's falling so close to Christmas, I won't be able to give you a definite answer until December 1, well past your November 10 deadline.
Show the reader that you understand his or her problem and do what you can to help with a solution.	I still hope to attend the convention and would be pleased to head the session, but because you need a firm commitment soon, I suggest that you ask Anthony Bishop of our St. Louis branch to head the session. As you already know, Tony is an excellent public speaker and would make a fine addition to the program.
The closing must be positive. Do not return to the negative aspect. An offer of "further" help sounds sarcastic.	The ideas you have outlined for the program look very good. The convention promises to be first rate. The results of your planning and hard work are already obvious—keep up the good work.

The foregoing example contains one business objective (refusing the request for the present) and one human objective (retaining the reader's goodwill). Frequently, negative replies to requests will contain more than one business objective. In addition to denying the request, you will often desire to retain the reader's business but in a way other than the way the reader has suggested. Whether you can accomplish the second business objective—retaining the reader's business—depends on how well you accomplish your human objective in the letter. Note the positive approach and the full explanation in the following example. The letter was written to an 18-year-old student who had requested that his insurance premium be reduced because his father's premium was lower.

Use a delayed beginning which agrees with something the reader has said.	Yes, Mr. Shull, we do make money on policies carried by good drivers like your father, and your father should be proud of the fact that he has not had an accident in 10 years.
Provide a full explanation for your decision.	Insurance companies keep careful statistics on different kinds of cars and drivers. These statistics are the basis for determining insurance rates.

Drivers with very few or no accidents, like your father, receive the lowest rates.

When possible, show that the refusal is based on impersonal evidence.

Because unmarried drivers under 25 account for the highest frequency of accidents of any age group, they are charged higher rates than any other age group. Also, the Cobra-Jet which you drive has had one of the highest frequency of accidents and is charged a higher rate than a car like your father's.

Avoid accusing the reader, and use positive language to subordinate the negative aspect.

The driving record of the individual driver is also one of the most important factors in computing the premium charged. The premium you received is correct for your age, car, and driving record.

Offer positive alternatives.

One way to lower your premium would be to drop the collision coverage on your car. But, should you have an accident that was your fault, you would have to pay for the damage to your car.

Your closing should be positive and forward looking.

I am happy to have your father as a policyholder, and I'm sure that you will be just as good a driver as your father. As you grow older and accumulate a few years of accident-free driving, your insurance premiums will drop accordingly.

Negative Replies to Claims

When a customer has written to you claiming that your product or service was deficient in some way, you obviously need to consider the situation carefully. Some companies have decided that it is in their best interests to act on the belief that the "customer is always right" and approve every adjustment requested. Other companies feel that unwarranted claims should be refused because it is unfair to make all their customers pay for the unreasonable requests of a few.

When you decide that a reader's request is unwarranted and should be refused, you need to be very careful to avoid accusing the reader of carelessness, misrepresentation, or fraud. Rather than assume that the reader is trying to cheat you deliberately, you should assume that your reader truly does not understand your service or the operation of your product. Your principal business objective is to refuse the request; your secondary business objective is to resell the product or service in question and, to show confidence, sell a new product or service at the same time. Your human objective is to retain the reader's goodwill. The following example refusing a refund for a tour illustrates these points.

Use a delayed beginning which agrees with something the reader said. As a last resort, thank the reader for having written.

You're right, Mrs. Paulson, to expect superior accommodations when you arrange tours through Adventure Travel. We do stake our reputation on providing the best accommodations available.

Explain the reasons for the refusal carefully.

Because you are a seasoned traveler, you know that different countries have different customs. Not all countries have the same concepts of courteous service as we have in this country. Do you remember how upset you were on your tour of Japan last year when you returned to your hotel only to discover that the hotel manager had moved you to a different room? When you discovered that being moved in that way is a common occurrence in Japan and shows no disrespect, you accepted your next unscheduled move like a native.

Subordinate the negative aspect by emphasizing the positive elements of the situation.

It is the same with Kenya and Tanzania. I'm sure you'll agree that your accommodations in Nairobi were as plush as you would expect to find in any major city anywhere in the world. When you signed up for the "Primitive Safari," we informed you that the journey around Lake Victoria would be under primitive conditions, and the materials we sent you before your trip described the emergency equipment required for the journey.

When possible, avoid saying **no** directly. Stress reader benefits.

As difficult as the journey was for you, I'm sure you'll agree that to be fully appreciated, the beauty of nature must be observed close at hand. You've had an opportunity, Mrs. Paulson, to see a part of Africa that few Americans will ever see, and to see it in a way that will be impossible in just a few years. Once you've rested more fully, you'll consider your "Primitive Safari" money wisely spent.

Your closing should be positive. Focus on future business.

Perhaps this next year you should consider a vacation a little less strenuous. We have several European tours scheduled that should appeal to you. The enclosed brochures describe the steamship lines, countries, and accommodations available.

Use the enclosed card to request further information. We'll be glad to complete all the arrangements for you.

Refusing Requests for Credit

In most respects a letter refusing credit is more a persuasive message than it is a negative message, because its objective is not so much to refuse credit as it is to obtain the customer's business on a cash basis. The human objective in a credit refusal is to show the reader that while a credit purchase might look attractive at the moment, it is in the reader's long-term interest to avoid risky credit obligations.

When refusing credit, you need to make clear why you are refusing it and suggest ways the reader can go about improving credit eligibility. Tell the reader what your requirements for credit are, and invite the reader to apply for credit again later. Do not, however, suggest that you will automatically extend credit the next time the applicant writes.

Because you still want the customer's business, but on a cash basis, much of your letter will consist of resale. Emphasize the advantages of doing business on a cash basis, but remember that these advantages are not reasons for refusing credit, so they should follow the refusal itself. The following structure applies whether you are writing an individual reply to a dealer who has ordered a large amount of goods on credit or a form reply to a customer who has requested a credit card.

1. **Delayed Beginning.**   Begin with something with which the reader can agree, such as the market conditions, the usefulness of the product(s), or the reader's choice of product(s). Include some resale to maintain reader interest in your product(s). Do *not* thank the reader for the order; to do so would sound selfish.

2. **Explanation.**   Explain your requirements for credit explicitly. Without sacrificing clarity, subordinate as much as possible the ways in which the reader does not meet your requirements. When you can offer useful advice (a local bank loan based on collateral, for example) without sounding paternalistic, do so. Your reader will appreciate genuine helpfulness.

3. **The Refusal.**   Make clear that you will not extend credit at this time, but leave the door open for future consideration. Do *not* promise to extend credit later.

4. **Positive Alternatives.**   Use resale material to encourage completing the order or otherwise doing business on a cash basis. Help the reader as much as possible by stating cash discounts and other advantages of cash. Smaller orders, lay-away, and other helpful suggestions will encourage the reader to continue doing business with your company.

5. Positive Closing.   Make it easy for the reader to reply. Remember that the reader has the choice of continuing the business relationship, so you cannot take action until your reader decides. Make clear what you would like the reader to do, and end on a reader benefit.

NEGATIVE ANNOUNCEMENTS AND REMINDERS

When your negative message is written in reply to something the reader has requested, you at least have a logical starting point for your letter. Readers who have requested favors, adjustments, or credit expect your reply and know that there is some possibility that their request will be denied.

Negative announcements and reminders present a more difficult problem. Even when your readers know that they have not fulfilled some obligations, they do not fully expect to receive your announcement. Also, negative announcements and reminders are frequently prepared as form letters to keep their costs low. This makes personalization difficult.

If negative announcements and reminders are to be read at all, they must offer the reader something of value. When you can, offer real and specific benefits. At the least, you should offer to discuss the situation with the reader so that you can reach an agreement about a satisfactory solution for the particular problem.

Negative announcements and reminders frequently tempt writers to forget to approach the problem with a positive attitude. Compare the following sentences from letters to college students:

Poor:
> I regret to inform you that your admission to candidate status has been delayed until you complete the following requirements.

Improved:
> Before your admission to candidate status, you will need to complete the following requirements.

Poor:
> On March 3, we sent you the accidental injury forms and requested that you return the forms to the Health Center. It's now March 27, and we have not yet received your reply.

Improved:
> Before you can receive your check from Student Insurance, you will need to file the accidental injury forms we sent you on March 3.

Note the brevity and the positive approach of the following examples.

Use a delayed opening when the reader doesn't really expect bad news.	As you know from reading the daily newspapers, local business has been hit rather hard by the recession. Perry's Packaging has tried hard to retain all personnel during this difficult period.
Explain quickly because the negative message will be obvious. Personal information can be added to a form letter.	Because of another recent downturn in business, we find that some layoffs have become necessary if the company is to remain solvent. The layoffs were determined strictly by seniority. Because you have low seniority, George, your layoff will be for 90 days. Your work has been excellent, and the layoff is not a reflection of your abilities.
Focus on the future when possible.	Should the market improve soon, you can be sure that we'll notify you. We will be glad to have you back at Perry's as soon as possible.

When the fact that you're writing makes it obvious that the news is bad, omit the delayed beginning.

Account #_____ Due Date _____

Amount Due $ _____ Late Charges _____

Although your payment is overdue, your previous record indicates a sincere desire to keep your account up to date. We assume that something has happened which makes it difficult for you to pay. We'd like to help.

Offer whatever help you can.

Solving money problems, whatever they might be, is our business. If you do have a problem, chances are that it will be easier than you think to find a solution. We would like to help you protect your credit standing. So, please make your payment or let us hear from you soon.

Letters of reprimand also fall into this category. Such letters are usually preceded by less formal warnings, so the reader should be expecting the negative message. Even so, when circumstances require you to reprimand an employee for his or her behavior, delay the most negative aspects of the message until you have reviewed the facts. To help the person do a better job in the future, be specific about what the person has been doing wrong (too much absenteeism, too many personal phone calls, poor quality control, or other failures to meet job requirements). You should also specify in the letter what the person needs to do to perform satisfactorily. Use the following structure:

1. **State the expected behavior.**   Tell the reader exactly what should be done to correct the problem.

2. **Review the facts.** Use positive language to specify what the reader is doing wrong, and explain the reasons the reader should be aware that the behavior is wrong.

3. **State the consequences.** Tell the reader exactly what will happen — and when it will happen — if the behavior is not corrected.

4. **Offer to help.** Keep the communication channels open. Offer to discuss the situation with the reader. Ask the reader to come up with his or her own solution to the problem.

SUMMARY

Negative messages contain a business objective to which the reader will respond in a negative way. The reader's response determines whether the informational message is negative. When your message will hurt, anger, or upset the reader, you should use a delayed structure. The use of the delayed structure helps prepare the reader for the negative aspect of the message by placing the emphasis on the reasons for the negative decision and on the positive alternatives to the original course of action.

The general structure for all negative messages is (1) delayed beginning, (2) explanation, (3) subordinated refusal, and (4) positive close.

A negative acknowledgment of a request for goods, service, an adjustment, or credit is bound to upset the reader. You need to make the best of the situation by (1) working to maintain a positive human and business relationship and (2) making certain that the reader understands the reasons for your decisions and knows what other courses of action are possible.

Delays in filling orders and refusals of orders are caused by a variety of circumstances, some of which are the reader's fault and some of which are the writer's fault (or the fault of the writer's company).

Anytime you must refuse a request or claim, the human objective — retaining your reader's goodwill — should receive the emphasis. You should delay the presentation of the business objective — the refusal — until you've prepared the reader by stating your reasons.

When you decide that a reader's request was unwarranted and should be refused, you need to be very careful to avoid accusing the reader of carelessness, misrepresentation, or fraud. Your principal business objective is to refuse the request; your secondary business objective is to resell the product or service in question and — to show confidence — sell a new product or service at the same time. Your human objective is to retain the reader's goodwill.

In most respects a letter refusing credit is more a persuasive message than it is a negative message, because its objective is not so much to refuse credit as it is to obtain the customer's business on a cash basis.

The human objective in a credit refusal is to show the reader that while a credit purchase might look attractive at the moment, it is in the reader's long-term interest to avoid risky credit obligations.

Negative announcements and reminders are frequently prepared as form letters to keep their costs low. If they are to be read at all, they must offer the reader something of value. When you can, offer real and specific benefits. At the very least, offer to discuss the situation with the reader.

EXERCISES

Review

1. What makes a message negative? Give the general structure for all negative messages.

2. When the reader is at fault for not supplying complete order information, what is the writer's principal task? What is the writer's principal task when the writer is at fault?

3. Name three reasons you would decline an order from a dealer.

4. What do you need to avoid when refusing a reader's request for an unwarranted claim? What are your business objectives? Your human objectives?

5. Why is a letter refusing credit more of a persuasive message than it is a negative message? What should you make clear to your reader?

Problems

1. Mrs. Charles Dickens, your boss at Dickens and Jackson, 9411 Pico Blvd., Santa Monica, CA 90400, asked you to prepare for her signature a form letter to be sent to all customers who send incomplete orders for clothing to the department store. Dickens and Jackson is currently using a form postcard which contains neither resale nor new sales material. Mrs. Dickens thinks that a form letter will provide sufficient opportunity to build goodwill and will be worth the added cost.

2. Assume that when Mr. Frank Busey (see problem #1, page 120) wrote to you ordering the electrical wire, he failed to specify the gauge of the wire. Acknowledge his order by mail, but suggest that he call you collect with the necessary information.

3. Your company, William Orange Publishing, 901 West Benjamin Street, Richmond, VA 23284, just received an order for 100 copies each of seven books from the Campus Book Store, Tiffin University, Tiffin, OH 44883. You can send five of the books now. The listed prices are retail, and the wholesale discount is 20 percent:

> *You Can't Go Home Again*, Thomas Wolfe, $4.95 ea., paper
> *You Gotta Be Kidding*, Henry McKeown, 8.95 ea., cloth
> *The Prodigal Son*, Richard Milhous, 14.95 ea., paper
> *Moses and Monotheism*, Sigmund Freud, 2.95 ea., paper
> *Ain't No Way*, Aretha Franklin, 11.95 ea., cloth

For two books, however, *Psychology and Phraseology*, by Caryl Freeman, and *Fun with the Semantic Differential*, by Vern Marietta, the Campus Book Store failed to specify the cloth or paper editions. The hardbound edition of *Psychology and Phraseology* sells for $10.95, the paperback for $4.95. The hardbound edition of *Fun with the Semantic Differential*, sells for $15.95; the paperback, for $6.75. Write the Campus Book Store.

4. Your Wholesale Electronic Supply Company, 4270 Peach Street, Atlanta, GA 30330, has just received a rush order for 15,000 200-ohm precision rheostats built to specifications supplied by Anderson Manufacturing, 47 Bethel Street, North Newton, KS 67117. You would like to retain the order, but because you have just begun a special order for the U.S. Navy that will take 90 days to complete, you must decline the order for the present. However, you don't want to lose Anderson as a customer. While other companies are capable of building the rheostats, your company has been building electronic equipment to individual specifications longer than anyone else in the country. Write the letter.

5. As the manufacturer of Lennox Sewing Machines, you frequently receive letters from customers who would like to purchase the machine directly from you rather than through one of your dealers. Prepare a form letter you can send as a reply which will direct the readers to their local dealers. Rather than specify dealers in the letter itself, you will enclose a brochure listing all your dealers in the 50 states.

6. As the manufacturer of Cowan Color Televisions, 716 Coamo Street, Hato Rey, PR 00917, you have received a letter from Mr. Wilbur Cox, owner of Cox's Appliances, 3911 Murray Street, Hennessey, OK 73742. Mr. Cox would like to be a dealer for you. While you do not have a dealer in Hennessey (the closest dealer is in Enid), Cox's Appliances does not have the right image for high-quality (and high-priced) Cowan Color Televisions. You only merchandise through quality department stores, and Cox's Appliances is a rather strange

conglomeration of fix-it shop, small town hardware store, and junk shop. Write a letter refusing Mr. Cox.

7. As owner of the Fruit Basket, RR4, Orlando, FL 32810, you advertise special gifts of fruit in several national magazines. Because you've found it much more convenient to do business for cash only, you always include a complete description of the baskets available and their prices in your ads. Nevertheless, today you've received an order for your $200 basket from Mrs. Ronda Young, 986 Gaviotta Drive, Los Angeles, CA 90000, requesting that the basket be sent COD. A quick check of your records indicates that Mrs. Young has purchased a $200 basket each year for the past five years. This is the first time she's requested a COD shipment. You don't want to lose her business, but you must write to her and request payment before you can send the fruit basket to her.

8. Answer Mr. William Atkins (see problem #3, p. 120) with a negative reply. You would like to be able to help him, but your schedule is completely full for the next six months. If he would contact you earlier next year, you would be glad to consider speaking about business communication to the English classes next fall.

9. As an assistant professor of marketing at Franklin and Marshall College, Lancaster, PA 17604, you have just published your first book: *The Shrinking World and the International Market.* Already you've received letters from three of your former students requesting autographed copies. The letters don't directly say so, but their implication is that you are to send the books without charge from your limited supply from the publisher. Write a sample letter to John Keats, 712 Lamia Way, Syracuse, NY 13210, and refuse. John can obtain a copy of the book from Shelley Press, Englewood Cliffs, NJ 07632, for $11.95 (includes postage and handling), and you'll be glad to autograph it for him should he visit Lancaster, PA, or send it to you by special fourth-class insured mail.

10. Because of your new book, *The Shrinking World and the International Market* (see preceding problem), you have been invited to interview for an associate professorship at the University of Bridgeport, Bridgeport CT 06602. The offer is very attractive and includes a substantial raise, but you wish to remain at Franklin and Marshall College until you complete work on your second book, *Principles of International Marketing,* which will take about a year. Decline the interview for the present, but leave the door open for future negotiations.

11. As assistant to Mr. Herman I Brogg, Manager, Education and Training, Walla Walla Insurance Companies, One Walla Walla Plaza, Walla Walla, WA 99362, prepare a letter for Mr. Brogg's signature

refusing to sell a copy of Walla Walla's video program, "Effective Sales Techniques," to Dr. Sally J. Larkin, College of Business, North Central Bible College, Minneapolis, MN 55404. All of Walla Walla's training films are for intracompany use only because they are made with Walla Walla employees rather than professional actors and actresses.

12. Assume you're Douglas Downing, Credit Manager, Blair Radio Equipment, 501 Wellington Drive, Denton, TX 76201. You have on your desk a letter and credit application from Mark McMerill, 2678 Crandall Court, Austin, TX 78734. Mark wants to order a $300 Panasonic Tri-Mode Stereo Sound System complete with an 8-track tape player and full-feature record changer with dust cover. Your credit check on Mark tells you that he is slow in paying his debts. In fact, he has an outstanding balance of $500 with another creditor. Write Mark denying him credit. Try to sell the stereo to him on a cash basis.

13. You're Sam Harrison, owner of Harrison Department Store, One South Chicago Street, Searcy, AR 72143. Your store has been in the family for five generations and has a fine reputation in the city. The mayor writes you and requests a contribution of $30,000 for the new civic center which is to be built near your store. You'll be glad to contribute $5,000 of corporate funds and to solicit another $5,000 from your employees. Write a letter to the mayor of the city, Ms. Alice Walden, City Hall, 1540 Page Mill Road, Searcy, AR 72143.

14. You're the office manager of Hoffman-LaRoche Inc., 133 Glentree Drive, Madison, WI 53706, and today you receive a letter from an accounting student at the University of Wisconsin. The student (Jana Jefferson, 578 Sanford Drive, Madison, WI 53706) said her professor assigned a project of auditing a local firm's records for a three-month period. The student is requesting your permission. Because of the confidentiality of your financial records, you refuse. However, you'll be glad to let Jana tour the accounting department and interview several of your controllers.

15. As the personnel director of E.I. Liddy Pharmaceuticals, 4721 Montgomery Lane, Joliet, IL 60436, prepare a form letter you can use to inform job applicants that they have not been hired. Each letter will be individually typed, which will permit you to personalize the opening paragraph and the reasons for the refusal. Write a sample letter to Ms. Judith Senne, 819 Weber Street, Huron, OH 44839.

16. Ms. Janice Roberts, 22 Darlington Apts., Ponce, PR 00731, has applied to your bank, the Industrial City Bank, 10 Clinton Square, Ponce, PR 00731, for an auto loan. Ms. Roberts is recently divorced,

and when she was married she established credit in her husband's name only. Because she has no marketable skills (she told you that she needs the car to look for work) and no job, you decide to refuse her application for credit. Because recent court decisions have tended to support divorced women's claim to credit established when they were married, you will need to word your refusal carefully. Be sure to tell her that because of her previous experience with your bank, you'll be glad to extend credit as soon as she obtains a job.

17. Rewrite the following letter:

Dear Student

We regret that our records indicate that you have failed to meet the requirements for graduation.

Please notify the graduate office if you plan to graduate in _____. If we do not hear from you IMMEDIATELY, we shall place your original diploma application in your folder with the understanding that you will notify us when you wish to have it reactivated for a future commencement.

The Graduate College

Requirements Not Met:

18. When you accepted an invitation to speak for free to your local chapter of Parents Without Partners, it was with the understanding that if you later received an invitation to speak for your usual fee of $500, you would be free to cancel your engagement with Parents Without Partners. Such an opportunity has arisen. Send Mr. Wayne Dwyer, president of PWP, 157 Hillside Drive, Rosell, IL 60172, your notice of cancellation. Include whatever specifics (title of talk, time, place, or names of possible replacements) you think are necessary.

19. Rewrite the following letter:

I regret to inform you that your admission to candidate status has been delayed until you complete the following requirement:

_____

Please let us know when you have completed this requirement so that your application for candidacy can be considered for approval. Let me emphasize that your candidacy will be denied if you fail to complete this requirement.

Sincerely,

Eileen S. Dostal
Associate Dean

P.S. Let me remind you of the regulation that graduate students are required to elect six hours of credit after their application for candidacy has been approved.

20. One of your least pleasant jobs as a department head is reprimanding members of your staff. Naturally you try to reprimand in as nice a way as possible: You begin by referring to the employee's deficiency in casual conversation, focusing on ways of improving job performance. Only when the situation is critical do you put anything in writing. Today you must write and deliver a letter of reprimand to Abraham Fenwick, who works for you in the Advertising Department. Your staff of professionals is composed roughly of half men and half women, who must work together closely. Fenwick, unfortunately, is unable to accept the women's professional competence. While he is not outright insulting, he manages to get in enough digs to ruin the harmony of your office. You've mentioned Fenwick's churlish attitude to him several times now, and each time he has promised to cooperate more fully with everyone in the office. This morning, however, Fenwick disrupted office procedures for what must be the last time. When Ms. Arlene Farrone, your best copywriter, was in the middle of presenting a new campaign to corporate management, Fenwick told her to go get coffee for everyone. Ms. Farrone continued her presentation in a professional manner, but, as she told you later, she found the remark extremely offensive. You've determined that the next time Fenwick fails to acknowledge the professionalism of the women on your staff, he will be fired. Prepare his letter of reprimand.

9. Persuading Your Reader to Act

Objectives

After you have read this chapter, you should be able to

1. Apply the general structure used for all persuasive messages.
2. Write persuasive messages in a way that will overcome reader resistance.
3. Write persuasive requests for favors, adjustments, credit, and funds.
4. Write solicited sales letters, direct-mail advertising, and soft-sell letters.
5. Write letters to collect debts.

To the extent that all messages attempt to influence behavior and thinking, all messages are persuasive. Almost everything we've said about letter writing thus far pertains as much to your need to "sell" a favorable image of yourself or your company as it does to communicating a particular idea. Persuasive messages, however, differ from the other message types we've discussed so far in that their purpose is to produce a specific behavior in a reader who is likely to ignore or resist either your message or the suggested behavior.

Because it is more difficult to communicate with people who are likely to ignore or resist your message, you run a greater risk of failing to communicate in persuasive situations than you do in informational situations. In communication situations involving positive information, your business objective and human objective are both served by communicating your message clearly. In communication situations involving negative information, your business objective includes not only communicating your message clearly but also having your reader accept your message. In negative situations, you cannot achieve your business objective without taking your reader's feelings into account and emphasizing the human objectives of the negative message.

In addition to the problems presented by negative messages, communication situations requiring persuasion present the problem of the reader's simply not caring about or actively disagreeing with your message. Persuasive messages, like negative messages, require a delayed structure because the writer must prepare the reader for the business objective by focusing on the human objective first.

Before you can ask your reader to take a particular action, you must convince your reader that your message has something worthwhile to offer and that what you say is true. Furthermore, you must achieve these objectives in spite of the fact that your reader may well already expect persuasive messages—yours included—to be less than fully truthful.

READER RESISTANCE AND APPEALS

Because readers are likely to ignore or resist your persuasive message, you will need to be especially careful to analyze your reader according to the principles we discussed in Chapter Three. Also, you will need to evaluate your reader's perception of you and the subject of your message and compare these with your reader's probable self-interest.

What the Reader Perceives

Several factors will influence your reader's reception of your persuasive message; while you don't need to understand fully the current theories of how persuasion works to be able to write an effective message, you will need to consider the following factors:

1. **Your credibility as an authoritative and reliable source.** Your ability to persuade will depend heavily on whether the reader perceives you as an expert on the topic of the message and on whether the reader believes that you are honest. You can have
   a. *Long-term credibility*—you're a well-known authority, and you've always been honest before.
   b. *Short-term credibility*—you offer facts and figures to prove that you're an expert, and your evidence is sound.
   c. *Carry-over credibility*—you know a lot about one subject and have been honest about it, so you will probably be honest about a new subject, too.
   d. *Official credibility*—your particular position or office shows that you should be credible.
2. **The reader's degree of interest in the subject of your message.** You can't expect someone who has no interest in your subject to be persuaded by even a first-rate letter. To paraphrase Lincoln, you can persuade all of the people some of the time and some of the people all of the time, but you can't persuade all of the people all of the time. Whenever you write persuasive messages, your success rate can be calculated as a percentage. While a typical

success rate is impossible to predict, in some instances, a "success percentage" of 4 or 5—with 4 or 5 out of every 100 readers being persuaded to act—would be an excellent response.

3. **The content of your message.**   The same arguments and appeals will not work equally well with all people, nor will they be equally successful for all products and services. You will have to select the approach and information based on your perception of your reader's wants and needs.

What the Reader Wants

More so than with other messages, a reader's main concern with a persuasive message is an answer to the question, "How will this message benefit me?" You will need to provide an answer to that question quickly, interestingly, and believably if you are going to overcome your reader's natural resistance to your persuasive message.

To be able to answer that question, you need to look at the communication situation from your reader's point of view. Your reader will be likely to resist your message for one of three reasons:

1. **Negative previous experience.**   Your reader may have had a bad experience with you, your idea, your company, a similar product or service, or with other persuasive messages.
2. **Time.**   Your reader may not wish to take the time to read an unexpected message, or your message may require the reader to spend time in a way he or she would not normally choose.
3. **Money.**   Acting on your message may cost the reader (or the reader's company) money that the reader would rather spend in some other way.

Unless a reader has had some positive experience with the suggested behavior, he or she will be inclined to focus on the negative aspects of previous experience and on the associated costs. To overcome the reader's tendency to accept the negative in the absence of a strong belief in the positive, you will need to appeal to the reader's self-interest. You will need to convince your reader that the action you are suggesting will prove desirable and will be more beneficial than the many other ways that the reader's time and money could be spent.

Because appeals to the reader's self-interest are more convincing when they are practical and specific, we recommend that you base your appeals on people's needs for *health*, *wealth*, *pleasure*, and *curiosity*. Undoubtedly the psychologists who have pointed out that human needs are hierarchical—with some being more important than others—are right. And, as a letter writer, you will naturally want to base your appeal on the strongest need you can associate with the behavior, idea, or product you are suggesting. You must, however, begin by selecting your appeals from the standpoint of what the suggested behavior, idea, or product will do for someone rather than by examining the range of human needs. You cannot simply assign attributes to the behavior, idea, or product because people might respond to those attributes.

Begin by asking yourself how the suggested behavior, idea, or product will contribute to your reader's health, wealth, pleasure, or curiosity. List as many appeals as you can think of for each category. Your appeals can be either positive or negative. Figure 9-1 illustrates the possibilities.

	HEALTH	WEALTH	PLEASURE	CURIOSITY
Positive:	Acting will make your reader feel better or live longer.	Acting will help your reader earn or save money or time.	The reader will enjoy acting, or action will make the reader think better of himself or herself.	Acting will answer questions the reader would like answered.
Negative:	Not acting will make your reader feel worse or die sooner.	Not acting will cost your reader time or money.	Not acting will deprive the reader of enjoyment or make the reader think worse of himself or herself.	Not acting will leave important questions unanswered.

Figure 9-1.   Possible appeals.

The general rule is that positive appeals, which focus on what the reader will gain, are more successful than negative appeals, which focus on what the reader might lose. Negative appeals have been effective in selling life insurance and some related concepts, and they are currently being used to promote seat-belt use and the 55 mile an hour speed limit. Unless the threat of loss is perceived as both real and fairly immediate, however, readers frequently ignore negative appeals. For example, negative appeals have been unsuccessful in persuading people to stop smoking. The threats of disease and an earlier death are too remote for most people to concern themselves with.

Appeals are also classed as either emotional or rational, depending on whether they appeal primarily to the reader's emotions or reason. Emotional appeals display the following characteristics:

1. **They use emotionally laden words.**   Two persuasive messages may contain the same factual elements, but one may use words that appeal to the reader's emotions and the other may use words that appeal to the reader's sense of logic.

Emotional: You can quit wasting precious fuel and pol-
luting the air by switching to modern,
pollution-free electrical heat.

Rational: An all-electric home gives you clean, efficient heating.

2. **They use explicit and implied analogies as proof.** Analogies—
comparisons—can be either emotional or rational, depending on
how they are used. When analogies are used as proof, they are
emotional. When they are used to illustrate and explain, they are
logical. The following examples are taken from recent magazine
ads:

Example: The GLC's instrument panel looks like an
instrument panel you'd expect to see in a
car costing a grand more.

Analysis: The analogy implies that the instrument
panel is high quality.

Example: Like a fine musical instrument, Marantz
(stereo equipment) is designed to be at
one with the music.

Analysis: The analogy implies that the product is
able to reproduce music with the same
quality of sound as the original instru-
ments.

Example: The U. S. Environmental Protection Agency
reports that charcoal is the best available
method for filtering water. It's also used
to mellow the taste of the finest bourbons.
Plain white filters remove taste. Tareyton's
charcoal filter actually improves flavor.

Analysis: The analogy implies that the charcoal filter
on the product will filter smoke as well as
EPA says it filters water and that the
charcoal will mellow the taste of cigarette
smoke the same way it mellows the taste of
bourbon.

Example: Let Arthur (Ashe), Tom (Watson), and Roger
(Stauback) tell you how to improve your
grip: "Get Armstrong Tires. They grip the
road!" On the court, on the course, and on
the field, the right grip gives these win-
ners the control they need. On the road,
the Armstrong grip does the same thing.

Analysis: The analogy implies that there is a high
degree of similarity between holding a
tennis racquet, a golf club, or football
and holding the road.

3. They appeal to the physical senses.   Messages that focus on seeing, smelling, tasting, hearing, and touching are emotional. Messages
that focus on ideas are rational.

Emotional: `Don't tell me taste isn't everything.`
`Taste. And only Winston gives me the taste`
`I like. Winston is all taste all the time.`
`And for me, taste is everything.`

Rational: `The Trimlite 28 camera has a sharp f/9.5`
`lens, sliding lens cover, electronic`
`shutter that goes from 1/160 to 1/30 second,`
`CdS meter for automatic exposure control and`
`a low-light signal.`

4. They omit steps required by logic.   A logical argument proceeds
carefully from point of proof to point of proof. An emotional argument draws conclusions without providing the complete evidence.

Example: `If your schedule (is busy), it's probably`
`hard for people to get hold of you. So you`
`have two choices. You can become a hermit`
`and camp by your telephone. Or you can get`
`yourself a Code-A-phone.`

Analysis: `The writer of the message has omitted`
`telling the reader why it's necessary for`
`the phone to be answered every time it`
`rings. The reader's third choice is to`
`assume that people will call back if the`
`message is important.`

Emotional appeals, as you can see, tend to manipulate the reader.
They lead the reader to draw conclusions based on insufficient evidence
or for the wrong reasons. Emotional appeals also tend to be more effective for achieving certain kinds of short-term persuasion. Emotional
appeals work best for inexpensive products and intangible services
which would be attractive to the reader primarily because of the momen-
tary pleasure they would provide.

For most situations, however, the best approach is to combine emotional appeals with more-logical arguments. The most persuasive argument you can provide for an idea, a product, or a service is the truth. An
emotional appeal may be useful to create reader interest in your message,
but a clear presentation of facts—accompanied by their real reader
benefits—is the most persuasive argument you can use.

In addition to a firm grounding in truth, successful persuasive messages
concentrate on one primary appeal based on the writer's analysis of the
reader's principal want or need. Secondary appeals are used to support
and supplement the primary appeal but are not fully developed.

GENERAL STRUCTURE AND CHECKLIST

The general structure for all persuasive messages is as follows:

1. **Attention.**   In a business letter it is impossible to persuade someone unless that person will pay attention to your message. You can
   get a reader to focus attention on your message by stating a
   problem that affects him or her or by promising something of benefit. Emotional appeals frequently catch attention better than
   rational appeals. The attention elements should introduce the primary appeal. Questions that cannot be answered *yes* or *no* (beginning with *what*, *how*, *why*, and *when*) usually make the best
   openings for persuasive messages. *Yes* or *no* questions are a second
   choice for an opening, as are statements of reader benefit.
2. **Interest.**   You can maintain reader interest by showing your reader
   that a solution to a problem is possible or by picturing your reader
   enjoying the benefits promised. Answer the questions asked in the
   attention element. Use the interest element to provide a clear transition from the attention element to the conviction element.
3. **Conviction.**   The conviction part of your persuasive message consists of the facts, figures, testimonials, tests, samples, guarantees,
   or other proof your proposal requires. A descriptive brochure
   (referred to late in the letter) may help keep your letter from being
   too cluttered. The conviction element should fully develop the primary appeal and perhaps contain secondary appeals as well.
4. **Action.**   The close of a persuasive message should tell the reader
   exactly what action to take, give a reason for acting promptly, and
   provide a postage-paid reply envelope or other aids to make that
   action easy. The action element should contain a reference to the
   primary appeal.

PERSUASIVE REQUESTS

Whenever you are writing to someone who has no special interest in
doing as you ask—or even in replying—you need to write a persuasive
letter. How persuasive you need to be depends on how obvious it will be
to your reader that he or she stands to benefit from action in the manner
you suggest. Persuasive requests fall into four basic categories: favors,
adjustments and claims, credit, and fund-raising letters.

Favors

Asking a favor by mail is *not* the same as asking a favor from a friend in
person. Friends do favors out of friendship and because they know that,

as the relationship continues, the favor will probably be returned. When you write to someone requesting a favor—which will usually cost the reader either time or money—you must offer the reader a benefit that will serve as a substitute for a continuing friendship.

Because your reader will need to have your persuasive request placed in a specific communication context quickly, it's important that you introduce the reason you are writing early in the letter. You should, however, mention the main reader benefit (health, wealth, pleasure, or curiosity) *before* you make the nature of your request clear. Be sure to keep the reader in the picture as you explain why the favor is necessary. Your closing should ask the reader to make a specific commitment by a specific date, and it should reiterate the main reader benefit.

Attention. Open with a question about a common concern or with a statement about a common problem. Avoid high-pressure openings and bribes.

How many accountants actually understand the principles of business communication? Your article in The Journal of Business Communication pointed out some rather serious shortcomings in letters and reports written by accountants.

Maintain reader's **interest**. Specify the problem, the benefit (reader's pleasure), and the request in general terms.

The Associated Chicago Accountants agree with you that the typical accountant writes cold, formal letters which can be understood only by other accountants. We'd like to change that, and your expert opinion would be a big help in persuading our members to write better letters.

Conviction. Keep the reader in the picture as you provide all the necessary details.

As the speaker at our annual accountants' banquet, you'd have the pleasure of presenting your ideas to 150 very receptive accountants who would be willing to share their letter-writing problems with you.

You'll be our guest at the magnificent banquet, which will be more than just another convention meal, to be held at the Palmer House at 6 p.m., Saturday, 14 September. The schedule for the program is

Cocktails:	6:00-6:30
Dinner:	6:30-8:00
Presentation:	8:00-8:45
Questions and Answers:	8:45-9:00
Entertainment and Dancing:	9:00-1:00

Specify the compensation in positive terms, even when what you can offer is less than the

Greater than our $50 honorarium is our sincere appreciation for your contribution to the education of our accountants. In addition to the $50 honorarium, we'll reimburse you for air travel and hotel accommodations at the Palmer

reader expects. Do
not apologize for
insufficient com-
pensation.

House. We'll have someone waiting for
you at O'Hare if you'll just let us
know your arrival time.

Action. Set an end
date and justify it.
Mention the reader
benefit once more.

Because the program must go to the
printer on 15 August, we'd appreciate
receiving your decision before that
date. Use the enclosed postage-paid
reply card to let us know. The Associated Chicago Accountants look forward
to hearing your expert presentation of
the principles of business communication
when we meet 14 September.

Adjustments

Most claims and requests for adjustment can be handled as immediate,
informational messages (see pp. 91-97). Sometimes, however, you will
need to write a persuasive message to get the results you desire. You
may, for example, have written one request as an informational message
and received an unsatisfactory reply. Or you may feel that your reader
will be inclined to ignore or resist your message because of the circumstances involved.

In requesting an adjustment, you can appeal to your reader's

1. Sense of fair play (an appeal to psychological pleasure),
2. Desire for customer goodwill (an indirect appeal to wealth),
3. Need for a good reputation (an appeal to continued wealth), or
4. Sense of legal or moral responsibility (an appeal to wealth or
   pleasure).

When writing a persuasive request for adjustment, you need to remember
that your goal—your business objective—is to have the adjustment
granted. You may be angry with your reader and tempted to accuse and
insult, but your reader will be more inclined to grant your request when
you present your case in a calm, logical manner. That doesn't mean that
you can't let your reader know how you feel. Your disappointment with
the products, policies, or services provided by the reader or the reader's
company may well be the most important part of your argument.

The main part of your argument, however, must be a clear and logical
presentation of the facts. Your reader must know exactly what you expect and why you expect it if you are to receive the adjustment.

Attention. State the
problem from the
reader's point of
view.

What better advertising could Scandi
have than satisfied customers? Just
as satisfied customers say nice
things about Scandi cars, those who
aren't satisfied like to talk about
their problems.

Interest. Introduce the problem. Remember that your reader is not personally responsible for your trouble.

That's why I'm writing to you. Right now I'm very unhappy with my Scandi because of the unusual difficulties I've been having with it. Since I purchased the car in August 19_, I've had practically the entire car replaced or rebuilt. In the first 12 months the car required a new water pump, new fuel pump, two new fuel injectors, new disc brakes, and a new battery. Also, the transmission had to be rebuilt. The warranty covered everything except my cab fare, inconvenience, and loss of time.

Conviction. Give specific dates, figures, and other facts to prove your point.

But last month the warranty ran out. Just 19 days after the warranty expired, the Scandi dropped a valve. As you know, when a car drops a valve, the engine must be overhauled completely. The dealer says that he's sorry I've had so much trouble, but the bill will be $395.49.

Under usual circumstances, Scandi's 12-month, 24,000-mile warranty should be sufficient for defective parts to turn up and be replaced. In the case of my dropped valve, however, a part that obviously had been defective for some time didn't reveal itself for 12 months and 19 days. Had my car not been in the shop so often the first year, I would have driven it more than the 12,000 miles it now has, and the defective valve would have been obvious sooner.

Action. Ask for the specific action you desire. Come back to the reader benefit.

Because of the unusual difficulties I've had with my Scandi, I believe that Scandi Motors should extend my warranty to cover the dropped valve. Your check to me for $395.49 will restore my faith in Scandi's reputation for fine cars and fair dealing.

Persuasive Requests for Credit

Persuasive requests for credit must be based on circumstances that genuinely warrant the extension of credit in spite of the requestor's inability to pass certain credit tests. For example, you may be opening a new store and need to purchase inventory on terms longer than your supplier's usual terms. Or you may be refused a credit card at a department store when you believe that your record indicates that you are fully capable of meeting credit card obligations.

Persuasive requests for credit need to demonstrate to the reader that the writer has a good understanding of how credit works, the intention of fulfilling credit obligations, and the ability to pay. Be sure to cover the following points:

1. **Attention.** Place the message in context by referring to previous correspondence ("Your letter refusing my application for credit came as a surprise. . . .") or by focusing on the way the reader can benefit from extending you credit (primarily, increased sales). Normal interest on a loan is *not* enough of a benefit because if there were not a greater than usual risk, you would be extended credit on the basis of your ability to pass normal credit tests.
2. **Interest.** Show your reader that you understand that credit is a privilege, not a right. Be positive and confident even if you've been refused credit once already.
3. **Conviction.** Explain your financial position and the method by which you expect to pay. Be specific. List credit references, employment and income, any assets and outstanding obligations, and other pertinent facts. Show how the reader will benefit by extending credit.
4. **Action.** State your request specifically and confidently.

Requests for Funds

Raising funds by mail can be a rather specialized business. Many service orgainzations providing welfare and health care to those who need it require donations to stay in business. Many churches, schools, and colleges would operate at a loss were it not for the generosity of those to whom the organizations turn for donations. Though you may not choose to work for an organization that makes a regular practice of soliciting funds by mail during your lifetime, you may belong to several nonprofit organizations that could benefit from a few extra dollars—fraternities, sororities, social clubs wishing to undertake worthy causes, youth clubs, and senior-citizen groups are a few examples.

People who respond to requests for funds fall into two general categories: (1) major givers (wealthy donors, foundations, corporations) and (2) most people. Major givers respond primarily to rational appeals. They wish to have a full explanation of how the money will be used, and they will want to see a detailed operating budget. Major givers will expect you to demonstrate a real need. Most people, however, give primarily for emotional reasons. They give because they want to help others who are less fortunate then they are; they give because they can see an opportunity to spend a little of their money doing good for others.

Like all persuasive messages, requests for funds must be carefully considered from the standpoint of cost effectiveness. Each letter will cost you printing and postage, but not everyone will respond. Your mailing list should be selected carefully on the basis of what audience will have a special interest in your particular project.

Requests for funds follow the same basic organizational pattern as other persuasive messages:

1. **Attention.**   State the problem in a way with which the reader can identify. Whether you are writing to a major giver or to the general public, use a people-oriented, personal beginning.
2. **Interest.**   Explain the problem in a way the reader can appreciate. Your main problem is to provide enough human interest to keep the reader reading.
3. **Conviction.**   Show what you will do with the money. Major givers are interested in your overall budget. Most people are interested in how you have helped (or will help) individuals. Consider enclosing a separate budget statement.
4. **Action.**   Ask specifically for a donation. If the donation is tax deductible, say so. Provide a postage-paid reply envelope to make the action easy, and remind the reader of the importance of the contribution. A postscript will frequently improve your return. In the postscript, mention a new reader benefit or a special benefit for acting promptly.

SALES LETTERS

From one point of view, every letter you write will be selling something. For example, requests sell your responsibility and credibility. Even letters conveying information may be said to "sell" a business relationship based on trust and fair play. When you are deliberately using a letter to sell a product or a service or are using the letter *only* to promote future business, your message requires a special strategy. In addition to analyzing your audience, you must know your product or service thoroughly before you can wite an effective sales letter. What will your product or service do for your reader? How will it satisfy your reader's need for health, wealth, pleasure, or curiosity?

Sales letters fall into three general, overlapping categories: unsolicited, solicited, and soft-sell. Unsolicited sales letters are also known as direct-mail advertising; they are a form of advertising sent by mail directly to the prospective buyer. Solicited sales letters are replies to inquiries about products or services. Soft-sell letters are special goodwill letters used to maintain cordial relations with important customers.

Unsolicited Sales Letters

Because many who receive unsolicited sales letters consider them "junk mail," your first objective must be to convince the reader that opening the envelope and reading the letter will be worthwhile. Consider using an "envelope teaser"—a few words on the envelope to suggest a reader benefit—to encourage the reader to continue. Remember that your main concern is with those poeple in your audience who are true

prospects—people who want your product or service and can afford to buy it. Write your letter to persuade those with a real interest in your product or service to buy it. Don't make the mistake of writing your letter to entertain everyone who may receive it.

Successful sales letters display the following characteristics:

1. **They emphasize the benefits** rather than the features of the product or service.
2. **They use active voice and personalize** the letter to the extent of making the reader the subject or object of many sentences. They picture the reader enjoying the use of the product or service.
3. **They focus on one main appeal.**
4. Unless the price is an obvious bargain, **they subordinate the price** by mentioning it after most of the benefits have been listed. They state the price in terms of small units ($2 a glass rather then $24 a dozen), compare the price with the cost of something else with which the reader is more familiar, or, when the price is high, suggest extended payments.
5. **They use enclosed brochures** to illustrate the product or service and to supplement the details presented in the letter.
6. **They are specific in their request for action**, specifying exactly what the reader should do (complete the order blank, send a check, or visit a dealer), making that action easy by providing simple order blanks and return envelopes, and encouraging the reader to act promptly.

The following letter written to home owners in Ohio, Michigan, and Indiana illustrates these points.

Attention. When the letter is a form, use a simulated inside address to catch the reader's attention.

> What can you do
> to reduce your rising
> fuel costs?
>
> The cost of heating homes in Ohio,
> Michigan, and Indiana has, as you know,
> increased tremendously in the past few
> years.

Interest. Keep the reader in the picture. Use lists and vary paragraph size to make the appearance of the letter interesting.

> Even with added insulation and a re-
> duced thermostat setting, your own bills
> have probably doubled since 1965. And
> there's no relief in sight for the in-
> creasing cost of fuel. Gas, oil, elec-
> tricity, and even coal are only going to
> cost more in the future.
>
> But Ajax Products has developed an in-
> expensive and completely safe solution
> to home heating problems. Our Energy-
> Savers can cut the cost of your winter
> fuel bill by as much as 31 percent, and
> you can install them yourself simply,
> easily, and without special tools.

Conviction. Provide facts, figures, and testimonials. Focus on one main appeal—in this case the appeal is to wealth.

Here's what some satisfied owners have had to say:

"Energy-Savers made a real difference in my bill." Iris Mannis, Butte, Montana.

"I should have had these years ago." Louis Schumacher, Yuba, Wisconsin.

"Cut the fuel cost in my store by 32 percent." Elmer Gantry, Chicago, Illinois.

The Engery-Savers can save you hundreds of dollars in heating costs next year—and every year thereafter—for only $7.95 each. All you need to do is place one or two Energy-Savers next to your heat sources. Energy-Savers should be placed behind radiators, above forced air outlets, and next to electrical heating elements. The self-stick backing makes them easy to install.

Made of a special ceramic substance, Energy-Savers are able to store and reflect heat in a much more efficient way than wall and ceiling plaster. Studies have shown that rooms with Energy-Savers stay warmer and require less fuel than rooms of the same size and shape without Energy-Savers.

After you've had the opportunity to read about the studies in the enclosed brochure, calculate the number of Energy-Savers you'll need for maximum heating efficiency this next winter according to the formula on page 4. You'll be amazed at how inexpensive it will be for you to reduce your fuel costs.

Action. Make it specific, make it easy, and encourage promptness.

To order, simply complete the order blank at the back of the brochure. Should you wish extended payments, complete and return the brief credit application at the same time in the postage-paid envelope provided. Your Energy-Savers will pay for themselves in no time—before next winter is over for typical homes—and you'll be more comfortable, too.

Cordially,

Alice Ajax

P.S. A postscript stressing benefits or advantages of ordering promptly will increase the letter's pull.

Order in the next 10 days, and we'll give you one free Energy-Saver for every 10 you purchase.

Solicited Sales Letters

In many ways it's easier to write a solicited sales letter than an unsolicited sales letter because your reader has invited you to send the letter. Because your reader expects your letter, you don't have to worry that your message will be ignored completely.

Whenever someone has written to you asking for information about your products or services, you have a fine opportunity to encourage that person to buy from you. Your message should display all of the characteristics of the unsolicited sales letter (see p. 158), but it should be prepared individually rather than as a form. Use the following structure:

1. **Attention.** Your reader is already interested in your product or service, so begin by answering one of your reader's main questions. Find the most important question in your reader's letter of inquiry which you can answer in a positive way. If you've been asked to make a recommendation, do it first.
2. **Interest.** Answer all of your reader's questions as clearly and specifically as you can. Subordinate negative answers. Adapt your letter to meet the needs expressed in the reader's inquiry.
3. **Conviction.** Supply the details and evidence that seem most appropriate for your individual reader. Use an enclosed brochure to keep the letter from becoming too cluttered.
4. **Action.** Just as in an unsolicited sales letter, you need to tell the reader exactly what to do to purchase, make the required action easy or *seem* easy ("visit your neighborhood dealer"), and encourage the reader to act quickly.

Soft-Sell Letters

Soft-sell letters are special goodwill letters, the purpose of which is to remind the reader that your firm provides a particular product or service. Because of the cost involved, soft-sell letters are primarily used at the industrial level to keep a company's name familiar to important clients and customers.

To be successful, soft-sell letters must be welcomed and appreciated by the reader. The reader must look forward to receiving and reading the message month after month. To create that kind of reader appreciation, you need to give the reader information of value or to provide entertaining material. The bulk of the letter consists of information or entertainment, and only at the end does the writer insert a reminder of the business involved.

Attention. Offer something of value or tell an interesting story.

WHY WASTE WORDS?

Ten years ago the average letter was 250 words long. Today the average is about 125 words. Yet the 125-word letter costs more to write.

Interest. Show the reader how to improve the way he or she does business or provide entertainment.

BE CONCISE...

You can generally tell your whole story in a few words and make the reader feel good about you and your company by concentrating on the essentials.

KNOW YOUR PURPOSE...

State the purpose of your letter in one clear, simple sentence. If the reader will welcome that sentence, put it first and explain later.

If the reader will resent that sentence, explain first to make the reader feel better, and follow the purpose sentence with some kind of positive advice.

If the reader will ignore or resist your purpose sentence, save it until near the end of your letter, after you've explained the situation thoroughly.

ELIMINATE NONESSENTIALS...

In addition to avoiding wordy expressions (the color red, square in shape, in the month of August, etc.) eliminate all words and sentences that do not help make your idea clear or make your reader feel better about you and your company.

Conviction. Briefly remind the reader of who your are and what you can do for him or her. Keep it simple.

Action. Remind the reader how to get in touch with you.

AND ASK THE EXPERTS...

When you have real communication problems, remember that COMMUNICA-TION CONSULTANTS INC., 2525 Wilshire Blvd., Los Angeles, CA 90000, is here to help. Whether your problems are letters, reports, interpersonal, small group, or labor-management, we can help you solve them. We're as near as your phone. Call us collect at (213) 389-9000.

Letters That Sell Ideas

Nearly everything we've said so far about selling products and services applies equally well to selling ideas. When you need to add a new person to your staff, convince higher management to adopt a new procedure, propose a feasibility study, or persuade your staff to conserve supplies, you should follow the same basic procedure you would use to sell a product: analyze your reader in the same way and select appeals based on the reader's needs. Also, selling ideas by letter requires the same kind of structural planning as that used for selling products and services. In addition to basing your argument on appeals to your reader's needs and structuring your message to overcome reader resistance, you need to take a few other precautions when you wish to persuade a reader to adopt your idea.

1. **Attention.** Not only do you need to begin with a problem of interest to your reader, but you must also begin with a premise your reader readily accepts. If the reader disagrees with your opening, he or she will be all the more inclined to resist the rest of your message.
2. **Interest.** How quickly you can develop your argument depends on your reader's degree of resistance. People usually have a vested interest in maintaining their current beliefs, and before they will adopt new ideas, they must be fully convinced that it is in their self-interest to do so. Corporations, for example, are notorious for accepting reports that agree with current policy and rejecting reports that disagree with current policy.
3. **Conviction.** Rely on truth and logic. When there are two sides to an issue, present both sides, You can emphasize your own side of the argument, but your reader will resent your message if you fail to mention other obvious possibilities. Always give your reader all the facts that might influence his or her decision. Long-range results are usually more important than short-range success (concentrate on winning the war, even if you must lose the initial battle).
4. **Action.** Let your reader know exactly what you expect. When your reader's resistance is high, it is better to persuade by degrees rather than to make your message an all-or-nothing proposition. Remind the reader of the benefits to be gained (or lost) by adopting (or not adopting) your idea.

COLLECTION LETTERS

Because doing business by credit always involves a certain degree of risk, it is sometimes necessary to persuade people who owe money to pay. While collection is quickly becoming an increasingly specialized business, everyone in business should have a basic understanding of collection procedures and letters because collection problems influence the entire operation of the organization. Because a sale is not complete until the seller is paid, and because a company's attitude toward its customers is influenced by the assumptions made about credit customers, you need a good working knowledge of collection procedures regardless of where you work in an organization.

As you will recall from our discussion of confidence (see p. 165), a letter writer should always assume that the reader is going to do the right thing until it's been proven otherwise. When customers are slow to pay, letter writers are sometimes quick to forget this important principle.

The collection procedure is one of gradual escalation in forcefulness. When a bill becomes overdue, the writer should first assume that the reader intends to pay but has forgotten. If the reader does not respond to a reminder (or reminders) to pay, the writer should assume that the reader is not paying because of financial, personal, or medical problems. The writer can help the reader solve his or her problems by making new financial arangements that will ease the reader's burden. Only after these efforts have been made, should the writer assume that the reader will have to be persuaded to pay.

Reminders

Reminders of overdue bills usually consist of

1. Duplicate copies of the original bill,
2. Duplicate copies of the bill stamped "Reminder" or "Past Due," or
3. A short note (usually a form) specifying the amount due, the due date, late charges, and the account number.

A company usually sends one or more reminders to a customer because most people who are going to pay will do so when they are reminded gently. Sometimes companies choose to combine a final reminder with an inquiry about the reasons for not paying. Reminders of overdue bills are negative messages, an example of which is presented on page 138.

Inquiries

Before the writer decides that the customer needs to be persuaded to pay, the writer should try to discover whether special circumstances are preventing payment. Many people are embarrassed when they can't pay their bills, and instead of taking positive action to solve their financial problems, they hope that if they ignore their problems long enough, they will solve themselves. When the writer demonstrates a genuine willingness to help the readers solve their financial difficulties, most will respond by agreeing to new terms that will allow the company to collect its money and the customers to remain solvent. Inquiries are written with the assumption that it is better to collect your money a little late than not to collect it at all.

Inquiries are divided into two categories: first and second. A first inquiry can be as simple as the example on p. 158; a second inquiry may contain an appeal for a prompt partial payment and some suggestions for taking care of the obligation in ways other than the original agreement called for. Keep inquiries positive: do *not* suggest that reader dissatisfaction with your goods or services might be responsible for late payment.

Appeals

When the reader has failed to respond to one or more reminders and to one or more inquiries, the writer must assume that the reader will not pay unless he or she is persuaded—perhaps even forced legally—to do so. Because you would not be writing an appeal unless you had gone through the reminder and inquiry stages, you should assume that the reader is going to be well prepared to resist your message. Should you choose to send more than one appeal, you can begin with at least one positive appeal, such as an appeal to cooperation, fair play, or pride. Because the reader has failed to respond to your earlier messages, however, the chances are that unless you can give the reader a very good reason for paying, he or she will continue to ignore your efforts to collect. We, therefore, recommend that your letter of appeal be a strong one, appealing directly to the reader's self-interest.

Because the reader has failed to respond several times, negative appeals are usually required at the appeal stage. The reader should be told that by not paying, he or she is likely to lose the following:

1. Credit privileges
2. The goods or services not paid for
3. Additional money or property
4. Reputation and self-respect

Attention. Resell the goods or services; remind the reader what he or she is currently enjoying.

Remember how thrilled you were the day we installed your General Appliance color television set? Your wife and children just couldn't wait to see their favorite shows in full color.

Interest. Review the facts for the reader.

When you agreed last August to purchase the $698 General Appliance television set for $42 a month, we were glad to allow you a generous $75 for your used Zephyr in trade to help you qualify for our monthly payment plan.

Conviction. Remind the reader that the consequences for nonpayment are unpleasant.

We were glad to give you the benefit of the doubt because we had faith in you. And we knew that you and your family would enjoy your television viewing more with a new color set.

You are now more than 90 days behind in your payments, and you must think about this each time you sit down to watch television. That can't be very enjoyable. As a favor to yourself and to your family, take care of this credit obligation before the situation becomes more serious.

Action. Tell the reader what you expect and when you expect it.

Right now you can solve your problem by using the enclosed envelope to send us your check for $140 to take care of the amount past due plus the charges for late payment. Send us your check today, and you'll enjoy your television viewing more tonight.

Should your readers fail to respond to your appeal (some companies send more than one letter, but we question the cost-effectiveness of doing so), you should give them one more opportunity to pay at the same time you notify them of the action you will take if they don't pay. This final letter is known as the ultimatum. Your assumption must be that the reader will have to be forced to pay. In this last effort to collect, you should review the facts, set an end date, and notify the reader that on that date you will turn the debt over to a collection agency or to your lawyer. Do not threaten the reader, and do not accuse the reader of personal shortcomings. Even at this point you may be able to retain your reader's goodwill and cash business, so remain fair, reasonable, and logical throughout.

SUMMARY

To the extent that all messages attempt to influence behavior and thinking, all messages are persuasive. Persuasive messages differ from the other message types we've discussed so far in that their purpose is to produce a specific behavior in the reader when the reader is likely to ignore or resist either your message or the suggested behavior.

The following factors will influence your reader's reception of your persuasive message: (1) your credibility as an authoritative and reliable source, (2) the reader's degree of interest in the subject of your message, and (3) the content of your message. Your reader will be likely to resist your message for one of three reasons—negative previous experience, time, or money.

You will need to appeal to the reader's self-interest to overcome a negative previous experience or to convince your reader that the action you are suggesting will be more beneficial than the many other ways the reader's time and money could be spent. People's needs fall into four general categories: health, wealth, pleasure, and curiosity. Your appeals to these needs can be either positive or negative.

The general structure for all persuasive messages is attention, interest, conviction, and action.

Persuasive requests fall into four basic categories: favors, adjustments and claims, credit, and fund-raising letters. When you write to someone requesting a favor, you must offer the reader a benefit that will serve as a substitute for a continuing friendship. In requesting an adjustment, you can appeal to your reader's sense of fair play, desire for customer goodwill, need for a good reputation, or sense of legal or moral responsibility. Persuasive requests for credit must be based on circumstances that genuinely warrant the extension of credit in spite of the requestor's inability to pass certain credit tests.

Requests for funds must demonstrate a real need. Before major givers will make a donation, they need to see a logical explanation of need— including a sample of your budget. Most people, however, give for emotional reasons and prefer to see your need expressed in terms of help for particular individuals.

Sales letters fall into three general categories: unsolicited, solicited, and soft-sell. Unsolicited sales letters are also known as direct-mail advertising. Solicited sales letters are replies to inquiries about products or services. Soft-sell letters are special goodwill letters used to maintain cordial relations with important customers.

Collection letters are necessary to persuade people who owe money to pay. The collection procedure is one of gradual escalation in forcefulness. When a bill becomes overdue, the writer should first assume that the reader intends to pay but has forgotten. If the reader does not respond to a reminder to pay, the writer should assume that the reader is not paying because of financial, personal, or medical problems. Only after an inquiry has been ignored should the writer assume that the reader will have to be persuaded to pay.

EXERCISES

Review

1. When is a persuasive message necessary?

2. Give the general structure for all persuasive messages.

3. What factors should you consider before writing persuasive messages?

4. Name the four general categories of self-interest. Explain how they can be either positive or negative.

5. Name the four characteristics of emotional appeals.

6. What are persuasive requests?

7. Why is the following statement true? "Every letter you write will be selling something."

8. Name the three categories of sales letters.

9. Why are collection letters important to business?

10. Explain the statement: "The collection procedure is one of gradual escalation in forcefulness."

Problems

1. As a doctoral student in the Department of Business Education and Administrative Services, Kent State University, Kent, OH 44240, Bruce Bailey, 224 Laurel Lane, Kent, OH 44240, needs to send out 600 letters to personnel directors asking them to complete a one-page questionnaire on job requirements for initial office employment. Write the cover letter for Bruce.

2. As Ms. Anita Sullivan (148 Sixth Street, Knoxville, TN 37916), fund-raising committee chairperson for a local charitable organization (name one of your choice), write a letter inviting friends to a $10 a plate dinner. To persuade friends, tell them what the funds will be used for (use your imagination). To entice them, you might want to mention what the mouth-watering menu will be. You might mention that the Vagabonds (choral group from a local university) will provide entertainment during the meal.

3. As Chris Wanamaker, president of Pi Omega Pi (a national honorary business education teacher fraternity), write a letter inviting school board member Charles Overton, 503 Fifth Avenue, Meriden, CT 06450, to speak for about 30 minutes to your organization of 50 students next Monday on academic freedom in the classroom.

4. You're Bill Thompson, 9087 South Gate Street, Orono, ME 04473, and you have just been graduated from the University of Maine. You decided you no longer will need your IBM electric typewriter, and you wish to sell it. You learn from a friend that Jill St. John, a freshman at the University, needs a typewriter. Write her a letter describing your typewriter and emphasize the benefits of owning an electric typewriter.

5. As the direct mail writer for *Psychology Today*, P.O. Box 2990, Boulder, CO 80323, you (Harold P. Crandall) have been asked to prepare a form letter that will be sent to former subscribers. Your letter will be an inducement for them to subscribe to the magazine once again. Be sure to give plenty of reader benefits (You might want to look at a copy in the library to see what the magazine offers.) You can offer four issues free to those who subscribe within ten days.

6. You're in charge of sales for the branch office of the Utah Insurance Company, 5089 Warner Road, Akron, OH 44325. The home office just announced a new sales incentive program. If you can sell $500,000 worth of insurance within a six-month period, you'll be eligible for a two-week vacation in Hawaii. You decide to write a letter to the parents of newborn babies (as listed in the birth announcements in the local newspapers) persuading them to buy additional coverage based on their new family responsibilities. Prepare a letter that can be used as a sample, and send it to Mr. and Mrs. Arden Farquhar, 10727 Sprague Avenue, West Haven, CT 06516.

7. As sales director for SweepPower (manufacturers of vacuum cleaners), 498 Stanford Avenue, Newark, NJ 07106, answer Ms. Karen Cayo's (1876 Beverly Drive, Metairie, LA 70002) inquiry about the SweepPower, an upright vacuum cleaner. SweepPowers move with only the slightest touch of the hand; a motor does the work. SweepPowers sell for $185 each. SP Motor: powerful 2-speed motor delivers 53 air power. Cleaning features: motor-driven vinyl beater brush revolves 4500 rmp. The SP has seven adjustment positions. Construction: hi-impact plastic housing. Push-button suction speed controls. Attachments: rear-mounted attachment port. Electrical information: 20-ft cord with automatic rewind. UL Listed; 110-120 volts. Order will be processed within ten days of receipt of order. Enclose a brochure for a more detailed description and illustrations.

8. As president of the Student Association at Boise State University, 1910 College Blvd., Boise, ID 83725, you're planning a week's sun-sea-sand vacation to Bermuda for all students during the Easter break. The $600 package trip includes the following:

   Airfare by United Airlines DC10
   Six nights in Bermuda's Surf Hotel
   Special area sightseeing tour
   All airport transfers
   All baggage handling
   All tips and taxes
   Complimentary meals and beverages enroute

   The trip originates from your campus on April 16 and returns on April 22. Reservations are made through the Student Association Tour Committee, Student Services Bldg. Write the creative letter that will be used as an ad in your school's student paper. Interested students may pick up a brochure and more information in the SA office.

9. As promotion manager for Sonneville Sisters Department Store, 736 Leland Road, Ellisville, MS 39437, write a form letter to your charge

customers encouraging them to do their Christmas shopping at your store. You'll be having daily specials for the week of December 12-17.

Monday	— Gifts for the toddlers to teens
Tuesday	— Gifts for him
Wednesday	— Gifts for her
Thursday	— Gifts for the teens
Friday	— Gifts for those who have everything
Saturday	— Gifts for the home

10. As Mr. Todd Thompson, credit manager of Mascolini's Department Store, 1092 Main Street, Baltimore, MD 21224, you write a letter to your charge customers who have not used their accounts in six months. If they make a $5 charge purchase within the next three weeks, you'll give them a free gift—a 14" x 15½" x 6" softly grained vinyl tote bag in a color of their choice (red, orange, grey, green, or gold) with top zipper and tuck lock. You might want to mention your new store hours—daily from 10 a.m. to 10 p.m. and on Saturday from noon until 6 p.m.

11. Write a letter to the superintendent of your local school system persuading him or her to add a course in business communication to the high school curriculum.

12. Write a letter persuading the mayor of your city to take action on an important local issue (for example, install a traffic light at a dangerous intersection, repave a particular street, increase pay for fire fighters, etc.).

13. As Jason Holland, 394 Meadowbrook Lane, Huron, OH 44839, you recently wrote a claim letter to Cold Air Refrigerators, 309 Berwick Road, Columbia, SC 29210, explaining that you wanted reimbursement for the $30 door gasket you had to replace on your one-month old refrigerator. You were refused your request. You decide to write a persuasive request. This time you mail the original gasket to the company by certified mail. In your letter you explain that obviously the gasket was contaminated by a petroleum product during manufacture.

14. Assume that your friend, Ms. Rose B. Tully, 806 South Highland Avenue, Forest City, IA 50336, has asked you to help her with a claim. Six months ago Rose purchased a 45-piece service for eight Royal China "Chantilly" from Pier 4 Imports, 5133 Glentree Drive, San Jose, CA 95129. She received the service for eight, but instead of the Royal China, she received Royal Ironstone. While the Royal Ironstone is very nice, Rose wants the Royal China. She wrote once and was told by Pier 4 that because the Royal China and Royal Ironstone are of equal value, company policy would not permit an exchange. Write a letter for Rose's signature that will secure the exchange.

15. Write a series of soft-sell letters (two, four, or six) appropriate for the kind of company you plan to join when you've finished your education. On a separate sheet explain to your instructor the kind of company involved and the specific audience for your soft-sell campaign. Remember that soft-sell letters are expensive, so you must restrict them to important clients or customers.

16. As president of Goldenrod Pharmaceutical, 206 Berwick Road, Columbia, SC 29210, you've been asked to write a letter to your employees on behalf of the United Fund's annual fund-raising drive. All the money collected will be used locally for a variety of good causes—Heart Fund, Cancer Society, The Family Counseling Center, Boy Scouts, Girl Scouts, and the YMCA. The goal for Goldenrod is $18,000. If each person would give just one percent of his or her annual income, Goldenrod would exceed that goal easily.

17. Assume that you are Ms. Janice Roberts (see Problem 16, p. 143). You believe that as a responsible, adult woman who has done business with the Industrial City Bank for nearly 15 years, you should receive the $2,300 you need to buy a car. While you are willing to concede that you were not gainfully employed during your 15-year marriage, you learned many job-related skills (how to organize, supervise, delegate, and manage) doing volunteer work. You are sure that you can use these skills to find a job, and you have already several interviews lined up. Having the car—which would be yours just as soon as the loan goes through—would make it easier for you to make it to interviews on time.

18. Because of your abilities as a business-letter writer, you've been asked to write a letter for your local Animal Shelter. Each year people bring you more than 3,000 dogs and cats (and a couple hundred rabbits, hamsters, turtles, and snakes—and one three-foot alligator) and expect you to find homes for the animals they don't want or can't care for. You receive some city and county funds, but to meet your operating expenses you must rely on the donations you receive from animal lovers. This year the Animal Shelter will add a direct-mail campaign to its other fund-raising efforts. Prepare letters for (1) major givers—including local businesses and the town's wealthy citizens who have an established reputation for giving and (2) the general public. Describe the enclosure you would include with each of the letters.

19. Assume that you have been on a particular job for five years. Your company, like many others, is fighting inflation. One of the ways it intends to fight is by not giving salary increases unless the increase can be fully justified in writing. Support your claim for an increase in a memo to your immediate supervisor.

20. As Ms. Aretha Flack, write to Wee Ones Inc. and request a donation of Wee One Wetless Disposable Diapers for use at your charity auction. The names of the donors will be listed in the *Yorkshire Record*, your local newspaper, and the money earned at the auction will be used to support a Family Christmas program, which sees to it that families unable to afford presents for their children receive something good for Christmas.

21. Because your job requires a great deal of travel and entertaining, you have a company expense account. Your company, Orlando Construction and Land Development, 113 Meadowlark Drive, Santa Fe, NM 86501, is very good about paying for travel in advance, but its current method of handling your car rental and entertaining expenses is to reimburse you for money actually spent. You must use your own credit cards and then request reimbursement from the company. The company has resisted providing company credit cards because once one person has one, everyone else will want one to maintain status. You're getting awfully tired, however, of having to delay paying some of your bills until the company check arrives. Write to Ms. Helen Orlando, the president of your company, and persuade her to issue you a company credit card.

22. You've been hired by Jake's, a local department store, to write a letter of welcome which will be sent to all newcomers in your community. The letter will be soft-sell, emphasizing useful information and stating that Jake's (118 Cambridge Street, Fairfield, CT 06430) is a friendly, helpful member of the community.

23. Assume that you are the manager of the Credit Department for Grantos Boutiques, a Wisconsin based string of stores featuring fashions for women. Design form letters that can be used to collect overdue revolving charge accounts. You'll need at least

    a. a 30-day reminder,
    b. a 60-day inquiry,
    c. a 90-day appeal, and
    d. a 120-day overdue ultimatum.

Design your form letters so it will be easy for you to insert the personal information required to make the letters convincing.

10. Writing Letters with More than One Purpose

Objectives

After you have read this chapter, you should be able to

1. Analyze complex situations, establish priorities, and place communication components into the mixed-message structure.
2. Apply the general structure used for all mixed messages.
3. Write letters combining positive and negative information.
4. Write letters combining negative and persuasive information.
5. Write letters combining positive, negative, and persuasive elements.

As you can tell from a quick glance at the objectives for this chapter, some letters combine more than one business objective. When those objectives will cause different reactions in your reader, the letter is called a **mixed message**. You need to write a mixed message when, for example, your reader will consider part of your message good news and another part of your message bad news.

Mixed messages are fairly typical in business situations, and while our earlier discussion of the communication context (Chapter Three) and the discussion of the preceding specific message types (Chapters Six through Nine) imply a methodology for handling mixed messages, certain kinds of mixed messages occur often enough to merit specific treatment.

Most mixed messages involve some kind of unexpected change. That is, the writer has changed or is going to change something, and the reader is not going to like it. Even though the change may benefit the reader, the general objective of a mixed message is to overcome the resentment or resistance that the unexpected change is likely to create. Because mixed messages always deal with some aspect of resentment or resistance, the human objectives are as important as the business objectives in your consideration of the structure of the message.

GENERAL STRUCTURE AND CHECKLIST

While the specific structure for mixed messages will vary depending on the components included, the general pattern is as follows:

1. **Benefit.**   The best beginning for a mixed message is a reader benefit. When you don't have a specific benefit to offer, begin with something the reader will respond to favorably that will also place the communication in its proper context. Positive information, a statement of agreement, or an acknowledgment of a common problem will help establish empathy between reader and writer.
2. **Information.**   Like all explanations, the informative part of the mixed message belongs in the secondary position because it is less interesting. To help overcome resentment and resistance, provide justifying reasons for the change that is involved. In addition to saying what you want or what the reader must do, say *why* such an action is necessary. When a compromise is involved, explain and justify the reasons for the compromise before stating the compromise itself.
3. **Requested action.**   Because mixed messages always require the reader to make a decision or change a behavior, you should make sure that the reader knows exactly what to do and when to do it, and you should make the action seem as easy as possible by providing clear instructions, blank forms, and other aids so that the requested action will be as easy as possible. Be sure to connect the action to the reader benefit. When the reader has a choice, however, make sure that you do not take that choice away.

MIXED MESSAGE PRIORITIES

In earlier chapters we considered communication situations in which the reader's response to your message would fall into one of three specific categories—the reader might *welcome*, *resent*, or *resist* your message. Not all letter-writing situations fall neatly into one of these categories, however. Some fall into more than one category at the same time.

A mixed message is one to which the reader's response will be mixed. Such messages present a special hazard for the business communicator because people have a special propensity for perceiving what they want to perceive. In a mixed message, the reader is likely to overlook the aspect of the message that causes the resentment or resistance. You must present both business objectives clearly without neglecting the human objectives.

As you can tell from our discussion of negative and persuasive messages, when your reader is likely to resent or resist the subject content of your letter, you must emphasize the feeling content to retain the reader's goodwill and ensure accurate communication. Until you meet the human objective of establishing empathy with your reader, you cannot achieve the business objective.

In the case of a mixed message, problems with structuring occur because the writer has conflicting goals. He or she wants to accomplish more than one business objective, and one of those objectives will cause the reader to resent or resist part of the message. While it's generally true that negative aspects should be subordinated by being placed in the middle of the letter, it is not always possible to arrange the subject content of a mixed message according to the general formula for subordination.

Because mixed messages always involve some kind of change which the reader will neither expect nor welcome, the writer must choose between business objectives and human objectives in ways that don't occur in single-purpose messages. For example, when you convey negative information to your reader, you try to do so as nicely as possible and to retain the reader's goodwill. Your main objective, however, is to convey the negative information. When the situation forces you to choose between conveying the negative information and retaining the reader's goodwill, you state the business objective clearly even at the expense of failing to achieve the human objective.

When your analysis of the communication situation as outlined in Chapter Three indicates that you will need to write a mixed message, you must still begin with a list of priorities for your message. Essentially you need to know which is more important: the business objective or the human objective. To help clarify your goals, ask yourself the following questions:

1. How will my reader feel about the change I am suggesting? How will the change affect my reader's business? How will the change affect my reader's self-image?
2. Is it more important to make my reader happy than it is to achieve a particular business objective?
3. When my reader's happiness is more important than my business objective, what can I offer to make the business objective more attractive?
4. When the business objective is more important than my reader's happiness, what can I say to help my reader save face or accept the business objective?

Your answers to these questions will help you determine the best structure for communicating your message. While it is impossible to anticipate the wide variety of letter-writing situations that will fall into the mixed-message category, illustrations of three common types will show you how to proceed.

COMBINING POSITIVE AND NEGATIVE INFORMATION

Communication situations involving compromise require mixed messages. Whenever you suggest a compromise to your reader, you have two business objectives: (1) you want to show the reader that his or her proposal is not fully acceptable, and (2) you want the reader to accept your counterproposal. Your reader will resent and resist these objectives. When you present your counterproposal in a logical, positive way, however, the reader may be willing to overlook the negative aspect and accept the compromise.

In presenting a compromise offer, you have to choose between assigning greater importance to the business objective or to the human objective. The objective you choose to emphasize is the objective you're more likely to achieve, as the following comparison makes clear. Use the following structure when you want to place the **emphasis on the business objective**:

1. **Delayed beginning.** Because the reader will be disappointed that you are refusing the original request, find some aspect of the situation with which you and the reader can agree.
2. **Explanation.** Give your reasons for not being able to accept the reader's proposal or request. Use your reasons and your counterproposal to imply the refusal. Make your counterproposal sound logical and reasonable. Don't be paternalistic ("we are willing to grant you," "we can permit you") or humble ("we can only offer," "the best we can do in this case"). Include all the reader benefits associated with your counterproposal.
3. **Action.** You need to convince the reader to agree to your counterproposal, but you must avoid taking choices away from your reader. When your reader has a choice, take no action without your reader's permission.

Use the following structure when you want to place the **emphasis on the human objective**:

1. **Immediate beginning.** Grant the reader's request or agree to the original proposal. Offer the reader everything he or she has asked for. Avoid apologies, and do not admit to a mistake.
2. **Explanation.** Even though your opening shows your willingness to let the reader have his or her way, your explanation should make clear your belief that your counterproposal is more reasonable, logical, and equitable than the reader's proposal or request. Include all the reader benefits associated with your counterproposal.

3. Action. While you need to make clear that the choice is the reader's, encourage the reader to reject your original offer and to accept your counterproposal by emphasizing the reader benefits associated with the counterproposal.

The same communication situation can be handled in either way. The following letters illustrate the different approaches.

Emphasis on business objective	Emphasis on human objective
You're right to expect quality when you buy Moonbeam products. Thank you for returning the toaster for our examination.	The enclosed refund check for $39.95 is our way of saying that we want to treat you right, Ms. Muchel. We want you to know that we stand behind the guarantee that you receive with Moonbeam products.
For your Moonbeam toaster to work properly, the two thermostats must both be set properly. The one thermostat lets you adjust the toaster to your own taste, from very light to very dark. The other thermostat, located inside the clean-out plate, is the main control. The main control on your toaster, Ms. Muchel, malfunctioned because the toaster had evidently been cleaned with a knife or other sharp instrument, which removed the insulation from some of the wires and caused a short.	(Same paragraph as other letter)
We've replaced and adjusted the main thermostat in your toaster, and it now works perfectly. It will continue to provide years of trouble-free service as long as the cleaning and operating instructions provided with each new toaster are followed. Because the cleaning instructions did not specifically prohibit scraping with a knife, we'll let you decide the best course of action.	(Same paragraph as other letter)
While we're perfectly willing to refund your money as you requested, we believe that you'll want the toaster back now that it is working perfectly. The Moonbeam toaster can provide you with reliable service—and toast the way you like it—for years to	The enclosed check shows you that we want you to be entirely satisfied, but now that your toaster is working perfectly, we think that you'll want it back. The Moonbeam toaster can provide you with reliable service—and toast the way you

come. Should you choose to have the toaster back, we'll pay your shipping charges. Please use the enclosed card to let us know your decision.

like it—for years to come. Should you choose to have the toaster back, we'll gladly pay all your shipping charges. With your repaired toaster, you'll receive a new, one-year guarantee. To receive your toaster, simply return the check to us in the envelope provided.

Whether the letter is structured to emphasize the business objective or the human objective, the basic content of the letter will be essentially the same. In the foregoing examples, however, the letter that encloses the refund check is more likely to make the reader happy. It is also less likely to encourage the reader to ask for the toaster back. Once the reader has the refund check, it is unlikely that he or she will decide to return the check and ask for the return of the toaster. The letter that emphasizes the business objective subordinates the possibility of the refund and encourages the reader to request the return of the toaster; but at the same time, it is more likely to make the reader feel that the company is taking advantage of her or him.

Which is the better letter? That depends on your primary objective. Do you believe that your company will be better off in the long run if you demonstrate conclusively that you stand behind your guarantee, or do you believe that your company will be better off in the long run if you can persuade the reader to give the toaster one more try? As long as the compromise you offer is honest, fair, and reasonable, either approach should prove successful in achieving the human and business objectives.

COMBINING NEGATIVE AND PERSUASIVE INFORMATION

Because people usually resist change even when that change may prove beneficial for them in the long run, messages announcing changes are frequently mixed messages. How much persuasive information you need to include in these messages depends on how resentful the reader will feel about the announced change, how much resistance your message will encounter, and how important your relationship with your reader is to you.

Unlike situations in which you have a compromise to offer, situations that require the combination of negative and persuasive information are those in which no real compromise is possible. The reader may have a legitimate choice, but it usually is an all-or-nothing choice in terms of the relationship between the reader and writer. If the reader doesn't accept what the writer is offering, the only alternative is to go elsewhere. A company may decide, for example, to install a new computer system. Company employees—and customers—will have to adjust to whatever new procedures the computer requires. Messages written to explain these procedures would be mixed messages. Changes in billing dates, changes in report procedures, and cancellation of certain courtesy privileges would also require mixed messages, which would attempt to convince the reader that the change will prove beneficial for both the writer and the reader.

When you have decided that you can neither give the reader what he or she wants nor offer a compromise or choice, your main concern is to present what you can offer in a way that will persuade the reader to accept the proposed change. Obviously you would not be proposing the change if it did not offer you and your business advantages, some of which you should be able to pass on to your reader. Whether you are selling a substitute product for the one a reader has ordered or selling an alternate procedure, the basic structure of your message is essentially the same.

1. **Benefit.**   Because you are going to offer something other than the product or procedure that the reader expects, you need to mention a benefit associated with the change before the reader can guess that you aren't doing as expected. Be sure to begin close enough to the subject to place the message in its proper communication context.

2. **Explanation.**   Remember that your reader has a vested interest in the original idea, product, or procedure. To achieve your business objective, you will need to present your alternative without calling your reader's judgment into question. Avoid the negative words *substitute* and *substitution*. Rather than disparaging the original idea, product, or procedure, concentrate on the positive aspects of the alternative. Although to be fair you should state the disadvantages associated with the alternative (they would become clear to the reader later anyway), you should subordinate them as much as possible without sacrificing clarity.

3. **Action.**   When the reader has a choice, make sure that choice is clear, and don't take unasked-for action (sending a substitute product, for example) unless you can do so without placing a burden on your reader. When the reader has no choice (to continue doing business with you, the reader must follow a new procedure, for example), make the action you expect clear, but subordinate it by re-emphasizing the reader benefit in closing.

One typical situation that calls for this kind of mixed message is the selling of a substitute product, though the process is the same whether you are dealing with a product, an idea, or a procedure. When you can't offer the product a customer has ordered (perhaps because you carry a different brand) but you can offer what you feel is a perfectly adequate alternative, your message to your reader has two business objectives: (1) to inform your reader that you can't sell the product ordered, and (2) to persuade your reader to purchase the alternative.

Your reader may resent your inability to sell the product ordered and may resist your effort to persuade him or her to purchase the alternative, so you will need to emphasize the feeling content of the message and achieve the human objective before you can accomplish your business objectives.

Use a delayed beginning that stresses a benefit. Place the message in its specific communication context, but do not mislead the reader into thinking that he or she will receive the product ordered.

Your recent order for one dozen electric typewriters shows that you've been satisfied with the office equipment we've provided you in the past. Electric typewriters will certainly improve the appearance of your business correspondence and reports, and their increased speed and efficiency will make life easier for your secretaries, too.

Begin your explanation before the reader starts to wonder why you haven't said that the product is on its way. Minimize and subordinate references to the product originally ordered. Give your reader the information required to make a logical decision.

In our continuous effort to provide only the best equipment at the lowest possible cost, we now carry the MNO Correctomatics exclusively. Our customers have reported that the MNO typewriters need fewer repairs and do high-quality work longer without adjustments than the Corone Electrics you ordered. While the Corone Electrics are still available from Hatch Distributors in Denver, Colorado, we believe you'll find that the MNO Correctomatics are a better buy.

Handle the sales information on the alternative product as you would were you writing an invited sales letter (see pp. 157-60).

The solid steel frame and a powerful but quiet heavy-duty motor that are standard on the MNO Correctomatics enable us to offer you an unusual five-year warranty on these typewriters.

Use a brochure to keep the letter from becoming too cluttered. When the price is higher or there is some other negative factor, subordinate it as much as possible.

After you're read the complete description of the Correctomatics in the enclosed brochure, we think you'll agree that the superior performance and construction of the MNO Correctomatics more than justify their slightly higher purchase price. The reliability and longevity of the MNO Correctomatics make them a sound investment.

Make the reader's choices clear, but emphasize the reader benefits associated with the decision you want your reader to take. Make the action seem easy.

Because we're so convinced that you'll prefer the MNO Correctomatic, we'll be glad to send you one on a trial basis. Our representative in your area could set it up and demonstrate it for you on 15 August. Please use the enclosed card to let us know your decision. We'll hold your check until we hear from you. To complete your order for one dozen MNO Correctomatics, simply return the card with your check for an additional $140.77 in the reply envelope provided.

Your closing should be positive. Do not take unasked for action. Let the reader decide the best course of action, but show confidence in the future of the business relationship.

Whatever your decision, Haas Office Equipment will always strive to bring you the best products at the lowest possible cost. For your convenience, we're sending a copy of our latest catalog by parcel post.

COMBINING POSITIVE, NEGATIVE, AND PERSUASIVE INFORMATION

When communication situations are complex, writers frequently need to make some difficult decisions about the best organizational patterns for accomplishing a variety of business and human objectives. In general, the basic structural pattern presented on page 173 will provide a useful guideline. Sometimes, however, the nature of the communication situation will require a chronological arrangement or a problem-solution presentation. In such cases, writers need to remember their obligation to present the information in a manner that is clear, courteous, concise, confident, correct, and conversational.

In some situations calling for a mixed message of this kind, the writer can subordinate the negative aspects and arrange the message to meet both the business and human objectives effectively. An example would be an acknowledgment of an order for which the writer can send some items immediately, needs to delay shipment on others, can't provide some of the items at all, and would like to substitute for yet other items. In acknowledgments of this sort, the organizational pattern is fairly predictable:

1. Begin by sending those items you can send. Be specific.
2. Explain the delay according to the principles presented on pp. 128-31.
3. Give the reasons that you can't supply certain items, and tell the reader where the items might be available.

4. Sell the substitute items according to the principles presented on pp. 157-61.
5. Ask the reader to confirm the required choices, and close by emphasizing the benefits the reader will receive by deciding in your favor.

When the nature of the communication situation requires a chronological arrangement or a problem-solution organizational pattern, you need to remember that your primary responsibility as a writer is to be clear. Your second responsibility is to be courteous. While you should subordinate those aspects of your message that will cause your reader to feel resentment, you should do your best to structure your message to reduce your reader's resistance to announced changes or to your counterproposals. In complex situations of this sort, remember that your message will be most effective when you

1. Adequately present and discuss all sides of the situation.
2. Distinguish and clearly label facts, opinions, and value judgments.
3. Emphasize points of agreement *before* you discuss points of disagreement.
5. Find and emphasize the benefits the reader will receive by accepting your point of view or course of action.

SUMMARY

Mixed messages are those that combine more than one business objective when those objectives will cause different reactions in your reader. You need to write a mixed message when your reader will consider part of your message good news and another part of your message bad news. Most mixed messages involve some kind of unexpected change. Even though the change may benefit the reader, the general objective of a mixed message is to overcome the resentment or resistance that the unexpected change is likely to create.

The organizational pattern for a mixed message is (1) benefit, (2) information, and (3) requested action. When you don't have a specific benefit to offer, begin with something the reader will respond to favorably that will also place the communication in its proper context. The informative part of the mixed message belongs in the secondary position because it is less interesting or negative. Make sure that the reader knows exactly what to do and when to do it.

When your reader is likely to resent or resist the subject content of your letter, you must emphasize the feeling content to retain the reader's goodwill and ensure accurate communication. Until you meet the human objective of establishing empathy with your reader, you cannot achieve the business objective.

Communication situations involving compromise require mixed messages. Whenever you suggest a compromise to your reader, you have two business objectives: (1) to show the reader that his or her proposal is not fully acceptable and (2) to persuade the reader to accept your counterproposal. In presenting a compromise offer, you have to choose between assigning greater importance to the business objective or to the human objective. Whether one structures the letter to emphasize the business objective or the human objective, the basic content of the letter will be essentially the same.

Because people usually resist change even when that change may prove beneficial for them in the long run, messages announcing changes are frequently mixed messages. Situations that require the combination of negative and persuasive information are those in which no real compromise is possible. Whether you are selling a substitute product for the one a reader has ordered or selling an alternate procedure, the basic structure of your message is essentially the same: (1) benefit, (2) explanation, and (3) action.

When communication situations are complex, writers frequently need to make some difficult decisions about the best organizational patterns for accomplishing a variety of business and human objectives. In general, the basic structural pattern will provide a useful guideline. Sometimes, however, the nature of the communication situation will require a chronological arrangement or a problem-solution presentation. In such cases, writers need to remember their obligation to present the information in a manner that is clear, courteous, concise, confident, correct, and conversational.

EXERCISES

Review

1. What is a mixed message?

2. Give the general pattern for all mixed messages?

3. Whenever you suggest a compromise to your reader, you have two business objectives. Name them.

4. In a compromise offer, what structure should you use when you want to emphasize the business objective? the human objective?

5. When you can't offer the product a customer has ordered but you can offer an adequate alternative, you have two business objectives. Name them.

6. When a complex communication situation requires you to combine positive, negative, and persuasive information, what factors govern the message's organizational pattern?

Problems

1. As customer relations manager for Edison Electronics, 82 Poe Avenue, Roxie, MS 39661, answer a letter from Roger Dutton, 22 Gaviotta Way, San Francisco, CA 94126. Mr. Dutton complains that the AM-FM portable radio he purchased by mail from your sale catalog has not worked since it arrived, and he demands his $42.75 back. When you examine the radio, you discover that the only thing wrong with it is a dead nine-volt battery. You believe that the radio, which usually sells for $59.95, represents a real bargain and that Mr. Dutton will want it back. Placing the emphasis on the business objective, offer to return Mr. Dutton's radio.

2. Using the information provided in the preceding case, write a letter to Mr. Dutton and place the emphasis on the human objective.

3. Ms. Mary Shelley has complained that her new Nota automobile, purchased from Frank's Automobile Center, 42 N. 73d Street, Gainsville, FL 32603, is getting only eight miles a gallon. She reports that two different mechanics have told her that the carburetor is defective but "not bad enough to replace under the warranty." Ms. Shelley wants the carburetor replaced. As Customer Relations Manager for Nota, you have called Frank Fitzsimmons, owner of Frank's Automotive Center, who told you that he had checked the carburetor himself, and that while it wasn't as good as it should be, it was within specified tolerances. You think that poor driving techniques may account for part of Ms. Shelley's bad gas mileage, but in the interest of goodwill you are willing to provide a new carburetor if Ms. Shelley will agree to pay for the cost of installation.

4. Dr. Janice Lester, a professor of international marketing at Indiana University, Bloomington, IN 47401, has written to Ms. Linn Andrews, the president of your company—Andrews Manufacturing Inc., 143 Lakefront Avenue, Holland, MI 49423. She proposes that your company finance a field study of the market potential for the new kind of flame retardant, permanent-press fabrics your company produces. Dr. Lester wants $30,000 to study the market possibilities in England, France, Germany, Italy, and Japan. While you think that the study might well open new and valuable markets for your company, you don't want to finance a luxury vacation for Dr. Lester, either. Based on what you know of Dr. Lester's work, you are willing to make an outright grant of $5,000 and match any funds she is able to receive elsewhere. You are also willing to pay legitimate expenses associated with the study itself (design and printing of questionnaires, computer analysis time, shipping of sample materials, taxi fares, and the like). Prepare a letter for Ms. Andrews' signature that will make Dr. Lester want to accept your counterproposal.

5. When you installed the Sol-Craft solar heating unit on Mr. L. H. Molzan's swimming pool at 401 W. 46th Street, Indianapolis, IN 46201, you told him that the heating unit would maintain a water temperature of 82 degrees only if an old maple tree, which prevents the afternoon sun from hitting the solar heating unit, were removed. You thought that Mr. Molzan had agreed to remove the tree, but now you receive a letter saying that the solar heating unit is insufficient. Mr. Molzan wants you to install a propane supplemental heater (which you manufacture). Mr. Molzan agrees to pay for the propane heater, but he wants you to pay for installation because the solar heater isn't doing the job. Write Mr. Molzan and explain that the solar heater alone will do the job from early June through the end of September provided the old maple tree—which probably won't live much longer anyway—is removed. Tell him that if he prefers, you'll add the propane supplemental heater but that he will have to pay the full cost for the heater and installation ($354).

6. Mr. Raymond J. Johnson, owner of Johnson Jewelers, 986 Stanford Plaza, Menlo Park, CA 94025, writes to you, owner of Jade & Things, 1492 Columbus Avenue, Tempe, AZ 85281, saying that the large order ($2,500) of silver and turquoise pendants, belt buckles, rings, and earrings arrived too late for Johnson Jewelers to take advantage of the annual Indian fair held in Menlo Park. Johnson requested that the jewelry be sent air express, but because of an oversight in your shipping department, the order was sent by United Parcel Service. As a result, much of the order remains unsold. While the mistake was yours and you are willing to take the order back, you think that it would be better—primarily for you but also for him—if you gave Johnson permission to hold a sale on your merchandise (something you've never done before) and split the advertising costs with him. Johnson would be able to sell most of the jewelry quickly and make necessary room for Christmas specialty items, and you would avoid having to handle the jewelry again. Emphasize the human objective in writing to Johnson.

7. Using the information in the preceding case, write to Johnson and stress your business objective.

8. As sales manager for Wyland Electronics, 1200 Newkirk Street, Baltimore, MD 21244, acknowledge an order from Ms. Lois Lane, 1780 Hudson River Road, Monsey, NY 10952. Ms. Lane has ordered your Model QT 12 All-channel CB radio for use in her customized Chevy van. Because of the change from 23 channels to the new 40-channel units, you have discontinued the Model QT 12 and replaced it with the Model QT 14. In addition to its extra communication capabilities, the QT 14 offers several features not available on the QT 12. It has a built-in automatic noise limiter, an illuminated meter

to indicate sending and receiving signal strength, and a frequency synthesizer to eliminate crystals. Like the QT 12, it provides four watts of power for a strong signal, it has a 100 percent solid-state chasis for long life and reliability, and it has an adjustable squelch control. It includes a bracket for mounting under the dash and a complete instruction manual. The QT 14 does cost more; Ms. Lane will have to send another $37.50 for it. Hold her check for $149.50 until she lets you know her decision.

9. Until recently, your company, Wilcox and Rogers, Investment Counselors, 2954 Helber Street, Flint, MI 48504, sent a monthly newsletter, "Financial Planning for Families," free to anyone who asked for it. The idea behind the newsletter was to provide useful advice and to establish cordial contact with those who received it. Because of the increased costs of publishing and mailing the newsletter, you now send one free issue as a sample, but subscribers must pay $6 a year or maintain a $1,000 account with your firm to remain on your mailing list. Answer a letter from Ms. Elizabeth Kranz, 67 Apian Way, Bloomington, IL 61701, requesting you to add her name to your subscription list.

10. Henrietta's Hardware Store, 101 W. Main Street, Duluth, MN 55815, ordered six Waste Queen Garbage Disposals from you, Electrical and Plumbing Supplies, 932 Portage Road, St. Paul, MN 55103. Because you specialize in products for the home handyperson and the Waste Queen requires installation by a professional plumber, you have received several complaints from dealers who purchased the Waste Queen to sell to do-it-yourselfers. You still have plenty of Waste Queen Disposals in stock, but you think that Henrietta's Hardware might prefer the new Grind-All Disposal, which has been especially designed for do-it-yourself installation. The Waste Queen and the Grind-All have many features in common. Both have solid steel construction, a ¾-horsepower motor, a foolproof safety inter-lock, and an automatic shutoff to prevent silverware and other metallic objects from damaging the disposal. The Grind-All comes with complete installation instructions and a short piece of a new kind of flexible, metal (not plastic) pipe to make installation easier. The Grind-All costs more—$12 more wholesale and $18 more retail. The retail prices are $79.99 for the Grind-All and $63.99 for the Waste Queen. Both the Waste Queen and the Grind-All come with a complete one-year warranty, and you'll be glad to sell Henrietta's Hardware either disposal. You do, however, want to make sure that the differences between the two are clear. Your terms are 2/10, n/30.

11. At the Hickory Nut, 4211 Maple Avenue, Albuquerque, NM 87100, you have received the following order from Mr. Hamilton Burr for

cheeses, candied fruits, flavored nuts, and specialty jams and jellies:

```
Five pounds smoked cheddar @ 2.79/lb        $13.95
Five pounds Monterey Jack @ 2.49/lb          12.45
Two four-pound packages of assorted
        candied fruits @ 9.95 ea             19.90
Six four-pound cans of barbequed
        almonds @ 10.99 a can                65.94
Three $9 packages of specialty jams
        and jellies                          27.00
```

                                       Total $139.24

              Tax and Shipping Charges   11.96

                                       Total $151.20

Write to Mr. Burr, 748 Arroyo Road, Los Altos, CA 94022, and tell him that you are sending the cheese and the specialty jams and jellies right away by United Parcel Service, that there will be a two-week delay for the candied fruits, and that because of a severe drought, the almonds are not available this year. In place of the almonds, sell Mr. Burr your barbequed walnuts at $6.76 for a four-pound can.

12. As director of sales for the Midwest Division of the American Cash Register Company, 1920 Clark Avenue, Raleigh, NC 27605, write a letter to your district sales managers informing them of a change in reporting procedures. Currently each district manager assembles the total sales figures each week and telephones them to you before noon each Monday. The telephone reports are followed at the end of the month by a written report specifying the sales by salesperson, district, purchaser, product, and price. The new procedure calls for a written report each month. As director of sales, you believe that because the new procedure will enable you to follow up on each sale more quickly, you will be able to establish a better relationship with your customers, which will lead to increased future sales.

13. Write a letter to your business communication instructor telling him or her

    a. What's wrong with the class.
    b. What you like about the class.
    c. What improvements should be made in the class.

14. As president of the local chapter of the National Secretaries Association, you recently wrote to Professors William Murphy and Catherine Jameson, who work at a nearby university, inviting them to conduct an all-day communication seminar for you. You offered them $500 for the seminar. In their reply, Professors Murphy and Jameson said that they would be glad to conduct the seminar but that their fee

would be $600 plus travel, accommodations, and material expenses. Write back to the professors suggesting a compromise: you'll pay the $600 and take care of their lodgings and meals.

15. You're Joseph Jencon, credit manager for Cyclists Inc., 42 East 53 Street, New York, NY 10016. You recently received a letter from Andrea Wilston, 917 Poplar Hill Road, Baltimore, MD 21210. She tells you that two weeks ago she purchased your Women's Model 5M 4892N 26-inch five-speed Midlight Bicycle for $98.99 as advertised in *National Sports*. She expresses much dissatisfaction with the five-speed bike. Because she needs to pedal uphill several times a day, she now prefers a ten-speed bike. She wants you to take it back at the price she paid for it and to send her a ten-speed bike. She says she only used the bike one week, and it is still as good as new. Because Andrea has used the bike, even though it was only for one week, it is still a used bike. She may trade the bike in for a ten-speed. You'll allow 75 percent of the original price of the five-speed bike as credit on the second purchase.

16. Mr. William Morrison, 14 Grand Street, Lynchburg, VA 24502, wrote to you as representative of the Last National Bank of Lynchburg, 458 Scott Street, Lynchburg, VA 24502, and asked whether he could change the date of his mortgage payments from the 1st of the month to the 15th. Because delaying the payment from the 1st to the 15th would change the amount of interest due and alter the amortization schedule, you would have to charge Mr. Morrison $30 for the change. A simpler—and less expensive solution—would be for Mr. Morrison to pay a month early and send his check on the 15th. Write a letter to Mr. Morrison and explain his options to him.

17. As manager of the Western Division of the Continental Oil Company, 111 Plaza Street, New York, NY 10002, you have general responsibilities for all West Coast operations. Recently, however, the main office has been putting a great deal of pressure on you to cut expenses—even though they are also insisting on increased exploratory drilling. Today you've received a letter—signed by Mr. Henry Hokezma, the company president—asking you to justify your recent expenditures for drilling equipment. All the equipment is necessary for you to meet company deadlines for your drilling operations on the 16 exploratory wells the company wants sunk in the next 60 days. In your reply, you will, of course, need to justify the expenditures on the basis of need, but you should also persuade the company to set some specific priorities so you can determine the relative importance of cutting back on expenses and maintaining normal drilling operations.

18. As manager of Zolad's Discount Store, write a form letter to all your charge customers announcing the installation of a new computer

billing system. Instead of receiving bills on the 1st of the month, customers will now receive their bills based on where their last name falls in the alphabet:

A-F will receive bills on the 1st
G-L will receive bills on the 10th
M-Q will receive bills on the 20th
R-Z will receive bills on the 30th

In addition to announcing the change in billing dates, caution your customers to watch for errors that are bound to happen with such a change in procedures and equipment.

19. For the last ten years, all executives working for American International have been issued American Express credit cards for charging legitimate expense-account items. Lately, however, the bills have far exceeded reasonable business expenses, and the Board of Directors has decided to recall all the credit cards. From now on, executives will have to use their own credit cards and submit a form requesting reimbursement. Write a form memo explaining the new policy. Be sure to set an end date for returning the credit cards.

20. As head of the Advertising Department (see Problem 20, page 145), you must write formal personnel evaluations once every six months until the employee has been with the company two years. It's time for you to rewrite Abraham Fenwick's formal review. In the past six months Fenwick has caused you a lot of trouble because of his sexist remarks and behavior. Fenwick has been improving, however, and he is obviously trying to overcome his rather strong prejudices against women colleagues. Other than the hard feelings Fenwick has caused, his work has been excellent. Your letter of review to Fenwick must mention his sexist behavior and remind him that such behavior will be cause for dismissal, but you should also mention his successes and encourage him to make every effort to acknowledge and accept the professional competence of his women colleagues.

11. Writing Letters about Jobs

Objectives

After you have read this chapter, you should be able to

1. Write a letter applying for a job of your choice.
2. Write a thank-you letter after you've been interviewed for a job.
3. Write a letter requesting more information about a particular job.
4. Write a letter requesting more time to decide about a job offer.
5. Write a letter accepting the job offer.
6. Write a letter refusing the job offer.
7. Write a letter of resignation.

Employment letters follow the same principles as those followed by other letters, but because they are of special importance to those writing them, they deserve separate treatment. We suggest that before reading this chapter, you review Chapter Two, "Appearance," and Chapter Three, "The Communication Context." Because employers usually receive a great number—sometimes hundreds—of applications for each available job, how your job letter looks will make a big difference in the attention it receives. Also, how well you understand your prospective employer's needs will make a big difference in how seriously your letter is considered *after* it is initially read.

For most people, job correspondence is an important part of the job-application process. Unless you are fortunate enough to know someone who can give you a job that satisfies you, you will need to communicate with potential employers by letter. Because the people who receive your job letters won't know you, their initial perception of you will be created by the image you present on paper. Before they invite you to an interview, prospective employers will have concluded from your job correspondence whether you are neat, courteous, well organized, confident, and competent.

For your job correspondence to be effective, you need to recognize that letters about jobs—like all business correspondence—have specific objectives. Letters written about jobs fall into two general categories: (1) those written to secure an interview and (2) those written after the interview has taken place. Letters written to arrange an interview are usually called letters of application (also called transmittal and cover letters). Follow-up correspondence includes thank-you letters, requests for information, requests for more time, and job-acceptance and job-refusal letters.

THE LETTER OF APPLICATION

Letters of application are almost always part of a job-application package which includes both the letter and one of the following: a data sheet, a resume (from the French, *résumé*), or a vita (Latin for "life"). The data sheet is the least sophisticated, usually presenting only the most fundamental facts without any accompanying interpretation. The resume offers more interpretation of the bare facts. The vita is much longer than either a data sheet or a resume, usually including a lengthy summary of professional accomplishments, publications, and the like. While one purpose of the letter of application is to transmit the resume to the reader, its main purpose is to persuade the reader to invite the applicant for an interview.

Because the letter's main objective is to persuade the reader to act in a certain way, it follows the basic organizational pattern for persuasive messages: *Attention, Interest, Conviction, Action.* Just as a sales letter is either solicited or unsolicited (see pp. 157-60), a letter of application is either invited or uninvited depending on whether the reader expects— and desires—to receive it. Whether your letter of application is invited or uninvited, you need to give careful consideration to what your reader already knows and expects and to what your reader (and your reader's company) needs.

Because all employers want employees who have demonstrated a willingness to work, the skills required to perform a required task, the ability to get along well with others, and sufficient potential to merit promotion, a letter of application cannot succeed unless it demonstrates that the writer possesses these qualities. To demonstrate these qualities in your letter, you need to assess the following:

1. **Your professional objectives.** What occupational goals have you set for yourself? Why do you wish to pursue these goals? Are your goals realistic? Are they flexible?
2. **Your education.** What has your education prepared you to do? How do your major and minor fields of study relate to one another? How do your major and minor relate to your professional objectives? Can you do what your education suggests that you can without a great deal of in-service training?
3. **Your experience.** Do you have work experience related to the kind of work for which you are applying? Have any of your jobs

taught you specific skills required for the kind of work you want to do? Do you have a well-developed work history? Does your previous experience show a willingness to work hard?

4. **Your personal qualities.**   Do you have any special personal attributes that make you especially well suited for the kind of work you are seeking? Do you enjoy working with people? with numbers? with books? Have any of your hobbies taught you something about the kind of work you're applying for? Did you work to finance your college education? Can you cooperate, follow instructions, and work as a member of a team? Have you demonstrated initiative in the past?

Obviously your answers to some of the foregoing questions will be more positive than your answers to others, and—as always—you will want to stress the information to which your reader will respond favorably and subordinate the information to which he or she will respond unfavorably. Regardless of whether your application is invited or uninvited, you should use the same basic organizational pattern:

1. **Attention.**   Place the message in its communication context right away by telling the reader that you are applying for a job. Subordinate that information to something of greater reader interest (a benefit perhaps) when possible. Invited letters of application should mention the source of the invitation, newspaper or journal ad, mutual friend, or special invitation. Uninvited applications should mention a way in which you can help the reader achieve certain job objectives.

2. **Interest.**   Show what you know about the reader's company. Show your reader how you would fit into the company structure. Show your reader that you understand the special language of the job you are seeking. Provide a transition to the proof you will give to convince your reader that you can do a particular job.

3. **Conviction.**   Use your education, experience, and personal qualities to show your reader that you can fill specific job requirements. Avoid lecturing your reader ("You need a person who . . .") and concentrate on showing your reader that you are qualified ("Because I am a person who . . . I could make a valuable contribution to . . ."). Because you will be using a resume as an informative enclosure, select and amplify those aspects of your background most appropriate for the company addressed. In invited applications, be sure to say something about each job requirement listed in the ad or other information source. In uninvited letters, say something about each job requirement you know applies to the work you're seeking. Omit negative factors your reader would have no way of knowing about, and subordinate negative information that will be obvious to your reader.

4. **Action.**   The business objective of the letter of application is to secure an interview. Ask for one. But keep in mind that your reader is not obligated to see you and will certainly resist seeing you at *your* convenience. When you have a specific time or day that would be convenient for you, suggest it. Do not, however, deny the reader the right to make choices. Be flexible, and let the reader suggest alternatives.

The letters shown in Figures 11-1 and 11-2 illustrate most of the previous points. Note that each of the letter writers has adapted the basic components of application letters to meet the needs and expectations of a particular reader. The salesperson's letter (Figure 11-1), for example, is more aggressive and "I" oriented than the communication specialist's letter (Figure 11-2).

```
802 West Green Street, Apt. 306
Urbana, IL 61801

February 15, 19__

Ms. Jean Major
Shull's Incorporated
45 Shady Lane
Atlanta, GA 30302

Dear Ms. Major:

I am interested in discussing career opportunities with Shull's.

Your company's recent growth indicates an expanding need for
young, aggressive college graduates--graduates with a strong
finance and marketing background, and with imagination and
leadership ability.  I have these qualifications.

And when you combine the enthusiasm and hard work I would put
forth in your executive training program with

 *    My educational background,

 *    My recent experience in retailing with Carson, Pirie,
      Scott & Co.,

 *    And my tremendous desire to excel,

I feel I would be able to make a significant contribution to
your management team.

Ms. Major, I would greatly appreciate your serious consideration
of my application and would welcome the opportunity to talk
with you.  I'll be looking forward to hearing from you after
you have evaluated the enclosed resume.

Sincerely,

Roger Martin

Roger Martin

enc
```

Figure 11-1.   Salesperson's letter.

1861 Darwin Place
Lawrence, KS 66045

7 March 19__

Mr. Anthony LeBarron
Personnel Director
Barrington Manufacturing Company
83 Lincoln Avenue
Lawrence, KS 66045

Dear Mr. LeBarron:

Please consider me for the job of Technical Information Officer you advertised
in the Lawrence Gazette.

My 12 years of varied working experience and educational background make me
especially well suited to develop and implement a total communication program
for the Barrington Manufacturing Company.

My administrative background gives me experience in program development and
implementation and the knowledge required to manage personnel and resources in
spite of limited budgets. My library training makes me a skilled researcher,
and my election to committees and positions of responsibility, combined with a
history of effective dealings with publics of widely varied educational levels,
demonstrates my well-developed oral and interpersonal communication skills.
My report and letter writing experience gives me excellent written
communication skills, as the enclosed sample of my copywriting shows.

My familiarity with the literature of communication, as is evidenced by my
publications, will ensure my quick adaptation to the special requirements of
your program. I also offer maturity, responsibility, common sense, and the
willingness to work hard.

In addition to the jobs listed on my resume, I have done free-lance work in
Lawrence, proofreading and editing for Behaviordelia Press.

Local people who are familiar with my abilities are

    Dr. Arno F. Knapper, School of Business, University of
       Kansas, Lawrence, KS 66045 (913) 864-3795

    Ms. Elizabeth C. Wolf, Editor, Behaviordelia Press, 411
       Parson Drive, Lawrence, KS 66045 (913) 867-3409

Dr. Knapper, Ms. Wolf, or any of the references listed on the enclosed copy of
my resume would be glad to verify my ability to develop and implement your
communication program.

I would be available for an interview on short notice and would welcome the
opportunity to discuss my qualifications with you.

Sincerely,

Marie Nelson

Marie Nelson

enc

Figure 11-2. Communication specialist's letter.

Each job letter you write, regardless of how many, should be individually prepared and typed. While you may wish to use the same basic letter to apply for several jobs, each of the letters should be personalized so that each person who receives it can see that you prepared the letter with one particular reader in mind. Note, for example, the way both of the letters use the reader's name or the name of the reader's company in the body of the letter. As a rule, your letter should be no more than one page long.

THE RESUME

Because your letter can't say everything about you without becoming so long that prospective employers would find it unreadable, you should put much of the general information about yourself in a resume, which you send with the letter as an informative enclosure. As an informative enclosure, your resume shows your prospective employer your ability to select important information, organize it in a meaningful way, and present it in an attractive, readable manner.

Your resume should be specific enough to show your sense of purpose, but avoid limiting yourself more than you have to. Your resume should be broad enough to be relevant to numerous organizations. Because your resume is an informative enclosure, you should have it printed or mechanically reproduced from a typewritten original—by offset or high-quality photocopy—not a ditto and *not* a carbon.

Your resume must cover four broad categories of information:

1. **Personal Details.**   Your name, address, and phone number, including the area code, should probably be listed first because most personnel directors expect to see them first. Height, weight, date of birth, and marital status (married or single, *not* divorced) are still expected. However, because Title IX of the 1972 Education Act which prohibits employers from discriminating against job applicants because of age, sex, race, and place of national origin, employers usually cannot ask for this information or for a photograph. Your spouse's name and occupation and the number and ages of your children should not be included. If the prospective employer wants to know, he or she can ask you during the interview. Because your height, weight, and other personal details don't say much about your qualifications for a job, that kind of information should be subordinated by allowing it as little space as possible or by placing it toward the end of the resume.
2. **Education.**   Unless you have four or more years of full-time experience in the kind of work for which you are applying, education will be your most important division. Emphasize your

advanced course work. Your letter should stress the courses that will be of special interest to a specific reader, so use the resume to emphasize the range and depth of your educational background. You should include schools attended, honors earned, grade-point average (if noteworthy), major and minor fields, activities, and the percentage of college expenses you yourself paid for.

3. **Experience.**   Stress job-related experience, but even if none of your working experience is job related, showing that you have worked is important. Be sure to tell where and when you worked and what you did. Interpret your job duties in a way that will have meaning for your reader, but don't state the obvious: if you worked as a typist, for example, you don't need to say that one of your job duties was typing. Mention special responsibilities (especially supervisory duties), whether the job was part-time or full-time. State what skills you learned in each job. Many employers expect to see your reasons for having left previous jobs. Include at least your last five positions.

4. **References.**   While some prospective employers do not feel that references are helpful on a resume, others insist on calling references before the interview. Listing academic and employment references may give you a slight edge in competing for some jobs. Be sure to get each person's permission before listing him or her as a reference, and give the person's courtesy title, full name, professional title, business mailing address, business telephone number, and connection to you (if not clear from title and position). References are always listed at the end of the resume.

In addition to the major categories, you may have other information which you'll want to include under an optional division. Some of the more common optional entries are as follows:

1. Professional objective
2. Honors
3. Awards
4. Military service
5. Publications
6. Offices held (elected offices)
7. Memberships
8. Special recognition
9. Special qualifications
10. Special licenses held (pilot, Federal Communication Commission, notary public, chauffeur)
11. Date resume was prepared

Most successful resumes are fairly conservative in appearance because the businesspersons who read job applications usually prefer resumes that establish individuality through content rather than appearance. Some fields (most notably advertising) require more innovation in appearance than others. Do not attempt to copy someone else's resume. Your resume should reflect *your* personality and style. Use the suggestions we've prescribed as guidelines rather than absolute rules.

```
MARY ANN PAGEL

Address until May 20                    Address after May 20
302 S. Fourth Street                    1411 Victoria Avenue
Athens, OH 45701                        Maurice, IA 51036
(216) 456-8795                          (712) 835-2340

Single      5'              120 pounds     Date of Birth  Jan 4 1956
```

JOB OBJECTIVE	To develop skills in assisting library patrons in use of library materials and service in a position that will encourage professional development and education.
EDUCATION Sep 19__ to present	Ohio University, Athens, OH. Will receive B.A. in Psychology in May 19__. Advanced courses include Experimental Techniques, An Introduction to Research, Behavior Modification, Abnormal Psychology, and Childhood and Society.
	<u>Library Science Courses</u> Introduction to Reference Service Literature of the Sciences Library Materials for Young Adults
EXPERIENCE Feb 19__ to present	Part-time student employee at Ohio University Interlibrary Loan Department, Ohio University, Athens, OH. Used main card catalog and serial record to find requested books' location in library system. Used shelf lists and circulation files in departmental libraries to find books in these smaller libraries.
Jan 19__	Receptionist at the Maurice Savings and Loan Association, 38 Broadway, Maurice, IA 51036, for Kelly Girl. Directed customers to appropriate banker.
Dec 19__ to Jan 19__	Manpower typist for special project at Armstrong Products, 345 Second Avenue, Maurice, IA 51036.
Summers 19__ 19__ 19__	Junior Clerk at Peoples Gas Light and Coke Company, Maurice, IA 51036. Typing and general office work in 19__ and 19__. Worked in the dispatch room in 19__. Took customers' complaints and radioed service personnel to answer them.
School Years 19__, 19__	Student Food Service Employee at Ohio University, Food Handler and Door Checker.
19__ to 19__	IBM card distributor at student registration at Ohio University.
Jun 19__ to 19__	Part-time clerk at Tischer's Pharmacy in Athens, OH.

MARY ANN PAGEL   2

HONORS
Mar 19__   Phi Kappa Phi Honor Society
May 19__   Psi Chi--National Psychology Honorary Society
Dec 19__   Alpha Lambda Delta Women's Honorary Society
Mar 19__   James Scholar
              Dean's list each semester

ACTIVITIES AND ORGANIZATIONS
Feb 19__   Secretary of Psi Chi local chapter
Oct 19__   Special Libraries Association Student Member
Mar 19__   Volunteer worker--started crafts program for girls
                 in Athens community center
Sep 19__   Krannert Center Student Association--tour guide for
    to   Krannert Center for the Performing Arts
May 19__
Sep 19__   Intramural sports--co-recreational--volleyball,
    to   softball, water polo
Dec 19__

REFERENCES
Mr. C. B. Puchalski, Superintendent, Central Shop, Peoples Gas
    Light and Coke Company, 1250 S. Kibourn Avenue, Maurice,
    IA 51036. (712) 345-8967.

Miss Lea-Ruth Wilkins, Assistant Professor, Graduate School of
    Library Science, Ohio University, Athens, OH 51036.
    (712) 345-4532.

Mrs. Elaine Albright, Librarian, Interlibrary Loan Department,
    Room 405 Library, Ohio University, Athens, OH 51036.
    (712) 345-4538.

Prepared June 19__.

Figure 11-3. Example of resume reproduced from a typewritten
original.

You should, however, make sure that your resume is well organized and easy to read. The important information should stand out, and the reader should be able to tell at a glance what you've accomplished in each category. Also, watch your use of space. Arrange your material so that you cover *all* of one page or *all* of two pages. Blank space on a resume has a negative implication. Your resume should not exceed two pages unless your career advancement requires a fully developed vita. Do not send a photograph unless the prospective employer asks for one.

The resumes shown in Figure 11-3, 11-4, and 11-5 are all real, successful resumes written by our students. Figure 11-3 is a sample of a resume reproduced from a typewritten original. Figure 11-4 is a sample of a two-page printed resume, and Figure 11-5 (which goes with the letter shown on p. 192) is an example of a one-page printed resume. You'll note that these resumes have much in common, but that each says something about the personality of its writer.

RICHARD G. LoPRESTI

Present Address	Permanent Address
604 Douglas Avenue	3757 Robina Avenue
Kalamazoo, MI 49007	Berkley, MI 48072
(616) 383-6900	(313) 544-2180

Single   5'10"   160 pounds   Born February 5, 1955

PROFESSIONAL OBJECTIVE

Using my Accounting major and my Administrative Communication minor, I would like a position as a financial communicator. My interest lies in being able to analyze and communicate accounting information from the accountants and financially minded people to the layman who doesn't completely understand the complexities of this information.

EDUCATION

Sep 1973 to Apr 1977
> College of Business, Western Michigan University, Kalamazoo, MI 49008. BBA degree April 1977. Overall GPA 3.25.

Major
> Accounting: 9 courses, 27 credit hours. Advanced courses include Auditing, Cost Accounting, Tax Accounting, Accounting Information Systems. Major GPA 3.0.

Minor
> Administrative Communication: 6 courses, 18 credit hours. Advanced courses include Business Communications, Organizational Communication, Advanced Business Writing, Communication Systems. Minor GPA 4.0.

EXPERIENCE

May 1976 to Aug 1976
> Factory press operator, Chrysler Corporation, Sterling Stamping Plant, Sterling Heights, MI 48077.

Jul 1975 to Aug 1975
> Factory press operator, Cavalier Manufacturing Inc., Madison Heights, MI 48071.

Sep 1974 to Apr 1975
> Student building supervisor, University Student Center, Western Michigan University, Kalamazoo. Position involved supervision of University Student Center two or three nights per week from 5 p.m. until 11 p.m. Job included supervising several employees, recording cash receipts for the day, and securing building at night.

May 1974 to Aug 1974
> Bank teller, Standard Federal Savings & Loan Association, Troy, MI 48084.

Richard G. LoPresti   2.

SPECIAL EXPERIENCE

Mar 1976 to Oct 1976
　　　　Career Day Chairman, Western Michigan University, Kalamazoo. Planned and organized a day-long Career Day conference involving 250 recruiters, faculty, and student organization representatives. On October 7, 1976, over 1500 students attended the conference to talk with representatives from 50 nationally known companies.

SPECIAL RECOGNITION AND OFFICES HELD

Alpha Kappa Psi:	President, Winter 1977
	V.P., Executive, Fall 1976
	V.P., Public Relations, Winter 1976
	Career Day Chairman, Fall 1976
	Social Chairman, Fall 1975

Who's Who Among Students in American Universities & Colleges:	Elected, Fall 1976
Dean's List:	Winter 1974, Winter 1976
Student Budget Allocations Committee:	Member, Fall 1975-Winter 1976
University Student Center Board:	Member, Fall 1974
Student Alumni Service Board:	Treasurer, Winter 1974-Fall 1974
French Hall House Council:	Member, Winter 1974-Fall 1974

CREDENTIALS

Official transcript and University Placement Service's data sheet may be obtained from

　　　　　　　　University Placement Services
　　　　　　　　Western Michigan University
　　　　　　　　Kalamazoo, MI 49008
　　　　　　　　(616) 383-1710

REFERENCES

Dr. Kimon Bournazos, Professor, Department of Business Education and Administrative Services, Western Michigan University, Kalamazoo, MI 49008 (616) 383-1908.

Dr. Joel Bowman, Assistant Professor, Department of Business Education and Administrative Services, Western Michigan University, Kalamazoo, MI 49008 (616) 383-1983.

Dr. F. W. Schaeberle, Associate Professor, Accountancy Department, Western Michigan University, Kalamazoo, MI 49008 (616) 383-4091.

Mr. Thomas Coyne, Vice-President for Student Services, Western Michigan University, Kalamazoo, MI 49008 (616) 383-1752.

Prepared February 15, 1977

Figure 11-4. Example of two-page printed resume.

ROGER A. MARTIN
802 West Green Apt. 306
Urbana, Illinois 61801
217-344-0515

Born on August 7, 1952
Single
Excellent Health
69 Inches
150 Pounds

Job Objective
Retail Management at Executive Level

Education
UNIVERSITY OF ILLINOIS, Champaign, Illinois—September 1972 to May 1974
Bachelor of Science in Commerce with specialization in Finance
Courses: *Finance*—18 hours including Investment Principles, Investment Banking, Real Estate and Urban Development,
    Income Tax Accounting;
    Marketing—12 hours including Marketing Principles, Retail Management, Consumer Behavior, Sales and Advertising
    Promotion;
    General Business—30 hours including Business Law, General Accounting, Statistics, Organizational Management
Activities: Marketing Club, Dean's List

ILLINOIS STATE UNIVERSITY, Normal, Illinois—June 1970 to June 1972
Courses: General Curriculum
Activities: Vice President of House floor; Union Board

SULLIVAN HIGH SCHOOL, Sullivan, Illinois—1966 to 1970
Activities: Jr. Class Magazine Sales Contest, 1st place; Co-Chairman for Jr. Prom; Chairman for float committee, jr.
    and soph. years

Experience
CARRIAGE LANE, Urbana, Illinois—August 1973 to May 1974
Division of Carson, Pirie, Scott & Co.
Worked as salesman in men's clothing department. Signature for checks, sales returns and house discounts.
Average sales expense—5.2 percent.

KAISER CHEMICAL CO., Sullivan, Illinois—June 1973 to August 1973
Operator of IBM System 360-Model 20 computer. Responsible for running all programs.

SULLIVAN COUNTRY CLUB, Sullivan, Illinois—1971 to 1973
Taught swimming at all levels to children ages 3 through 16 for three consecutive summers.

SULLIVAN DRIVE-IN THEATRE, Sullivan, Illinois—June 1972 to August 1972
Assistant Manager. Duties included supervision of snack bar and clean up crew, helped with food purchasing, and cashier
at gate.

LITTLE THEATRE-ON THE SQUARE, Sullivan, Illinois—December 1970 to August 1971
Worked as occasional valet to stars and in box office.

References
Ms. Priscilla Sanders, Mgr., Carriage Lane, 125 Lincoln Square, Urbana, IL 61801
Ms. Kay Miller, Mgr., Data Processing, Kaiser Chemical Co., Sullivan, IL 61951
Prof. Fred M. Jones, Dept. of Bus. Admin., 109 David Kinley Hall, University of Illinois, Urbana, IL 61801
Mr. Richard Harshman, Vice Pres. of Marketing, Tootsie Roll Ind., 7401 So. Cicero, Chicago, IL 60629

Figure 11-5. Example of one-page printed resume.

FOLLOW-UP CORRESPONDENCE

The objective of the job-application package, consisting of the cover letter and resume, is to secure an interview. The objectives of the interview are to (1) determine whether you want the job and (2) secure the job if you decide that you want it. Naturally, if your first application package to a particular company does not secure the interview and you are really interested in working for that company, you would send a second letter of application and resume to demonstrate your seriousness.

While your second letter requesting an interview should be essentially the same as the first (especially if several months have elapsed), you should mention that you are writing a second time because of your serious interest in the company and your belief that you can make a significant contribution to the organization's ability to achieve its objectives. The basic organizational pattern for a second application is the same as that shown on pp. 191-92.

Even though one objective of the interview is to secure the job for you, your task is not over with the interview. You should pursue your objective until you've been hired, rejected, or have decided that you would be better off working for another company. Correspondence after the interview has one or more of the following objectives:

1. To bring your name to the attention of the interviewer one more time.
2. To improve your interviewer's opinion of you by
   a. Expressing appreciation for the interview,
   b. Overcoming deficiencies discovered during the interview,
   c. Offering new information to strengthen your application.
3. To express continued interest in a particular job.
4. To find out more about a particular job or company.
5. To negotiate for
   a. More money,
   b. More time to decide about a job,
   c. A change in some aspect of the job,
   d. A more rapid decision about your status.
6. To accept a job offer.
7. To refuse a job offer.

Thank-You Letters

Thank-you letters are the most frequently used follow-up letters. Every interview you have—regardless of whether you still want the job and of how you were treated in the interview—deserves to be followed with a letter of thanks. Thank-you letters can be either simple or complex, depending on how much work they need to do. When you're no longer interested in the job, you could simply write

```
Thank you for discussing the junior accountant's job with me last
Tuesday. I was glad to meet you and greatly appreciated your
frank discussion of the duties involved.

As we agreed in the interview, I would be happier working for a
company that would expose me to a variety of accounting func-
tions. I did enjoy talking with you, and I'm sure you'll find
the ideal candidate for the job.
```

When you still want the job, and the interview went well (and you're fairly convinced that the company will offer you the job), a short thank-you letter expressing your continued interest will suffice. It's more often the case, however, that you'll need to improve your interviewer's opinion of you either by overcoming deficiencies that were discovered during the interview or by offering some new information which you believe will strengthen your application. In such cases you'll need to write a complex follow-up letter, which is essentially a mixed message (see pp. 172-82), according to the following organization pattern:

1. **Positive beginning.**   Thank the reader for having taken the time to interview you. Your thanks is a positive opening that places your letter in its specific communication context.
2. **Explanation.**   Deal in a direct manner with the deficiencies that came up during the interview. The damage was done during the interview, and your objective is to overcome the negative element by stating what you have done or are doing to correct the deficiency or by offering a fuller explanation for the problem than you did during the interview. Present any new information you have to offer (Have you completed or enrolled in additional courses or other training programs? Have you learned something new that would help you on the job?). Focus on the contribution you can make to the company based on what you learned in the interview.
3. **Action.**   Don't push. It's all right to assert yourself and to desire to know more, but don't be aggressive. Express your continued interest and ask whether you might answer additional questions.

The following example illustrates these points:

```
Thank you very much for the time you spent with me when you vis-
ited Purdue University last week. I enjoyed talking with you
about the possibility of working as the Personnel Director for
Communication Unlimited.

Since we talked, I've given further thought to the questions
you asked about my lack of formal training in communication.
As you stated in the interview, your main concern is to hire
someone who can handle the correspondence and face-to-face
communication the job of Personnel Director entails; and
though my formal training is limited to the three basic
courses offered at Purdue University, those courses were
thorough and demanding.
```

In addition to my formal training, my extracurricular
activities have called for well-developed communication
skills. In my role of Secretary of Pi Omega Phi, I wrote many
letters—including the most successful fund-raising letter in
the history of the fraternity—and chaired many meetings. I
would be able to bring this on-the-job experience with me to
Communication Unlimited. I am also following your suggestion
and reading several of the communication books you mentioned.

I believe that I can make a valuable contribution to
Communication Unlimited, and I would appreciate it if you
would let me know if there is anything else I can do or tell
you about myself to help you decide about my application.

Inquiries and Negotiations

While your initial thank-you letter following the interview may easily and
naturally contain questions about aspects of the job which you weren't
able to learn during the interview, it's more difficult to write and ask job-
related questions when your letter has no other purpose. Also, our
current tight job market makes it difficult to negotiate with a prospective
employer for more money, more time to decide about taking a job, a
change in some aspect of the job, or a more rapid decision about your
application.

Requesting more information about a company or a particular job may
seem awkward because the writer assumes that questioning the interviewer (or interviewer's company) further would be viewed as criticism.
Actually, the reverse is true. As long as your inquiry is legitimate—about
something you should know before accepting a job with the company or
about something for which the information isn't readily available elsewhere (the company's annual report, for example)—it will demonstrate
your real interest in the company and place your name before the
interviewer one more time. Treat inquiries about job matters the same as
you would other inquiries, and use the organizational pattern presented
on pp. 91-100.

Negotiations also present problems. Every negotiation is a risk, and
when you negotiate, you should be prepared to lose. By asking for more
money or a change in some job duties, for example, you run the risk not
only of not getting what you want but also of creating resentment in your
reader and reducing your chances of getting the job at all. For this reason,
most letters of negotiation are mixed messages with two or more business
objectives. Because each letter of negotiation will contain information
that the reader will resent and/or resist, it should also contain enough
positive information to prevent the writer from losing what he or she has
already gained. Suppose you received the following letter:

Thank you for the prompt return of the completed application
form. This expression of your continued interest is sincerely
appreciated.

We are very interested in your background and would like to

```
consider you for our September 10 Sales Management Development
training class. However, since your graduation isn't until
August, I would like to delay further consideration until
July. If this presents a problem, please drop me a note.
```

You really want to work for this particular company, but other good companies have made you more definite and attractive offers already, and they require your answer by mid-June. How do you answer the letter? Here's the way one of our students handled the situation:

```
Thank you for your letter.

Because I am particularly interested in the job you described
at Steele, I would be grateful if you would make a final
decision on my eligibility for your Sales Management Develop-
ment class by early June.

As you probably know, I am at present interviewing with
several other companies, and I have been asked to give these
companies my decision by the middle of June. While Steele is
the company for which I would prefer to work, I would like
to know what my opportunities with Steele will be before I
refuse other offers.

Please let me know if another interview would help you decide.
The University of Illinois has spring vacation from April 14 to
April 23, and I could see you anytime during the week. With
only a short notice, I could visit La Crosse at any other
time convenient to you.
```

Note that the student does not explicitly state that the situation requires an "either/or" decision, but the letter implies that if the Steele Company doesn't make a definite job offer by early June, the student will have to accept one of the other job offers. This illustrates a basic premise of negotiations: you can't negotiate unless you have something with which to negotiate. In this case, the student had other job offers. When you negotiate for more money, you must be able to offer tangible evidence that you are worth more money. When you negotiate for more time to decide about a job or for a change in some aspect of the job duties, you must be able to provide evidence to support your request. In any case, don't negotiate unless you are prepared to lose.

Job-Acceptance and Job-Refusal Letters

Job-acceptance letters rarely present problems. They use the immediate structure, beginning with the acceptance itself. Their structure is the same as for other immediate messages and is shown on pp. 104-05. Because the letter offering the job and the letter accepting it will constitute a contract, you need to make sure that you understand exactly what is being offered before you accept. Also, your letter of acceptance should include those aspects of the job, its responsibilities, and rewards that you consider essential parts of the offer.

Yes, I do want to work as Executive Secretary for the
Anthracene Coal Company, and I'm glad to accept your offer.

The conditions specified in your letter of November 15, 19_,
including the $13,000 salary, the six-month probation, and
your overtime policy, are all agreeable to me. I've completed
and enclosed the insurance and medical forms you sent. Should
I do anything else before reporting for work?

I will be glad to see you at 8:00 a.m. Monday, January 3, when
I report for work.

Job-refusal letters are negative messages and use the delayed structure shown on pp. 127-28. The reader undoubtedly has other qualified applicants to choose from, but his or her feelings can still be hurt by your refusal. Try to keep the reader on your side. Base your refusal on reasons that leave the door open for possible future employment with the company, and express continued interest in the firm. Do not, however, imply that you will be leaving the company whose offer you are accepting.

Discussing the job of District Sales Manager of Resartus In-
dustries with you was one of my more interesting interviews.
You make the job at Resartus sound very challenging, and I'm
sure that the opportunity is a good one. Thank you for giving
me such serious consideration.

As you know from our interview, in addition to my interest in
sales, I also have a strong interest in management motivation.
Because I believe that I can be most useful in a job that will
permit me to spend most of my time working on problems of employee morale and motivation, I have decided to accept a job
with the Carlyle Conglomerate which will allow me to work on
such problems.

Thank you for the time you spent with me.

Letters of Resignation

Like job-refusal letters, job-resignation letters are delayed messages and use the structure shown on pp. 127-28. In most cases, you will announce your resignation orally, and the letter will be useful primarily as a matter of record. Even when your employer knows in advance that you are resigning, you should use the letter to help retain good feelings between you and your employer in spite of the fact that you are resigning. You can do this by

1. Showing that you learned something while working for the company.
2. Providing ample notice (depends on the job level—the higher the job level, the more notice is required).
3. Expressing willingness to train a replacement.
4. Explaining your reasons for leaving.
5. Offering constructive suggestions when possible.

SUMMARY

Letters written as part of the job search fall into two general categories: (1) those written to secure an interview and (2) those written after the interview has taken place. Letters of application are almost always part of a job-application package which includes both the letter and the resume. While one purpose of the letter of application is to transmit the resume to the reader, its main purpose is to persuade the reader to invite the applicant for an interview.

Because all employers want employees who have demonstrated a willingness to work, the skills required to perform a required task, the ability to get along well with others, and sufficient potential to merit promotion, a letter of application cannot succeed unless it demonstrates that the writer possess these qualities. To demonstrate these qualities in your letter, you need to assess the following: (1) your professional objectives, (2) your education, (3) your experience, and (4) your personal qualities. Regardless of whether your application is invited or uninvited, you should use the same basic organizational pattern: (1) attention, (2) interest, (3) conviction, and (4) action.

Because your letter can't say everything about you without becoming so long that prospective employers would find it unreadable, you should put much of the general information about yourself in a resume, which you send with the letter as an informative enclosure. Your resume must cover four broad categories of information: (1) personal details, (2) education, (3) experience, and (4) references. In addition to the major categories, you may have other information which you'll want to include under optional divisions.

The objective of the job-application package, consisting of the cover letter and resume, is to secure an interview. The objectives of the interview are to (1) determine whether you want the job and (2) secure the job if you decide that you want it. Even though one objective of the interview is to secure the job for you, your task is not over with the interview. You should pursue your objective until you've been hired or have decided that you would be better off working for another company.

Thank-you letters are the most frequently used follow-up letters. Every interview you have deserves to be followed with a letter of thanks. Requesting more information about a company or a particular job may seem awkward because the writer assumes that questioning the interviewer further would be viewed as criticism. Actually, as long as your inquiry is legitimate, it will demonstrate your real interest in the company and place your name before the interviewer one more time. Treat inquiries about job matters the same as you would other inquiries and use the organizational pattern presented on pp. 91-100.

Most negotiation letters are mixed messages with two or more business objectives. Because each letter of negotiation will contain information that the reader will resent and/or resist, it should also contain enough positive information to prevent the writer from losing what he or she already has.

Job-acceptance letters use the immediate structure, beginning with the acceptance itself. Because the letter offering the job and the letter accepting it will constitute a contract, you need to make sure that you understand exactly what is being offered before you accept. Your letter of acceptance should include those aspects of the job, its responsibilities, and rewards that you consider essential parts of the offer.

Job-refusal letters are negative messages and use the delayed structure shown on pp. 127-28. Base your refusals on reasons that leave the door open for possible future employment with the company, and express continued interest in the firm.

Like job-refusal letters, job-resignation letters are delayed messages and use the structure shown on pp. 127-28. Use the letter to help retain good feelings between you and your employers in spite of the fact that you are resigning.

EXERCISES

Review

1. What are the two general categories of job-search letters?

2. What are the two purposes of a letter of application? What is its organizational pattern?

3. In the letter of application you need to assess four general areas to demonstrate your qualities for the job. What are they?

4. Why is a resume included with the letter of application?

5. What four categories should be included in the resume?

6. Give seven reasons for writing follow-up letters.

7. When you need to write a complex follow-up letter, what organizational pattern would you use?

8. Why would you write a letter of inquiry to a company after an interview?

9. Why are letters of negotiation a risk?

10. How do you retain the good feelings between you and your employer in a letter of resignation?

Problems

1. Using your current qualifications or the qualifications you expect to have when you finish school, prepare a letter of application and resume for the company and job of your choice.

2. Assume that you have interviewed for the job you applied for in the preceding problems.

   a. Write a thank-you letter based on a smooth, successful interview and your continued interest in the job.
   b. Write a thank-you letter based on your continued interest in the job and on an interview in which the interviewer expressed concern about your lack of formal education in report writing.
   c. Write a thank-you letter based on an interview in which you discovered that you are not really interested in the job.

3. Assume that two months have gone by since your interview and you have heard nothing. Write to your interviewer and persuade him or her to make a faster decision.

4. Assume that you have been offered the job you applied for in Problem 1 and that your prospective employer wants your answer in one week. You are already committed to interviewing with a competing firm, and that interview won't take place until the day of your deadline. Write to the firm that offered you the job and request an additional week to make your decision.

5. The company has just offered you the job but for $2,000 a year less than the usual rate for people at your level in your line of work. You have no other job offers at the moment, but you do have several promising interviews coming up in the next two weeks. Negotiate for a higher salary.

6. You've been offered two jobs at a suitable salary. Providing the specific details appropriate for your line of work, write to one company and accept its offer.

7. Write to the other company in Problem 6 and refuse.

8. Assume you have worked for the company for five years and wish to accept a much better paying job that offers more challenges with a new company. Resign your job giving 60 days' notice.

APPENDIX A
Supplemental Problems

1. Answer an inquiry from Mr. Art Capriotti, Western Tape, P. O. Box 69, Mountain View, CA 94042. Mr. Capriotti is inquiring about Ms. Sally VanHoven, who is seeking employment as an administrative assistant. As Sally's former employer, you write and say that for the two years that Sally worked for you, she was dependable, trustworthy, and accurate. She seemed to get along with her supervisors, her peers, and her subordinates. Sally was an energetic person who was always eager to learn.

2. You are Ryland Hoskinson, owner of Candles Galore Inc., 756 Hogate Street, Milwaukee, WI 53222. You receive a letter from new retirees, Mr. and Mrs. LaRue Truball, 9800 El Manor Avenue, Los Angeles, CA 90045, who have leased space in a newly opened shopping mall. They want you to let them have $5,000 worth of candles and candle accessories (holders, wreaths, etc.) on credit. You must turn them down. Because this is their first business venture, they may be a poor credit risk. Write a letter that will keep their friendship. Suggest local financing and business on a cash basis.

3. You have just learned that your school is going to discontinue the program you are majoring in. Budget restrictions are going to result in several faculty members being dismissed. Write a letter to the president of your school persuading him or her to reinstate your major and find other, more equitable ways to reduce expenses.

4. You're Mrs. William Kennard, Credit Manager for Kennard's Leather Shop, 8 Farrier Street, Charleston, WV 25306. One of your customers, Michael Robertson, 50 Herkimer Street, Trenton, NY 08609, who has a $900 outstanding balance with you for previous purchases, sends an order for 12 five-inch Samsonite attaché cases, $35 each (four black, four brown, four gray). Write Mr. Robertson and tell him you're glad he likes your products and you appreciate his order. Also explain to him that as soon as his account is paid in full, you'll be glad to ship him the items he ordered.

5. As a professor of business communication, write a letter to the president of the Kiwanis Club, Mr. Herbert Keenan, 3098 Kingsgate Street, Memphis, TN 38118, telling him that you accept his invitation to speak on "Writing Winning Letters" at the September 12 club luncheon meeting. You'll need an overhead projector and screen for your presentation. You plan to speak for 45 minutes and to allow 15 minutes for questions and answers.

6. As director of sales, Midwest Insurance Company, 5167 South Main Street, Charleston, IL 61920, you are concerned because the independent insurance agents who sell your policies have let their sales lag over the last three months. Your sales are off by about 15 percent. In investigating the problem, you've discovered that several of your competitors have initiated new sales incentive programs. For the

agent with the most sales each month, one company offers a weekend in Las Vegas and another offers a weekend at Disney World. You decide to give a 19″ color television each month to the agent with the most sales. Persuade the independent agents to sell more of your life, homeowner's, fire, auto, accident, and health insurance packages.

7. As president of General Cereals, 670 Post Drive, Battle Creek, MI 49000, you've been receiving many complaints from parents who are concerned that one of the television shows you sponsor, "The Assassins," is too violent. The parents are fairly well organized, and their most recent move, a boycott of your products, is hurting your sales. "The Assassins," however, is sufficiently popular that you don't wish to quit sponsoring it completely. Write a letter to the producers of "The Assassins," TMT Inc., 1427 Hillcrest Drive, Hollywood, CA 90028, and persuade them to tone down the violence without destroying the artistic integrity or impact of the show. Also, prepare a form letter to mail to those who write to complain about the show—justify the inclusion of some violence, explain that the shows will be less violent in the future, and convince them that your sponsorship of the show does not mean that you approve of violence as a means of solving problems.

8. As a faculty member of the physical education department, you have been asked by the sponsors of the cheerleaders to judge the tryouts. Twelve men and women are trying out, and you and two other judges need to select four persons for next year's squad. Write a letter to the sponsors, Dr. and Mrs. Bruce Kemel, Foothill College, 12345 El Monte Road, Los Altos Hills, CA 94022, saying that you'll be happy to be a judge.

9. As Alan Archincloss, Credit Manager of Crepe's, 35 Clarkson Street, Des Moines, IA 50300, you need to write Mrs. Sylvester Balboa (see Problem 2, page 120). Mrs. Balboa has reached her credit limit of $500 and wants to charge another $200 on her account. This would raise her charges to $700. Because Mrs. Balboa does not always pay on time, you decide not to raise the $500 limit. Write Mrs. Balboa telling her this.

10. Write a letter to a Member of Congress or another government official persuading him or her to change an opinion or to take a particular action on a controversial issue. Submit a copy of the letter to your instructor.

11. As a result of the new sales incentive plan and the improved national advertising campaign you instituted at Midwest Insurance Company (see Problem 6, page 211), your sales have increased by 75 percent in the last six months. Your staff of three—one assistant and two secretaries—can no longer handle all the work. You wish to hire an administrative assistant who has been trained to operate an IBM Mag

Card II typewriter. Rent and supplies for the Mag Card II would cost about $350 a month, and the salary for the administrative assistant would be about $1,000 a month. Because yours is a small company, only the president can authorize that kind of an expenditure, and she is taking an extended leave. Write to Ms. Gloria Wade, Oceanside Hotel, 80 Bayview Drive, San Diego, CA 92182, and persuade her to authorize the expenditures.

12. A friend just wrote to you asking how he or she should go about writing a letter requesting a replacement for a defective cassette tape recorder just purchased through the mail. Using your own words, describe the general procedure your friend should use to obtain a replacement. Put your description into proper letter format.

13. You are chairperson of the Suggestion Committee for your company, American Cheese Products Inc., 2112 W. Layton Avenue, Milwaukee, WI 53221. Greg Sims, a student employee at the Urbana, Illinois, plant submitted a suggestion for replacing the metal trays for packaging your company's frozen dinners with polystyrene plastic for use in microwave ovens. Greg's suggestion is dated 14 May. You've also received essentially the same suggestion dated 16 May from Roger Greenberg, the Vice President of Production for your Midwest Division. As chairperson of the committee, you have a vote only in case the four members have a tie vote. The committee thinks that the idea is an excellent one and wishes to award a $2,000 bonus for it. They feel, however, that it would be in the company's best interests to award the bonus to the executive rather than to the student employee. They feel that the student would quit work as soon as he received the money. By a vote of 3 to 1, your committee decides to award the bonus to Mr. Greenberg. Write the letters to Greenberg (525 Jeffery Street, Calumet City, IL 60409) and Sims (105 Grand Avenue, Urbana, IL 61801) on behalf of the Suggestion Committee.

14. Mr. Rodney Stipes, 1441 Banbury Lane, Austin, TX 78700, wrote to you because the fine bone china imported tea set he purchased through your store (Pier 4 Imports, 1700 Aberdeen Street, San Francisco, CA 94133) was broken in shipment. The tea set (valued at $400) was insured, and you are immediately sending a new set. Because of your experience with Mr. Stipe's set, you will use an improved carton and additional packing for all future shipments.

15. As Personnel Director, Midwest Insurance Company, 5167 South Main Street, Charleston, IL 61920, write a form letter to send to the beneficiaries of life insurance policies held by your company. The beneficiaries may collect the money from the policy in either one lump sum or monthly installments. Or, if the beneficiary prefers, you will hold the money—invested at 6 percent a year—until the beneficiary wishes to collect. Such an arrangement can help with children's college expenses or the beneficiary's own retirement.

16. As president of the Newcomer's Club, 45 Dudley Avenue, St. Paul, MN 55108, you write a letter to Schaffer's Bakery, 976 Lincoln Avenue, St. Paul, MN 55108, asking for free coupons for 1-lb. loaves of their famous whole wheat bread that you will present to newcomers of St. Paul. When one of your members calls on the newcomers, he or she gives them various coupons from merchants in St. Paul. The newcomers then visit the stores to redeem the coupons and to become familiar with the stores. This is a fine opportunity for Schaffer's to meet prospective customers.

17. Prepare a letter for the director of admissions at your school, which will inform applicants that they have been denied admission.

18. As the administrative assistant for Cain and Cogdel Insurance, 99 Race Street, Fayetteville, AK 72701, write a letter to Mrs. Miriam Webster, 765 Frontage Road, Fayetteville, AK 72701, reminding her to submit the paperwork required to complete the claim she filed after her auto accident about a month ago. Because the accident was Mrs. Webster's fault, there is a good chance that her rates will be raised and that may be the reason for her delay. Even if her rates are raised, she should complete the claim and have her car fixed.

19. As the director of public relations for Majestic and Taylor's, write a form thank-you letter to be sent to your regular charge customers around the country. Because you have stores in 15 major cities, you will need to avoid regionalisms—references to particular cities, climates, or styles appropriate for one region only. Majestic and Taylor's specializes in fine fashions for men and women.

20. Trout Equipment, 165 State Street, Chicago, IL 60612, manufactures fishing gear. The company received a $950 order for various fishing supplies from Don Hampton, 300 Oakland Street, Topeka, KS 66601. Pat Sheehan, your salesman, said that Hampton, a former client of his, recently opened his own shop. Pat reports that Hampton has an excellent reputation in his community and has invested his life savings in the business. Write Hampton and suggest that he cut his order in half and pay cash less a 2 percent cash discount. As soon as his business is well enough established that his ratio of assets to liabilities has stabilized at about 2:1, you'll be glad to extend him credit. Point out to him that because you can guarantee delivery in three days, he doesn't need to maintain a large inventory. Send him your new spring catalog.

21. As the president of H & B Rock, CPAs, 350 Doming Street, Billing, MT 59102, write a letter to Mrs. Ila Todd, owner of Todd's Gravel Pit, RR 2, Billings, MT 59102, informing her that her financial records indicate that her bookkeeper, Mr. Henry Palmore (whom you know to be her nephew), has embezzled more than $7,000 from her company over the past two years. Palmore's scheme was clever, and that's why

you missed it during your audit last year. Palmore was using regularly scheduled maintenance on equipment to create the cash flow necessary for defalcation. He had set up a dummy corporation, Machine Parts Inc., and as chief accountant he would complete the paperwork authorizing the purchase of unnecessary repair parts. The checks payable to Machine Parts Inc. constituted a small amount compared with the total maintenance costs, and because the parts ordered were not really needed, no one missed them. You missed this scheme in your audit last year because none of the transactions with Machine Parts Inc. was included in your samples. This year you've discovered that Palmore is the owner—and only stockholder—of Machine Parts Inc., and in checking further, you've discovered that none of the parts ordered and paid for was actually delivered. When you write to Mrs. Todd, keep in mind that Palmore is her nephew.

22. As president of DeRamus Jewelers, 1405 Vernon Avenue, Batesville, MS 38606, write a form letter to your 100 employees announcing your bankruptcy. The company's assets will be sold to pay outstanding obligations, and you cannot pay salaries for the last two weeks until the major creditors have been satisfied. Your employees will need to look for work elsewhere, and you'll pay them what you can in about six weeks.

23. You've just opened a restaurant, Pasqual's Pizza, 41 Coamo Street, Greenville, NC 27834, specializing in Italian food two blocks from Pitt Technical Institute, Greenville, NC 27834. You know that the combination of pizza and beer will go over well with the students, but you'd like to make a hit with the faculty, too. Prepare a form letter to be sent to the Pitt faculty announcing your opening and stress your "Family Fare." Enclose a sample menu and offer one free meal of equal value for each meal purchased during the week of May 15.

24. As the communications coordinator for William Morris Toy Company, 3761 Pleasant Valley Road, Mobile, AL 36609, you have the job of writing the form letters the company uses to communicate with customers. It's your company policy to replace any toy a customer complains about—all the customer has to do is return the toy, and you'll send a new one. Prepare a form letter that you can use to notify customers that you'll send a new toy as soon as they return the original one.

25. As Henry Bixby, owner of Bixby Imports, 703 Linck Street, Cazenovia, NY 13035, you've just received a call from Mr. James Richards, P.O. Box 691, Indiana Hills, CO 80454, who told you that two months ago he ordered a Spanish silver serving tray for the 25th wedding anniversary of his sister and her husband, Mr. and Mrs. William Grady, 422 Summitt East, Seattle, WA 98102. Mr. Richards did not receive a bill for the purchase and became curious. Mr. Richards called his sister

to see whether the gift had arrived. It had—gift wrapped, accompanied by an anniversary card, and a bill for $297 plus $18 COD charges. Mr. Richards has sent the Gradys a check to cover the cost, and he wants you to send them a letter of apology and full explanation. You investigate and discover that the tray was sent COD because Mr. Richards' name did not appear on the order slip and the Gradys did not have a charge account with the store. You will redesign your order forms to show both the person to be billed and the person who is to receive the merchandise. Write letters to the Gradys and to Mr. Richards. Send Mr. Richards a copy of your letter to the Gradys and refund the COD charge.

26. Your boss has given you the following letter to answer:

```
Communication Consultants Inc.
2102 Randolph Street
Atlanta, GA 30300

Gentlemen:

I'm the owner of a small personnel agency, and lately my em-
ployees are having to write each letter twice to make them-
selves understood. This extra communication and the problems
unclear letters are causing are costing me a great deal of
money.

Can your company help? Can you give me some simple guidelines
to give my employees? Please let me hear from you soon.

Sincerely yours,


Faye Johnson
```

Although you're not sure what Ms. Johnson is asking for, you would like to *sell* her your company's services. Write the letter.

27. As Claims Adjuster, Department of Health Services at the University of Hawaii, Honolulu, HI 96822, you need to respond to a student, Jack Baker, 685 Luau Lane, Honolulu, HI 96822. Jack wrote you and said that he enrolled at the University as a part-time student because he wanted to combine his vacation with his education. While surfing the giant waves at Waikiki Beach, he slipped and suffered a sprained ankle. Jack sent you all the bills he incurred from his emergency treatment at the local hospital. Write Jack a refusal letter. Part-time students provide their own insurance (as specified in the college catalog) or pay the $20 insurance fee at registration. Jack did not take the insurance plan with the University. Return the unpaid bills to Jack.

28. As Robert Furgeson, Manager of Customer Relations, Moonbeam Products Inc., 3809 Lakeway Lane, Denver, CO 80200, refuse the following request from Mr. Howard Quillan, 234 Hilda Street, Tucson, AZ 85700.

The blender in the attached box needs repairs. It worked fine
for about six months and then quit for no good reason. Because
your guarantee is for five years, the blender should be fully
covered. May I receive the repaired blender in about ten days?

Your examination of the blender reveals that the blender has been used to mix paints rather than to mix foods. Evidently Mr. Quillan had repeatedly allowed paint to dry around the blender's rotor shaft, which put an additional strain on the motor. The extra strain caused the motor to burn out. You can replace the motor, but mixing paint is definitely an abuse of the blender, which nullifies your warranty. Actually, it would be okay for Quillan to mix latex paints with the blender as long as he cleaned it thoroughly with soap and water (following all your directions) after each use. Oil base paints and turpentine would ruin the blender's rubber seals. Offer to replace the motor for Mr. Quillan at cost ($14.99). Explain that the blender is guaranteed only when it is used in the ways specified in the directions. Should Quillan use it to mix paints, he does so at his own risk.

29. As Personnel Director, Indiana State Bank, Bloomington, IN 47401, write to Ms. Mary Lou Berard, 469A Nobles Hall, Bloomington, IN 47401. Ms. Berard is an honors graduate in finance and banking from Indiana University in Bloomington, and you want to invite her to an interview. You wish to see her at 10 a.m. on June 2. You'll interview her and then introduce her to the officers of the bank. At noon, you and the bank president will take her to lunch.

30. As sales manager for Hyland's Furniture Company, 3490 Lebanon Street, Stratford, CT 06497, you obtain the names and addresses of future brides from the society section of your local newspaper, *The Stratford Gazette*. You write a letter to each prospective bride inviting her and her fiance to come to your store and see your fine display of furniture for every room in a house. You carry well-known brands— Henredon, Drexel, and Ethan Allen. During August you'll be having a special sale on all bedroom furniture, with reductions up to 50 percent. You'll offer a special 2 percent discount to all newlyweds, over and above the sale prices.

31. As the general manager of Insty Prints, 946 Garnsey Avenue, Corvallis, OR 97331, you receive a letter from Ms. Charlene Fuller, owner of The Ceramic Shop, 4982 Southfield Road, Klamath Falls, OR 97601, who placed a rush order for 500 business cards several weeks ago. Ms. Fuller asked that the cards be printed using brown ink on light gold 65-lb.-weight card stock. When she received the business cards, she noticed that the cards were printed on brown paper and the printing was done in gold ink. Also, her name was incorrectly spelled as "Charleen." Ms. Fuller needs the cards by the end of the week; otherwise, she will have to go to another printer. Write Ms. Fuller and tell her she will receive the cards by the end of the week.

32. As chairperson of the Management Department, Mississippi State University, Mississippi State, MS 39762, write a letter of reprimand to a staff member, Dr. Darlene Bush, who has frequently missed classes the last two semesters. You have spoken to Dr. Bush about the missed classes three times, and each time she promised to meet all future classes unless she were sick. After each of these talks, Dr. Bush met classes regularly for a while, then began missing — at first once every two weeks, then once a week. After awhile there were times when she would miss as many as four or five of her scheduled classes a week. When writing to Dr. Bush, tell her that a copy of this letter of reprimand will become part of her official university records and will be considered when she is evaluated for promotion and tenure.

33. Mr. Patrick Foley, RR 4, Topeka, KS 66600, sent a check for $298 and ordered a gasoline-powered, 1-horsepower irrigation pump from your firm, Oakley Fuel and Pipe Company, 383 Drake Road, Wichita, KS 67213. Because the 1-horsepower pump proved inadequate for most irrigation purposes, you've discontinued manufacturing it although you still have some in stock. You now manufacture irrigation pumps with 2½- and 5-horsepower motors. The 1-horsepower pump will deliver up to 35 gallons of water a minute, whereas the 2½-horsepower pump delivers up to 60 gallons a minute, and the 5-horsepower pump delivers nearly 140 gallons a minute. You will still sell Mr. Foley the 1-horsepower pump, but because you've discontinued the model and can offer only a one-year warranty and parts replacement for five years, offer to sell it for $219. The 2½-horsepower pump costs $374, and the 5-horsepower pump costs $429. Both come with a complete five-year warranty. Hold Mr. Foley's check until you hear from him.

34. As president of Act II, manufacturers of quality clothing for women, write a form letter to the stores that handle your products announcing a 20 percent increase. The increase is necessary because of the higher prices you must pay for materials and labor.

35. As sales promoter for Libermann's Jewelers, 340 Spring Street, Huntsville, AL 35807, you obtain, for a small fee, a list of the names and addresses of the parents of all the June graduates of Jefferson High School, Huntsville, AL 35807, from the superintendent of schools. You write a letter to the parents of these graduates inviting them to visit your store and see your fine selection of gifts for graduates — rings, necklaces, chains, tie tacks, and a special collection of watches: Lucien Piccards, Hamiltons, Elgins, Walthams, and Seikos. For coming in and browsing, the parents may register for the free drawing of a $250 Seiko solid state quartz digital watch for the young male or female graduate. Write a sample form letter and send it to Mr. and Mrs. Stephen Pompykala, 1521 Merriman Drive, Huntsville, AL 35807. Their son Andrew is a member of the June graduating class.

36. Write a letter designed to sell a product or service of your choice. If you have difficulty in choosing a product, select an item from a mail-order house catalog. If your instructor requests it, design a brochure to enclose with the letter.

37. When you opened your general contracting business (Miller Construction Company, 2098 Terrace Drive, Gainesville, FL 32601) 20 years ago, you were short of capital so you enlisted Mr. Rodney Clements as a partner. Clements invested $45,000 and worked hard to make the company grow. Your contracting business is now worth nearly a million dollars, and you'd like to buy Clements out. In the last five or six years Clements has made several costly mistakes because of excessive drinking during working hours, and you've gradually had to restrict his activities, which he greatly resents. Because of his resentment, Clements wants to charge you an outrageous amount for his share of the business. Today you've received a letter from Mr. Peter Johnson, owner of Johnson Contracting, 902 Ocean Drive, Orlando, FL 32800, expressing an interest in hiring Clements as a senior estimator and supervisor. Clements would be well qualified to do the work if he would quit drinking, and perhaps the change in jobs will provide the challenge he needs to have more interest in life. You haven't met Johnson, but you know that if your letter about Clements is misleading, the word will spread quickly, and it could hurt your business. Still, if Johnson can hire Clements away from you, you'd probably be able to buy Clements' share of the business for a reasonable amount. Write the letter to Johnson. Johnson said that Clements had applied for the job a few days ago and stated that you were not giving him sufficient responsibility.

38. As Rocco Fumento, owner of Fumento Construction Company, 4371 North 57th Street, Oakland, CA 94600, write a letter to Dr. Laura Manis explaining that the bill for $6,538 she received and paid for the addition to her house at 319 Beaumont Plaza, San Pedro, CA 90731, was incorrect because of an error in addition. The itemization on the original bill was correct; only the total was wrong. The full price, $7,538, is still less than the written estimate of $8,000 you gave her before you began work. Collect the $1,000 she still owes you.

39. As the president of General Watch Works, 77 Sheila Street, New York, NY 10001, you've just discovered that several of your dealers have been taking the parts from your less expensive Chronomatic watches and placing them in the more expensive Oldsake watch cases. While the Chronomatic parts are perfectly all right and keep good time, they are not as well made as the Oldsake parts. The Chronomatic parts are noisier and not quite so accurate. Write a letter to all your dealers explaining that the substitution is unethical and, in some states, illegal. Should a dealer continue to substitute parts, you will have to discontinue doing business with him or her.

40. As the U. S. distributor for Renabbit Automobiles, write a form letter to purchasers of your 1977 cars informing them of a potentially dangerous defect in the braking system which requires immediate attention. They are to phone their local dealers for an appointment to have the problem corrected.

41. Yesterday, one of your employees, Mr. Francis Bacon, had a heart attack at work. The heart attack was very serious and only the quick thinking of Ms. Sara Eldridge, his secretary, saved his life. She called the rescue squad and performed mouth-to-mouth resuscitation and heart massage until help arrived. Mr. Bacon had just recently separated from his wife, Frances, to whom he has been married for 27 years. He moved out of the house they had shared for the past 16 years (address: 47 Shakespeare Circle, Falls Church, VA 22043) and into a room at the YMCA. Mr. Bacon was very depressed about his marital problems and had been working long hours to take his mind off his troubles. Because of your conversations with him, you know that Bacon would like nothing better than to patch things up with his wife. Write the appropriate letters. If your instructor requests it, submit a separate analysis justifying your selection of messages.

42. Mr. Bacon (see preceding problem) has died after 16 days in the hospital. Write the appropriate letters. If your instructor requests it, submit a separate analysis justifying your selection of messages.

43. On your last two visits to Nichols' Department Store, you've been treated rudely by the sales clerks. On Monday, 27 October, you went in the store to buy a pair of shoes. You tried on several pairs but found none that you liked. As you were leaving, the clerk said, "Thanks for wasting my time." On Thursday of that same week, you went in to return a set of towels because the towels had been packed in such a way that you were unable to see that one of the towels was defective, having an orange stain on it. When you requested an exchange or a refund, the clerk said, "Don't you think that you're being awfully picky?" Only after several minutes of arguing were you able to obtain a refund. Write a letter of complaint to Mr. Roger Nichols, owner of the department store.

44. Select a company with whose products or services you are familiar. Prepare form correspondence to send to those people who write to the company complimenting it on its products or services. Also, prepare form correspondence to send to those people who have complaints about its products or services. For each form, prepare a separate sheet explaining how it should be used.

45. As the manufacturer of glass and aluminum containers, your company, Spartan Bottle and Can Company, 83 Lincoln Avenue, Hammond, LA 70401, receives a great many letters from ecology-minded

people who complain about the harmful effects of your throw-away bottles and aluminum cans. They complain about the waste of glass and metal resources and the waste of energy caused by continual production of new containers which will be used only once and thrown out. Until recycling technology improves, however, manufacturing new containers is less expensive than recycling, and most consumers prefer the convenience of no-deposit, no-return containers. Your company does not condone littering or other misuse of your products. Write a form letter to send to people who write letters of complaint about your lack of concern for the environment.

46. Mrs. Betty Cinq-Mars wrote to you and complained that she found a dead mouse in a box of your Roasties Wheat Cereal. Unfortunately, she called her local TV station, which interviewed her and photographed your cereal and the dead mouse. The story was picked up by the national TV networks and appeared in *Time, Newsweek,* and *People.* Write the appropriate letters. If your instructor requests it, submit a separate analysis of the situation justifying your decision.

47. Write to a company of your choice and request information about a service or particular line of products. Along with your letter, submit to your instructor the company's reply and your analysis of its effectiveness.

48. In recent months, several small children (ages 3-6) in your community have been seriously injured or killed when large trash containers of the sort used by apartments, stores, and schools have tipped over on them. As the parent of a three-year-old girl, you are quite concerned about this unnecessary hazard. Most of the new containers are sufficiently stable and will not tip over even if children climb on them. Write to your state legislators requesting that the unsafe containers be made illegal.

49. As the manager of a 300-unit apartment complex, prepare a form letter for your tenants outlining rules for using the apartment's swimming pool during the summer. The rules you will need to include are as follows:

    a. The pool will open for the season on May 31 and close the day after Labor Day.
    b. The hours for the pool will be from 10:00 a.m. until 10:00 p.m. daily.
    c. All swimmers (men and women) must wear bathing caps and bathing suits. No cut-offs are permitted.
    d. No food or drink is permitted in the pool area.
    e. Children under 12 must be accompanied by an adult.
    f. Children under 5 must be out of the pool at 6:00 p.m.
    g. Tenants must accompany their guests.

h. Guests are permitted only one visit every 30 days.
i. Tenants may bring only one guest on any Friday, Saturday or Sunday.
j. No rough play will be permitted in or around the pool.

50. Write a letter to the authors of this book and tell them

a. What's wrong with the book.
b. What you like about the book.
c. What improvements should be made in the book.

Submit a copy of the letter to your instructor.

APPENDIX B
Correction Symbols

CORRECTION SYMBOLS

Ab   **Abbreviation.**   Do not use abbreviations in formal communication. With the exception of commonly used abbreviations (US, YMCA, NASA), spell out the term the first time it is used with the abbreviation enclosed in parentheses.

Ac   **Accuracy.**   Be sure that names, addresses, and other details are correct.

Adapt   **Adaptation.**   Adapt your message to your reader's level. Write your message for a particular individual.

Agr   **Agreement.**   Subjects and verbs agree in number and in person. Pronouns and antecedents agree in number, person, and case.

Amb   **Ambiguity.**   Statement has more than one meaning; it is not clear.

Ap   **Appearance.**

Apos   **Apostrophe.**   Use apostrophes correctly.

Awk   **Awkward.**   Reword the sentence for a more natural flow.

Cap   **Capitalize.**

Case   **Grammatical case.**   Use subject, object, and reflexive cases as required.

Chop   **Choppy construction.**   Use a variety of sentence structures and make transition between sentences clear.

Cl   **Clarity.**   Message is not clear.

CM   **Confidence in your message.**   See p. 67.

Coh   **Coherence.**   Writing should flow smoothly from one idea to another. Watch transition between sentences, paragraph unity, and transition between paragraphs.

Con   **Conciseness.**   Eliminate all unnecessary words and phrases.

Coop   **Cooperation of equals.**   Feelings of either superiority or inferiority will interfere with the success of your letter. Avoid indignation, mistrust, paternalism, humility, and flattery.

CR   **Confidence in your reader.**   See pp. 66-67.

CS   **Comma splice.**   Two or more independent clauses must be separated by a period, a comma and a coordinating conjunction, or a semicolon.

CT   **Conversational tone.**   Use natural, modern language. Avoid jargon, clichés, and trite expressions.

D   **Diction.**   Word is used incorrectly. See your dictionary.

Emp   **Emphasis.**   Stress the idea indicated.

Enc   **Enclosure.**

Exp   **Expletive.**   Omit wordy and weak expressions, such as *it is* and *there are.*

F   **Format.**   Check margins, letter or report parts, and placement.

Fl   **Flattery.**   Legitimate praise is fine, but don't exaggerate.

Frag   **Fragment.**   Not a complete thought. Check for subject and verb.

Gob   **Gobbledygook.**   Garbled expressions or excessive use of technical jargon.

Gr   **Grammar fault.**

Imp   **Imply.**   Many negative and obvious ideas should be implied rather than stated explicitly.

Jar   **Jargon.**   Avoid words used just to impress the reader.

lc   **Lower case.**   Do not capitalize.

Log   **Logic.**   Check the relationships between ideas. Be especially careful with cause-and-effect statements.

MM   **Misplaced modifier.**

N   **Number.**   Use numbers rather than words.

Neg   **Negative.**   Accentuate the positive; eliminate the negative.

Obv   **Obvious.**   Omit or subordinate statements that the reader already knows.

OC   **Overconfidence.**   See pp. 67-68.

Org   **Organization.**   See appropriate general structure and check list.

P   **Punctuation.**   Use the marks of punctuation correctly.

// cst **Parallel construction.**   Use the same kind of grammatical struc-
            ture for related ideas. Ideas in a series should be expressed with
            the same parts of speech. Correlative conjunctions should be
            followed by parallel elements. Parallel construction should also
            be used to emphasize ideas of equal importance. See p. 169.

Pas   **Passive voice.**   Passive voice is usually weak and wordy. Use
            active voice to emphasize. Use passive voice to de-emphasize a
            reader's mistake.

PV   **Point of view.**   Be consistent with the point of view. It should
            usually be the reader's.

RB   **Reader benefit.**   Find and emphasize what the reader will gain.
            Emphasize the benefit, not the physical facts.

Red   **Redundant.**   Unnecessary repetition of words, similar expres-
            sions, or ideas.

Ref   **Reference.**   Incorrect or indefinite antecedent for pronoun.

RO   **Run-on sentence.**   Running two sentences together without a
            mark of punctuation.

SB   **Should be.**   Wording should be changed as indicated.

Sp   **Spelling error.**

Spec   **Specificity.**   Be specific. Use concrete words rather than abstract
            words. Use specific words rather than general words.

Sub   **Subordinate.**

Syl   **Syllabication.**   Divide words between syllables.

T   **Tense.**   Use correct tense.

TR   **Transition.**   Needs transition. Show relationship from one idea
            to another.

V   **Variety.**   Vary sentence length and type. Vary paragraph length.

W   **Wordy.**

WC   **Word Choice.**   Not a good word for your purposes because of its connotations.

X   **Obvious error.**   Proofread.

YA   **You-attitude.**   Keep the reader in the picture.

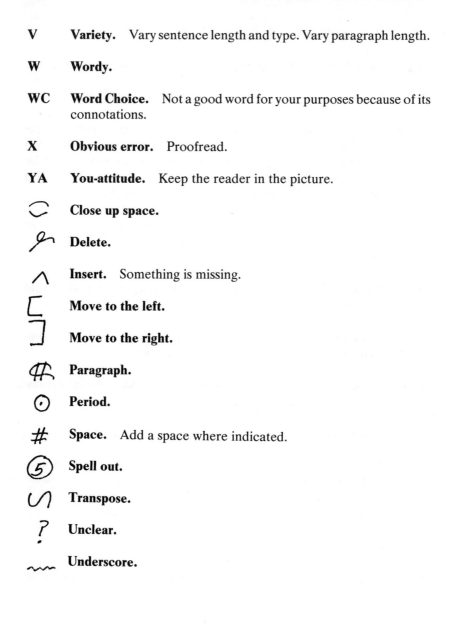

      Close up space.

      Delete.

      Insert.   Something is missing.

      Move to the left.

      Move to the right.

      Paragraph.

      Period.

      Space.   Add a space where indicated.

      Spell out.

      Transpose.

      Unclear.

      Underscore.

INDEX